The Constitutional Law Dictionary

THE CONSTITUTIONAL LAW DICTIONARY

VOLUME 1:
INDIVIDUAL RIGHTS
SUPPLEMENT 3

Covering the 1990-91, 1991-92, 1992-93,
and 1993-94 Terms of the Supreme Court

Ralph C. Chandler
Richard A.Enslen
Peter G. Renstrom

ABC-CLIO

Santa Barbara, California
Denver, Colorado
Oxford, England

Library of Congress Cataloging-in-Publication Data

Chandler, Ralph C., 1934–
    The constitutional law dictionary.

    (Clio dictionaries in political science ; #8)
    Vol. 2 has publisher: ABC-Clio.
    Vol. 2 without series numbering.
    Vol. 1 kept up to date by supplements.
    Includes indexes.
    Contents: v. 1. Individual rights—v. 2. Governmental powers.
    1. United States—Constitutional law—Terms and phrases. 2. United States—Constitutional law—Cases. I. Enslen, Richard A., 1931– . II. Renstrom, Peter G., 1943– . III. Title.
    KF4548.5.C47   1985   342.73   84-12320
                                347.302

    ISBN 0-87436-758-1

    00 99 98 97 96 95   10 9 8 7 6 5 4 3 2 1

ABC-CLIO, Inc.
130 Cremona Drive, P.O. Box 1911
Santa Barbara, California 93116-1911

This book is printed on acid-free paper ∞.
Manufactured in the United States of America

CONTENTS

A NOTE ON HOW TO USE THIS BOOK

Students of constitutional law know the extent to which the law is ever changing. With each new term of the Supreme Court the justices review their previous decisions and those of their predecessors in light of current legal and social circumstances. The changes that are made are frequently incremental: a nuance here and an adjustment there. The Court may simply wish to apply an established doctrine or more clearly define a standard in a particular case as it weighs real-world situations on the scales of justice. Sometimes it sweeps aside an entire line of precedent in a bold new interpretation of the Constitution. The system is constantly in flux. It is evolutionary, developmental, and responsive to human need. Thus it adds stability to the governmental system as a whole. A systems theorist would say constitutional law has a well-defined dynamic feedback loop.

These conditions create certain problems for writers and publishers of constitutional law books. Given the lead time necessary to prepare such a book, it is out of date in some particulars on the day it is published. In this case, *The Constitutional Law Dictionary, Volume 1: Individual Rights* was published in early 1985. Significant decisions rendered later than the middle of the 1983–84 term of the Court, plus, of course, those decisions coming since, were not included in the original volume. To remedy the need to keep the *Constitutional Law Dictionary: Individual Rights* current, this supplement is offered as the Court begins the 1994–95 term. This is the third such supplement we have prepared. The first, published in 1987, covered the 1983–84, 1984–85, and 1985–86 terms. The second supplement spanned the 1986–87, 1987–88, 1988–89, and 1989–90 terms. As with the two earlier supplements, the same guidelines remain:

(1) Chapters 1 and 8 of the original volume, the chapters on "Constitutionalism" and "Legal Words and Phrases," have not been revised.

(2) The other six chapters are moved up one chapter number each in the Table of Contents. In the original *Dictionary* the First Amendment was Chapter 2, following "Constitutionalism." In this third supplement it is Chapter 1, and so forth.

(3) All *See also* page number references are keyed to the original work. It is a good idea therefore to have the original *Dictionary* and the preceding supplements at hand when using this supplement.

(4) Rather than include parts of cases that have been modified since publication of the original volume and the earlier supplements, we have included the entire case representing the matter as it now stands in constitutional law. When a new case modifies or replaces an older one, the new standards are emphasized in the *Significance* section. The alphabetical list of cases at the beginning of the supplement assembles all the new cases appearing for the first time. There are 108 cases contained in this list that have not been discussed in either the original *Dictionary* or the two earlier supplements. The new cases are also listed at the beginning of the chapters in which they appear. The reader should bear in mind that in most instances the new cases are introduced in the earlier discussions of older cases, which are also listed at the beginning of each chapter with the new cases listed directly under them. Case names appearing in uppercase letters indicate complete new entries. There are 22 such new entries. These new entries represent decisions that overturned or substantially modified previous doctrine.

(5) In some instances the complete citation is unavailable because reference page numbers have not been assigned. This is particularly true of cases decided in 1994. The citation from the *Lawyers Edition* is included for every case.

(6) Supreme Court justices appointed since the last supplement have been added to Appendix C and Appendix D, which are reproduced in full in this supplement.

We are very grateful for the good reception *The Constitutional Law Dictionary: Individual Rights* has received, and we hope this third supplement will make it even more useful.

—Ralph C. Chandler
Professor of Political Science
Western Michigan University

—Richard A. Enslen
United States District Judge
Western District of Michigan

—Peter G. Renstrom
Professor of Political Science
Western Michigan University

ACKNOWLEDGMENT

The authors have discussed many of these same cases in *Constitutional Law Deskbook,* published by the Lawyers Co-operative Publishing Company of Rochester, New York. Lawyers Co-op has allowed us to use portions of text from that volume and other material edited from the annual supplements to the *Deskbook.* We greatly appreciate Lawyers Co-op's consideration and cooperation in the preparation of this volume.

ALPHABETICAL LIST OF NEW CASE ENTRIES

Capitalized cases are discussed in the definitional portion of a new entry. Cases listed in lowercase are discussed in the Significance sections of other cases.

The Constitutional Law Dictionary

1. The First Amendment

The Constitutional Law Dictionary

Free Speech

Free Press

Assembly and Protest

Association

ESTABLISHMENT OF RELIGION

Graduation Ceremonies

Lee v. Weisman, 505 U.S. __, 120 L. Ed. 2d 467, 112 S. Ct. 2649 (1992)
Prohibited clergy-led prayer at public school ceremonies. The Providence, Rhode Island, School Department conducts promotional and graduation ceremonies for its middle and high school students each spring. Invocations and benedictions offered by local clergy are allowed at these ceremonies at the discretion of the school principal. It is agreed by the School Department that the recitations by the clergy are prayers. Student attendance at these ceremonies is voluntary. In addition to the challenge to the ceremonial practice, it was anticipated that the case could provide the Court with an opportunity to reconsider the three-pronged test from *Lemon v. Kurtzman* (403 U.S. 602: 1971). An alternative to the *Lemon* criteria might permit greater presence for religion in public activities. The Providence Schools argued that the proper establishment test should hinge on whether the government coerces people toward some "official" view of religion. This coercion of religious belief test was seen as providing the appropriate balance between keeping government away from matters of conscience, but at the same time protecting a right of public expression of religious beliefs. The Bush Administration offered arguments in support of the Providence Schools' position. In a 5–4 decision, the Court ruled that prayers at these ceremonies were not allowed under the Establishment Clause. Justice Kennedy wrote for the majority of Blackmun, Stevens, O'Connor, and Souter. Because the state's involvement with religious content was so "pervasive" in this case, the Court found it possible to make a decision "without reconsidering the general constitutional framework" by which establishment issues are examined. Kennedy reviewed the choices attributable to the state in the Providence case. First, the school principal had authority to decide whether or not to have prayers. Second, the principal had the choice of the participating clergy. Finally, the principal provided the clergy with guidance as to the content of the prayers. It was the Court's conclusion

that such state involvement with these prayers violated "central principles" of the Establishment Clause. Kennedy stated, "One timeless lesson [of the First Amendment] is that if citizens are subjected to state-sponsored religious exercises, the State disavows its duty to guard and respect that sphere of inviolable conscience and belief which is the mark of a free people." If the prayers are allowed at these ceremonies, objectors would face the dilemma of "participating, with all that implies, or protesting." Primary and secondary level students ought not be forced to make such a choice. Voluntary attendance at these ceremonies was seen as insufficient to save them. High school graduation is "one of life's most important occasions." It is for this reason that the school district argued that prayer ought to be included. Kennedy countered that this "becomes one of the principal reasons why their argument must fail." The state is not allowed, he concluded, "to exact religious conformity from a student as the price of attending her own high school graduation." Justice Scalia issued a dissent joined by Rehnquist, White, and Thomas. He said the Court's decision to prohibit invocations and benedictions "lays waste a tradition that is as old as public school graduation ceremonies themselves...," and eliminates a component of an "even more longstanding American tradition of nonsectarian prayer to God at public celebrations generally...." The "deeper flaw," according to Scalia, was that no one was "legally coerced" into reciting or subscribing to the content of the officially sponsored nondenominational invocation and benediction read by the clergyman at these ceremonies. As a result, the dissenters saw no Establishment Clause violation. *See also* ESTABLISHMENT CLAUSE, p. 408; *LEMON v. KURTZMAN* (403 U.S. 602: 1971), p. 92.

Significance   The criteria currently used by the Court to determine if a government action violates the Establishment Clause were fashioned in *Lemon v. Kurtzman* (403 U.S. 602: 1971). The *Lemon* test requires that a State show that the action under review has a secular purpose, does not have a primary effect that either advances or inhibits religion, and does not excessively entangle government and church. Under *Lemon,* a government initiative is permissible only if all three parts of the test are met. The *Lemon* test has come under sharp criticism by several members of the Rehnquist Court who feel it too stringent; that it prevents even marginal contact of government and religion. Justice Kennedy, for example, said in his dissent in *Allegheny County v. American Civil Liberties Union* (492 U.S. 573: 1989) that the *Lemon* standard prevents even marginal contact of government and religion. Indeed, in his view the test produced outcomes that reflect "unjustified hostility toward religion." This view was generally shared by the Reagan and Bush administrations. Their preference was to substitute for the *Lemon* test a single criterion based on governmental coercion. The Bush administration argued in *Lee v. Weisman* that prayer at graduation ceremonies is not coercive and is nothing more than a "ceremonial acknowledgement of the heritage of a deeply religious people." Justice Kennedy was seen as the pivotal vote on retaining the *Lemon* criteria. Based on his dissent in *Allegheny County,* it was expected that he would vote to overrule *Lemon.* He did not do so. Rather, he concluded that the school district's role in organizing and sponsoring the graduation ceremony was so obviously barred by the Establishment Clause that reconsideration of *Lemon* was not necessary. The replacement of Justice White, one of the *Lee* dissenters, probably insures retention of *Lemon,* at least for the short term.

Public Access to Facilities

***Board of Education of the Westside Community Schools v. Mergens,* 496 U.S. 226, 110 L. Ed. 2d 191, 110 S. Ct. 2356 (1990)** Reviewed the Equal Access Act of 1984, which requires public secondary schools receiving federal educational funds to allow political or religious student groups to meet on school premises provided other non–curriculum-related groups do so. Under the act, a school need not permit any student group to use facilities beyond those related to the curriculum. If at least one group unrelated to the school curriculum has access, however, the school becomes a "limited open forum," and religious or political groups must be able to access the same facilities as well. The Court upheld the act against Establishment Clause challenge. The Court first determined that the school district allowed non–curriculum-related groups to meet. The school district had a formal policy recognizing that student clubs are a "vital part of the education program." About 30 student clubs voluntarily met on school premises at the time Mergens sought access for a Christian Bible club. As a result, the act's equal access obligations were triggered. The question then became whether the act violated the Establishment Clause. It was argued that if a school district permitted religious groups to use school facilities, it would constitute an official recognition or endorsement of religion. The Court disagreed. The Court had ruled in *Widmar v. Vincent* (454 U.S. 263: 1981) that an equal access policy was constitutional at the university level. After applying the three-pronged test articulated in *Lemon v. Kurtzman* (403 U.S. 602: 1971), the Court concluded that the "logic of *Widmar* applies with equal force to the Equal Access Act." Congress's reason for enacting the law was to "prevent discrimination against religious and other types of speech." Such a purpose, said Justice O'Connor, "is undeniably secular." Neither did access to facilities advance religion. There is a "crucial difference between government speech endorsing religion, and private speech endorsing religion." The Court concluded that high school students were "mature enough and likely to understand that a school does not endorse religion or support student speech that it merely permits on a nondiscriminatory basis." The proposition, O'Connor continued, that "schools do not endorse everything they fail to censor is not complicated." Indeed, Congress specifically rejected the contention that high school students are "likely to confuse an equal access policy with state sponsorship of religion." Furthermore, the act limits participation of school officials at meetings of student religious organizations and requires that meetings occur during noninstructional time. As a result, the act "avoids the problems of 'the students' emulation of teachers as role models' and 'mandatory attendance requirements.'" The Court acknowledged that the possibility of student peer pressure remained. It concluded, however, that a school can make clear that permitting a religious club to use facilities is not an endorsement of the club members' views. To the extent it does so, students will "reasonably understand that the school's official recognition of the club evinces neutrality toward, rather than endorsement of, religious speech." In addition, the district recognized a "broad spectrum" of organizations and invited the organization of more clubs. This "counteract[s] any possible message of official endorsement of or a preference for religion or a particular belief." Lastly, the Court found little risk of excessive entanglement in the situation. Although the act permits assignment of a school staff member to meetings for "custodial purposes," such oversight of a student-initiated religious group is "merely to ensure order and good behavior." This does not "impermissibly entangle government in the day-to-day surveillance or administration of religious activities." Justice Stevens dissented. He would have interpreted the act more narrowly, such that access could be restricted. In his view, the Court's ruling required an open-door policy for any group "no matter how controversial or distasteful its views may be." *See also* ESTABLISHMENT CLAUSE, p. 408.

Significance   *Mergens* once again gave the Court the opportunity to examine that zone of ambiguity between First Amendment expression and establishment of religion interests. As in *Widmar* before it, the Court chose in favor of the expression interests. In *Widmar*, a state university denied use of its facilities to a group wishing to use those facilities for religious worship and religious discussion. The Court held that the denial of access was unjustified. The Court found the university had "discriminated against student groups and speakers based on their desire to use a generally open forum to engage in religious worship and discussion." While religious groups may benefit from use of the university facilities, "enjoyment of merely 'incidental' benefits does not violate the prohibition against the 'primary advancement' of religion." That the benefits would be incidental was based on the Court's view that "an open forum does not confer any imprimatur of state approval on religious sects or practices." Furthermore, the facilities were available to a "broad class of nonreligious as well as religious speakers." The provision of benefits to "so broad a spectrum of groups is an important index of secular effect." While a state university must avoid any activity that would have the effect of advancing religion, the Establishment Clause does not provide a compelling enough interest to allow singling out religion for exclusion from access to university facilities. The Court considered a similar problem in *Lamb's Chapel v. Center Moriches Union Free School District* (124 L. Ed. 2d 352: 1993). New York law allows local public school districts to establish policies permitting use of school property after school hours. The statute sets forth ten specific purposes for which school property may be used, but does not include in the list the use of property for religious purposes. Under terms of this law, the Center Moriches School District fashioned rules allowing, among other things, use of its school facilities for social, civic, and recreational purposes. The District categorically prohibited use of school facilities by any group for religious purposes. A local church unsuccessfully sought access to school property to show a film series on family values and child rearing. A unanimous Supreme Court ruled that denying the church group access to the school facilities was unconstitutional on free speech grounds. The First Amendment forbids the government from regulating speech in ways that "favor some viewpoints or ideas at the expense of others."

That the District banned access to all religious groups did not make the policy viewpoint neutral. The film the religious group wished to exhibit dealt with otherwise permissible subject matter, and denial of access for its presentation was, said Justice White, "solely because the film dealt with the subject from a religious standpoint." The denial of access was thus discrimination on the basis of viewpoint. When school property is used by a variety of private organizations, there is "no realistic danger than the community would think that the District was endorsing religion or any particular creed." The content-based limitation on expression is particularly suspect. As the Court held in *Carey v. Brown* (445 U.S. 914: 1980), a case involving selective regulation of labor picketing, "government may not grant the use of a forum to people whose views it finds acceptable, but deny use to those wishing to express less favored or more controversial views." Content discrimination was the central factor here, too. The Court concluded that "selective exclusions from a public forum may not be based on content alone, and may not be justified by reference to content alone." Nevertheless, a state may be able to justify time, place, and manner restrictions on expression so long as they are not selective. In *Heffron v. International Society for Krishna Consciousness, Inc.* (449 U.S. 1109: 1981), the Court upheld a state fair regulation that limited the sale, exhibition, or distribution of printed material only to assigned locations. The Court found the regulation reasonable and applicable to all groups, not merely religious organizations.

Aid to Nonpublic Schools

Lemon v. Kurtzman, 403 U.S. 602, 29 L. Ed. 2d 745, 91 S. Ct. 2105 (1971) Prohibited salary supplements for nonpublic school teachers. *Lemon* involved a Pennsylvania statute which authorized reimbursement to nonpublic schools for expenditures "for teachers, textbooks, and instructional materials." The reimbursement was limited to "courses presented in the curricula of the public schools." A school seeking reimbursement needed to identify the separate costs of the eligible "secular educational service." The contested statute specifically prohibited reimbursement for "any course that contains 'any subject matter expressing religious teaching, or the morals or forms of worship of any sect.'" The Supreme Court struck down the statute in a unanimous decision (Justice Marshall not participating) on the ground that the statute fostered an "excessive entanglement with religion." In assessing the entanglement question, the Court indicated it must "examine the character and purposes of the institutions which are benefitted, the nature of aid that the State provides, and the resulting relationship between the government and the religious authority." The main problem was the "ideological character" of teachers. The Court could not "ignore the dangers that a teacher under religious control and discipline poses to the separation of the religious from the purely secular aspects of precollege education." Although parochial teachers may not intentionally violate First Amendment proscriptions, "a dedicated religious person, teaching in a school affiliated with his or her faith and operated to inculcate its tenets, will inevitably experience great difficulty in remaining religiously neutral." If a state is to make reimbursements available, it must be certain that subsidized teachers do not inculcate religion. The comprehensive and continuing surveillance required to maintain that limit itself becomes an establishment defect since the "prophylactic contacts will involve excessive and enduring entanglement between state and church." Ongoing inspection of school records is a "relationship pregnant with dangers of excessive government direction in church schools." Finally, the Court found entanglement of a different character created by the "divisive political potential of state programs." Continuation of such state assistance will "entail considerable political activity." While political debate is normally a "healthy manifestation of our democratic system, political division along religious lines was one of the principal evils against which the First Amendment was intended to protect." *See also* CPEARL v. NYQUIST (413 U.S. 756: 1973), p. 94; *TILTON v. RICHARDSON* (403 U.S. 672: 1971), p. 82; *WOLMAN v. WALTER* (433 U.S. 406: 1977), p. 96.

Significance   *Lemon v. Kurtzman* clearly reflected the decisive role of the entanglement criterion in establishment cases. The Burger Court's reliance on that criterion did not diminish. The Court again noted the difference between precollege levels of education and higher education as it had defined the distinction in *Tilton v. Richardson* (403 U.S. 672: 1971). Religious indoctrination is only an incidental purpose of education at the college level while educational objectives at the lower levels have a "substantial religious character." *Lemon* emphasizes that the Court sees programs at the elementary and secondary levels as inherently susceptible to entanglement problems. *Lemon* also casts serious doubt on purchase-of-service programs. Monitoring personnel, especially teachers, would be an ongoing obligation which would excessively entangle government and the church school. Transportation and books, on the other hand, have no content to be evaluated or they are subject only to a onetime review. Service items are much more difficult to fit into child benefit coverage than are books and transportation. *Lemon* involved an irresolvable establishment problem. Religion would obviously be advanced in violation of the purpose and effects criteria without the surveillance of teachers. At the same time, the maintenance of a monitoring system produces entanglement defects. *Lemon* added another dimension to the entanglement test. As nonpublic schools encounter greater financial difficulty, demands to retain or expand aid programs will grow and communities will be divided along religious lines. Such community divisiveness is an end the Establishment Clause must seek to avoid.

The Court reaffirmed the *Lemon* ruling in two shared time cases in 1985. In *Grand Rapids School District v. Ball* (473 U.S. 373) and *Aguilar v. Felton* (473 U.S. 402), it struck down programs in public school systems which sent teachers into nonpublic schools to provide remedial instruction. These programs were seen as advancing religion and fostering an excessively entangled relationship between government and religion. The Court said that state-paid teachers, "influenced by the pervasively sectarian nature of the religious schools in which they work," may subtly or overtly indoctrinate students with particular religious views at public expense. The symbolic union of church and state inherent in the provision of secular, state-provided instruction in religious school buildings "threatens to convey a message of state support for religion." The Court said the effect of the programs is to subsidize the religious functions of the parochial schools by taking over a substantial portion of the responsibility for secular subjects.

Ball and *Felton* returned to center stage in a case decided in 1994. The Village of Joel is a community in southeast New York populated exclusively by Satmar Hasidic Jews. The village was incorporated in 1977 out of what was formerly a portion of the town of Monroe. The Satmars are an extremely conservative Jewish sect. They wish to insulate themselves from interactions with nonresidents of the village as much as possible; virtually all of the school-age children of the village attend private religious schools. There are a number of village children, however, who are handicapped or disabled in some way and require special attention. At the time the village was incorporated, these students received state and federally funded special services at the religious schools from teachers and other staff of the Monroe-Woodbury School District. Several years later, the Supreme Court ruled in *Ball* and *Aguilar* that public school staff could not deliver any services at private religious school sites. The arrangement between the Monroe-Woodbury School District and the Satmar village fell within the reach of the ruling and was terminated. Hasidic parents then had to choose whether to send their children to public schools in order to receive the special services, or go without those services altogether. Most chose the latter, fearing that their children would be ridiculed because of their language (the students spoke only Yiddish), dress, and manner. In 1989, New York enacted a law establishing a separate public school district, Kiryas Joel Village School District (KJVSD), for the village. The sole function of the new district was to provide special education services to the special needs children of the village and other Hasidic communities located nearby. The law was challenged on establishment grounds. In a 6–3 decision, the Supreme Court struck down the law in *Board of Education of the Kiryas Joel Village School District v. Grumet* (129 L. Ed. 2d 546: 1994). Justice Souter said that the Constitution "allows the state to accommodate religious needs by alleviating special burdens." There is no doubt that there is "ample room" under the Establishment Clause for "benevolent neutrality" which permits religious exercise to exist "without sponsorship and without interference." Accommodation, however, is not a "principle without limits." What New York attempted here was an "adjustment to the Satmars' religiously grounded preferences that our cases do not countenance...." Souter emphasized that invalidation of this statute did not preclude accommodation. The problem with this statute was that it was "tantamount to an allocation of political power on a religious criterion...." Accommodation is possible as long as it is "implemented through generally applicable legislation." The Court's ruling, Souter repeated, did not "disable a religiously homogeneous group from exercising political power conferred on it without regard to religion." The line chosen for drawing the Kiryas Joel Village School District, on the other hand, was one "purposely drawn to separate Satmars from non-Satmars...." The Court in this case was "clearly constrained to conclude" that the statute failed the test of neutrality. The Establishment Clause precludes the government from treating people differently "based on the God or gods they worship, or don't worship." Accommodations may justify treating those who share a deeply held religious belief from those who do not, but such accommodations do not justify "discriminations based on sect." Justice Scalia said in dissent that the Founding Fathers would be "astonished" to find that the Establishment Clause could be employed to "prohibit characteristically and admirably American accommodation of the religious practices (or more precisely, cultural peculiarities) of a tiny minority sect." He again criticized the Court's recent Establishment Clause decisions. "Once this Court has abandoned text and history as guides, nothing prevents it from calling religious toleration the establishment of religion."

The "conveying a message" criterion was coupled with the "student benefit" doctrine in *Witters v. Washington Department of Services for the Blind* (474 U.S. 481: 1986). Witters suffered from a condition which made him eligible for state vocational rehabilitation assistance for blind persons. He sought such assistance to cover the costs of his studies at a Christian college where he was engaged in a program leading to a religious vocation. The aid was denied on the ground that public money could not be used to obtain religious instruction. The Court ruled, however, that such aid did not advance religion. The aid was given directly to Witters and any money which eventually gets to religious institutions in these circumstances comes as a result of the "genuinely independent and private choices of the aid recipients." That Witters chose to use the aid in this way did not confer any message of state endorsement of religion. The Court ruled in *Zobrest v. Catalina Foothills School District* (125 L. Ed. 2d 1: 1993) that a public school district could place a sign language interpreter for a deaf child in a parochial school without violating the Establishment Clause. He said that the First Amendment has never "disabled" religious institutions from participating in publicly sponsored social welfare programs. To the contrary, the Court has "consistently held that government programs that neutrally provide benefits to a broad class of citizens defined without reference to religion are not readily subject to an Establishment Clause challenge just because sectarian institutions also receive an attenuated financial benefit." Rehnquist observed that if religious groups were precluded by the Establishment Clause from receiving general governmental benefits, a church could not, for example, be protected by police or fire departments. The Court saw the service at issue in this case as a general government program that distributes benefits neutrally to any student qualifying as handicapped under terns of the Individuals with Disabilities Education Act (IDEA). Because IDEA "creates no financial incentive for parents to choose a sectarian school," said Rehnquist, "an interpreter's presence there cannot be attributed to state decision-making."

FREE EXERCISE OF RELIGION

Ceremonial Rituals

Employment Division v. Smith, **494 U.S. 872, 108 L. Ed. 2d 876, 110 S. Ct. 1595 (1990)**   Ruled that a state could withhold benefits from employees terminated from their jobs for use of peyote, a controlled hallucinogen. Oregon had refused to pay benefits because use of peyote was a crime in the state, and termination for its use constituted "misconduct," thereby making employees ineligible for benefits. The employees in this case had used the peyote in the sacramental rituals of the Native American Church and sought exemption on free exercise grounds. The Court ruled that while the state legislature could have established such an exemption, the Free Exercise Clause did not require it. "We have never held," said Justice Scalia, that an "individual's beliefs excuse him from compliance with an otherwise valid law prohibiting conduct that the State is free to regulate." As long as religion is not itself the object of the regulation, and any burden is "merely the incidental effect of a generally applicable and otherwise valid provision, the First Amendment has not been offended." To permit individuals to exempt themselves from such regulations would make "professed doctrines of religious belief superior to the land," and in effect "permit every citizen to become a law unto himself." In addition, the Court ruled that the balancing test set forth in *Sherbert v. Verner* (374 U.S. 398: 1963) was inapplicable here. The *Sherbert* test, said the Court, was "developed in a context that lent itself to individualized governmental assessment of the reasons for the relevant conduct." The test is not appropriate, on the other hand, for the challenge of an "across-the-board criminal prohibition on a particular form of conduct." The government's ability to enact and enforce generally applicable regulations of "socially harmful conduct cannot depend on measuring the effects of a governmental action on a religious objector's spiritual development." To make an individual's obligation to comply with a law "contingent on the law's coincidence with his religious beliefs, except where the State's interest is 'compelling,' contradicts both constitutional tradition and common sense." Justices Blackmun, Brennan, and Marshall applied the *Sherbert* balancing test and concluded that the failure of Oregon to make an exception for religious uses of peyote did not outweigh Smith's free exercise interests. *See also* FREE EXERCISE CLAUSE, p. 413; *SHERBERT v. VERNER* (374 U.S. 398: 1963), p. 103.

Significance   The Court's opinion in *Smith* emphasized two critical free exercise concepts. The first is that a law must have a secular purpose and, second, it must be applied generally. In other words, a law cannot regulate the actions of a particular religious group. An example of a law that does not meet these criteria is *Church of the Lukumi Babalu Aye, Inc. v. City of Hialeah, Florida* (124 L. Ed. 2d 472: 1993). The free exercise claim was asserted on behalf of practitioners of the Santeria religion. A basic tenet of the religion is the development of personal relationships with spirits (orishas). These spirits, while possessing substantial power under the religion, are not immortal. Rather, they are sustained by periodic ritual sacrifice of animals. In April 1987, the Church of the Lukumi Babalu Aye (Church) leased land in Hialeah, Florida and announced its intention to establish a Santeria church in the community. The prospect of a Santeria church in the area was "distressing" to many members of the Hialeah community. In September 1987, the City of Hialeah adopted ordinances that, among other things, increased the penalty for animal cruelty and prohibited "possession, sacrifice or slaughter" of certain animals within the city (licensed slaughterhouse were excepted). Sacrifice was defined as to "unnecessarily kill, torment, torture, or mutilate an animal in a public or private ritual or ceremony not for the primary purpose of food consumption." A unanimous Supreme Court supported the Church's free exercise challenge. The Court's review of the ordinances "confirm[ed] that the laws in question were enacted by officials who did not understand, failed to perceive, or chose to ignore the fact that their official actions violated the Nation's essential commitment to religious freedom." There was no doubt that Santeria is a "religion" entitled to First Amendment protection. Although animal sacrifice may be unacceptable or abhorrent to some, religious beliefs need not be "acceptable, logical, consistent, or comprehensible to others" to qualify for First Amendment protection. If the purpose of a law is to "infringe upon or restrict practices because of their religious motivation, the law is not neutral," and it is invalid unless the government can demonstrate that the law serves a compelling interest and is narrowly tailored in doing so. The design of these ordinances impermissibly targets the religious practices of the Church. The inquiry into the neutrality of the ordinance led the Court to conclude that they "had as their object the suppression of religion." The Court noted a pattern of "animosity" toward Santeria adherents and their religious practices. The ordinances were "gerrymandered with care" to regulate religious but not secular killing of animals. Furthermore, the ordinances suppressed "much more religious conduct than is necessary" in order to achieve the asserted ends. Essential to the protection of free exercise rights is the principle that government cannot "in a selective manner impose burdens only to conduct motivated by religious belief." Without precisely defining a general applicability standard, it was the Court's judgment that Hialeah's ordinances "fall well below the minimum standard" necessary to protect First Amendment rights.

FREE SPEECH

Hate Speech

R.A.V. v. St. Paul, **505 U.S. __, 120 L. Ed. 2d 305, 112 S. Ct. 2538 (1992)**
Struck down a local "hate crime" ordinance. The City of St. Paul, Minnesota, made it a misdemeanor to engage in speech or conduct likely to "arouse anger, alarm, or resentment in others on the basis of race, color, creed, religion or gender." The ordinance was challenged by a juvenile charged with violating the law by burning a cross on a black family's lawn. All nine members of the Court agreed that the ordinance violated the First Amendment, but the Court was deeply split on its reasons for that conclusion. Justice Scalia's opinion, joined by Rehnquist, Kennedy, Souter, and Thomas, regarded the regulation as facially unconstitutional because it prohibited speech solely on the basis of its content. Under the ordinance, expression containing "abusive invective" is permissible unless it "addressed one of the specified disfavored topics." The First Amendment, said Scalia, does not permit St. Paul to "impose special prohibitions on those speakers who express views on disfavored subjects." The ordinance had not focused on threatening expression. Rather, it proscribed "fighting words of whatever manner" that communicated intolerant messages about race, gender, or religion. "Selectivity of this sort creates the possibility that the city is seeking to handicap the expression of particular ideas." The question for these five justices was whether "content discrimination is reasonably necessary" to achieve a compelling interest. Their answer was "plainly not." The only interest served by the content limitations was the city council's "special hostility towards the particular biases thus singled out." Scalia concluded, "That is precisely what the First Amendment forbids." Justice White felt the ordinance was fatally overbroad, but was critical of the majority's "simplistic, all or nothing-at-all approach" to dealing with fighting words. White said Scalia's opinion signaled that "expressions of violence...are of sufficient value to outweigh the social interest in order and morality that has traditionally placed such fighting words outside the First Amendment." White felt regulation of all or some fighting words to restrict the "social evil of hate speech" could be crafted "without creating the danger of driving viewpoints from the market place." Similarly, Blackmun saw no First Amendment values "compromised by a law that prohibits hoodlums from driving minorities out of their homes...." To the contrary, he saw "great harm in preventing the people of St. Paul from specifically punishing the race-based fighting words that so prejudice their community." Justice Stevens said the Court "wreaks havoc in an area of settled law" by its disruption of a "rough hierarchy in the constitutional

protection of speech." They said the Court's holding that content-based regulations are "presumptively invalid" was a premise that has "simplistic appeal, but lacks support in our First Amendment jurisprudence." Stevens said conduct that creates "special risks or causes special harms may be prohibited by special rules." *See also* COHEN *v.* CALIFORNIA (403 U.S. 15: 1971), p. 114; FREE SPEECH CLAUSE, p. 416; OFFENSIVE SPEECH, p. 438.

Significance   The issue of what to do about hate speech presents difficult First Amendment problems. The City of St. Paul unsuccessfully tried to regulate "hateful" speech by banning it. A different approach was attempted in Wisconsin by authoring longer sentences for those criminal offenders who select their victims on the basis of "race, religion, color, disability, sexual orientation, national origin or ancestry." Todd Mitchell was convicted of aggravated battery, an offense that typically carries a two year maximum sentence in Wisconsin. Mitchell was sentenced to four years, however, because the jury determined that he had chosen intentionally his victim on the basis of race. The Wisconsin Supreme Court, citing *R.A.V.,* ruled for Mitchell. According to the state court, the Wisconsin legislature criminalized "bigoted thought with which it disagree[d]." A unanimous U.S. Supreme Court upheld the policy, however, in *Wisconsin v. Mitchell* (124 L. Ed. 2d 436: 1993). Chief Justice Rehnquist found the argument that the enhanced sentence punishes only conduct to be "literally correct," but not wholly dispositive. The Court, he said, has rejected the view that "an apparently limitless variety of conduct" can be labeled speech whenever a person engaged in the conduct "intends to express an idea." Accordingly, a physical assault "is not by any stretch of the imagination expressive conduct protected by the First Amendment." At the same time, the threshold condition for triggering the enhanced sentence is discriminatory motive in the selection of a particular victim. In other words, the Wisconsin law punishes someone more severely for conduct "motivated by a discriminatory point of view" than for the same conduct "engaged in for some other reason or for no reason at all." Rehnquist resolved the problem in the state's favor in two ways. He said state legislatures possess "primary responsibility for fixing criminal penalties." As a result, state legislatures may reasonably decide that bias-motivated offenses warrant more substantial penalties. Motive plays the "same role" in Wisconsin's statute as it plays in federal and state antidiscrimination laws—laws previously upheld against constitutional challenge. Furthermore, judges who are about to sentence criminal offenders have traditionally been able to consider a "wide variety of factors" beyond the evidence directly bearing on guilt in determining an appropriate sentence. One such important factor is the defendant's motive for committing the crime. He saw the definition of aggravating circumstances for capital crimes as analogous. Rehnquist then distinguished the Wisconsin law from the ordinance struck down in the St. Paul case. There the ordinance had selectively targeted speech deemed offensive and, thus, violated the prohibition against "content-based discrimination." The Wisconsin law, on the other hand, aims at "conduct unprotected by the First Amendment." In addition, the Wisconsin statute selected bias-motivated crimes for enhanced penalty because this kind of conduct is "thought to inflict greater individual and societal harm." The Court concluded that a state's "desire to redress these perceived harms provides an adequate explanation for its penalty-enhancement provisions over and above mere disagreement with offenders' beliefs or biases."

FREE PRESS

Libel

Masson v. New Yorker Magazine, Inc., **501 U.S. 496, 115 L. Ed. 2d 447, 111 S. Ct. 2419 (1991)** The question in *Masson* was whether fabricated quotations attributed to a public figure are recklessly false enough to go to trial in a libel action. Masson, a psychoanalyst, was the subject of an unfavorable article by Janet Malcom that appeared in *The New Yorker*. Before writing the article, Malcolm interviewed Masson extensively. Most of the interview sessions were taped. There were, however, several statements attributed to Masson for which there was no recording. Masson filed a libel action claiming that several statements enclosed in quotation marks were fabricated or deliberately misrepresented. The lower federal courts ruled for *The New Yorker,* concluding that while Malcolm had deliberately altered the quotations, the inaccuracies did not raise a jury question of actual malice. The Supreme Court reversed in a 7–2 decision. According to Justice Kennedy, the constitutional question, in the framework of a motion for summary judgment, was whether the evidence was sufficient to show a publisher "acted with the requisite knowledge of falsity or reckless disregard as to truth or falsity." Key to the Court's inquiry was the concept of falsity—whether the "requisite falsity inheres in the attribution of words to the petitioner [Masson] which he did not speak." Kennedy acknowledged that any "alteration of a verbatim quotation is false," but this falsity is only technical. The Court's view reflected a recognition of the difficulties faced by writers to "edit and make intelligible a speaker's perhaps rambling comments." Some alterations may only make minor changes to correct grammar or syntax. This kind of alteration clearly does not show actual malice. Indeed, the Court rejected the argument that a change beyond the correction of grammar or syntax proves falsity "in the sense relevant to determining actual malice." If an author, said Kennedy, changes a speaker's words but "effects no material change in meaning, including any meaning conveyed by the manner or fact of expression, the speaker suffers no injury to reputation that is compensable as defamation." The Court refused to make determination of the falsity of quotations as a special kind of libel inquiry. Rather, the Court applied its long-standing definition of actual malice. A statement is not considered false unless it "would have a different effect on the mind of the reader from that which the pleaded truth would have produced." A deliberate alteration of a speaker's words does not constitute knowledge of falsity, Kennedy concluded, "unless the alteration results in a material change in the meaning of the statement." Using quotation marks to attribute words not in fact spoken "bears in a most important way on the inquiry, but it is not dispositive in every case." Justices White and Scalia dissented. They found sufficient proof of malice in the knowing publication of false attribution. *See also* FREE PRESS CLAUSE, p. 415; LIBEL, p. 433; *NEW YORK TIMES v. SULLIVAN* (376 U.S. 254: 1964), p. 121.

Significance   *Masson* is important both for what it does and what it does not do. The question in this case was whether actual malice might be found when quotations are altered. The Court held that false attribution may or may not reflect such reckless disregard for the truth. The Court did rule that the First Amendment does not categorically insulate writers who choose to change quotations. Some changes may not materially affect content. In those cases, requisite malice cannot be found. More importantly, the Court refused to establish an independent set of review criteria for this kind of libel issue. Instead, the Court retained the actual malice rule established in *New York Times v. Sullivan* (376 U.S. 254: 1964). *Masson* did not substantially affect the public figure concept. While the decision did not rule out the recovery of damages for fabrication of quotes from public figures, it required the plaintiff to demonstrate actual malice based on alterations that produced "material change" in the meaning of the statement.

Royalty Forfeiture

Simon & Schuster, Inc. v. New York State Crime Victims Board, **502 U.S. 105, 116 L. Ed. 2d 476, 112 S. Ct. 501 (1991)**   Almost all the states have laws designed to prevent criminals from profiting from their crimes by selling their stories to book publishers or film makers. The Court's ruling in *Simon & Schuster* declared such laws unconstitutional. New York enacted such a law in 1977 soon after the arrest of David Berkowitz, an alleged serial killer. Berkowitz was popularly known as "Son of Sam," and New York's law became known as the "Son of Sam" law. Under terms of the law, any money earned by persons who admit to criminal conduct through their expressive works is placed in escrow and held for distribution to eligible victims for a five-year period. Initially, the New York law applied only to those convicted of a crime. Because Berkowitz was found incompetent to stand trial, the law was never applied to him. This case arose out of a contractual agreement between Simon & Schuster and an organized crime figure, Henry Hill, who had produced a book about his criminal life. The Crime Victims Board determined the book to be covered by the Son of Sam law, ordered Hill to turn over payments already received, and ordered Simon & Schuster to turn over all future money payable to Hill. Simon & Schuster brought suit seeking declaration that the law was incompatible with the First Amendment. A unanimous Supreme Court agreed with the publisher. Justice O'Connor said that a statute is "presumptively inconsistent" with the First Amendment if it "imposes a financial burden on speakers because of the content of their speech." The Court found the Son of Sam law to be such a content-based statute. The law "singles out income derived from expressive activity for a burden the State places on no other income, and it is directed only at works with a specified content." The financial disincentive of the law, said O'Connor, was placed "only on speech of a particular content." The Court acknowledged the state's compelling interest in ensuring that victims of crime are compensated by those who commit crime. Similarly, a state may attempt to make sure that criminals do not profit from their criminal conduct. O'Connor pointed to laws, including those in New York, which require forfeiture of the proceeds of criminal behavior. The Son of Sam law defined the state's interest more narrowly—to ensure that criminals "do not profit from storytelling about their crimes before their victims have a meaningful opportunity to be compensated for their injuries." The state's interest in targeting the proceeds from storytelling about their crimes in on "far shakier ground." As distinct from the compelling interest to compensate crime victims, the state has "little interest in limiting such compensation to the proceeds of wrongdoers' speech about the crime." Furthermore, the law was fatally "overinclusive." The law applied to works on "any subject, provided that they express the author's thoughts or recollections about his crime, however tangentially or incidentally." The law also reached crimes an author admitted to and then discussed whether or not the author was ever formally accused of such crimes. The Court concluded that such a law reached too "wide a range of literature" to pass First Amendment scrutiny. *See also* FREE PRESS CLAUSE, p. 415.

Significance   Regulation of the press requires that a "compelling" government interest is served or advanced. Even more problematic are regulations that apply differently to different subjects. Such differential regulations are "presumptively inconsistent" with the First Amendment because they may allow the government to censor certain material on a content basis. In *Simon & Schuster,* the Court found content-based burdens on expression to be excessive. Even if speech is otherwise proscribable, the New York regulation constituted content discrimination. The Court also concluded that the legitimate interest of compensating crime victims could occur in ways that are less burdensome on expression. The Court came to a slightly different conclusion in *Leathers v. Medlock* (499 U.S. 439: 1991). Arkansas taxed all sales of property or services with the exception of newspaper or magazine sales. The law was amended to include the sale of cable television services. The issue in this case was whether the state could tax some of the broadcast media while excepting the print media from similar taxation. The Court ruled that differential taxation of media does not in itself produce a First Amendment violation. The Arkansas tax was not seen as one that singled out the media nor did it intentionally target cable television in a "purposeful attempt to interfere with its First Amendment activities." Furthermore, there was nothing in the law that referred to the content of mass media communications. In other words, the tax did not discriminate on the basis of content, as was the case in *Simon & Schuster.*

Commercial Press

***Central Hudson Gas & Electric Corp. v. New York Public Service Commission,*
447 U.S. 557, 65 L. Ed. 2d 341, 100 S. Ct. 2343 (1980)** Struck down a state regulation prohibiting promotional advertising by electric utilities. In the wake of a fuel shortage, the Public Service Commission ordered electric utilities in New York to stop all "promotional" advertising—advertising intended to increase sales of utilities. The ban on promotional advertising was continued even after the fuel shortage had eased. The state's interest in conserving energy and fair utility rates provided the basis for the advertising ban. Throughout this period, the electric utilities were permitted to continue "institutional and informational advertising"—a category "inclusive of all advertising not intended to promote sales." The Court of Appeals of New York upheld the advertising regulation. With only Justice Rehnquist dissenting, the U.S. Supreme Court reversed. Justice Powell pointed to the long-standing distinction between "speech proposing a commercial transaction" and other kinds of speech. While commercial speech is protected, it is accorded lesser protection than other forms of expression. The protection that is extended to commercial speech is a function of the "nature both of the expression and of the governmental interests served by its regulation." Government may certainly regulate communication that is likely to deceive the public or

communication related to unlawful activity. If the regulated communication is neither misleading nor related to illegal activity, the government's power to regulate is "more circumscribed." The state must assert a "substantial interest" to be achieved by the regulation. Further, the method of regulation must be "in proportion" to that interest. Compliance with this requirement, said Powell, "must be measured by two criteria." First, the regulation must "directly advance" the state interest involved. Second, a regulation is excessive if a "more limited restriction" on commercial speech could serve the governmental interest. The Court concluded that the Commission ban did not meet these standards. The fact that Central Hudson held a monopoly on electricity sales in its service area did not, in itself, make the utility subject to regulation. Even in monopoly situations, the suppression of advertising "reduces the information available for consumer decisions," and thus "defeats the purpose" of the First Amendment. In addition, the asserted objectives of energy conservation and fair rates represent a "clear and substantial governmental interest." The "critical inquiry" in this case was whether the complete suppression of promotional advertising was more extensive than necessary to further the state's interests. The Court concluded that the Commission had not shown that a less restrictive regulation on promotional advertising would not be sufficient to adequately serve the state's interest in energy conservation. Indeed, the Commission's ban prevented Central Hudson from promoting services that would reduce energy use by diverting demand from less efficient sources. To the extent the order suppressed expression that in no way impaired the state's interest in energy conservation, it violated the First Amendment. *See also* FREE PRESS CLAUSE, p. 415.

Significance   The commercial speech doctrine had its origin in *Valentine v. Chrestensen* (316 U.S. 52: 1942), a decision that virtually put all commercial speech outside First Amendment coverage. While later decisions narrowed the *Chrestensen* concept of commercial speech, certain regulations were upheld. A representative case is *Pittsburgh Press Company v. Commission on Human Relations* (413 U.S. 376: 1973). Pittsburgh Press was found in violation of a local ordinance because it placed help-wanted advertisements in gender-designated columns. The Commission ordered the newspaper to end the gender-referenced layout of the advertisements, and the Supreme Court affirmed in a 5–4 decision. Pittsburgh Press Company argued that editorial judgment about where to place an advertisement should control, rather than its commercial content. The Court answered that "a newspaper's editorial judgments in connection with an advertisement take on the character of the advertisement, and, in those cases, the scope of the newspaper's First Amendment protection may be affected by the content of the advertisement." The kind of editorial judgment involved in this case did not strip commercial advertising of its commercial character. Even more crucial was the fact that the commercial activity involved was illegal employment discrimination. In the Court's view advertisements could be forbidden in this instance just as advertisements "proposing a sale of narcotics or soliciting prostitution" could be forbidden.

Following *Pittsburgh Press,* the Burger Court narrowed the definition of commercial press. In *Bigelow v. Virginia* (421 U.S. 809: 1975), the Court protected the publication of an advertisement by an organization offering services related to legal abortions in another state. The Court held the advertisement "conveyed information of potential interest and value to a diverse audience," not merely a commercial promotion of services. The next year, in *Virginia State Board of Pharmacy v. Virginia Citizens Consumer Council, Inc.* (425 U.S. 748: 1976), the Court struck down a statute that made advertising of prescription drugs a form of conduct possibly leading to the suspension of that license. The Court argued that even if the advertiser's interest is a purely economic one, such speech is not necessarily disqualified from protection. The consumer and society in general have a "strong interest in the free flow of commercial information." Such a free flow is indispensable in a predominantly free enterprise economy which requires many private economic decisions. *Central Hudson* was a logical continuation of the Court's thinking in *Bigelow* and *State Board of Pharmacy.*

The Rehnquist Court used *Central Hudson* criteria in two 1993 rulings. The Discovery Network is a private company that broadcasts educational and social programs. In addition, it publishes a magazine promoting its programming, but also containing information about current events. The magazines were distributed from freestanding newsracks, 62 of which were located by permit on public property in Cincinnati, Ohio. The city revoked the Discovery Channel's permit to place newsracks on public property. The revocation notice said the magazines were "commercial handbills" within the meaning of a city ordinance that prohibited the distribution of that class of material on public property. The Supreme Court ruled 6–3 against the prohibition in *Cincinnati v. Discovery Network, Inc.* (123 L. Ed. 2d 99: 1993). The Court concluded that Cincinnati had not "carefully calculated the costs and benefits associated with the burden on speech associated with the prohibition." The Court saw no "reasonable fit" between the city's purpose of "preventing visual blight" and its method for achieving it. Even thought the city had not acted with animus toward the content of the Discovery Network's publication, whether a newsrack was subject to the regulation was determined by the "commercial" content of the magazines in any newsrack. Cincinnati did not regulate newsracks generally. Rather, it sought only to eliminate newsracks containing commercial publications. The Court found no justification for such a prohibition other than the city's "naked assertion that commercial speech has low value." The absence of a neutral justification for the "selective ban" on newsracks precluded Cincinnati from "defending its newsrack policy as content neutral."

The State of Florida, through its Board of Accountancy, prohibited direct, in-person solicitation of prospective clients by certified public accountants. The Supreme Court, with only Justice O'Connor dissenting, ruled that the ban violated the First Amendment in *Edenfield v. Zane* (123 L. Ed. 2d 543: 1993). Justice Kennedy observed that while there are "detrimental aspects" to personal commercial solicitations under some circumstances, these detriments are "not so inherent or ubiquitous that solicitation of this sort is removed from the ambit of First Amendment protections." To the contrary, solicitation in the commercial context "may have considerable value." By banning such solicitation, Florida "threatens societal interests in broad access to complete and accurate commercial information" that the First Amendment is designed to protect. The "penultimate prong" of the *Central Hudson* test, said Kennedy, is direct advancement of the state interest. The burden of proof is not satisfied "by mere speculation or conjecture." Rather, a governmental body seeking to justify a restriction on commercial speech must demonstrate that the "harms it recites are real," and that its restriction "will in fact alleviate them to a material degree." Without this requirement, Kennedy continued, a state could with ease restrict commercial speech in the service of other objectives that could not themselves justify a burden on commercial speech. Finally, Florida sought to justify the ban in much the same way as the ban on in-person solicitation by attorneys was upheld by the Court in *Ohralik v. Ohio State Bar Association* (436 U.S. 447: 1978). It was the Court's judgment that solicitation by CPAs "poses none of the same dangers" as solicitation by attorneys. In particular, Justice Kennedy noted that CPA training "emphasizes independence and objectivity, not advocacy," the prospective clients of CPAs are typically "sophisticated and experienced business executives," the manner in which CPAs typically solicit business is "conducive to rational and considered decision making," and, because prospective clients of CPAs are generally in control of the meeting, invasion of privacy is "not a significant concern."

A recent case with the potentially greatest significance on commercial speech doctrine is *City of Ladue v. Gilleo* (129 L. Ed. 2d 36: 1994). Ladue, Missouri, had an ordinance banning all residential signs except those falling within 10 specified exemptions. Among the exemptions were "residence identification" signs, "for sale" signs, and signs warning of safety hazards. Commercial establishments, churches, and nonprofit organizations are allowed to place certain signs that are not allowed at residential sites. Margaret Gilleo placed a 2-foot by 3-foot sign in her yard expressing her opposition to the Persian Gulf War. She was informed that she was in violation of the sign ordinance. She first sought a variance from the ordinance from the city council. When she failed to obtain the variance, she brought action in federal district court and obtained a temporary injunction against enforcement of the ordinance. The city council amended the ordinance by eliminating the language allowing for variances and grandfathering signs already exempted under the original ordinance. Gilleo then amended her complaint and pursued a permanent injunction against the modified ordinance. In the meantime, she replaced her yard sign with a small ($8\frac{1}{2}$ inches by 11 inches) sign which was displayed in a second-story window of her residence. Local authorities judged that she was still in violation of the ordinance. In late 1991, a federal district court granted a permanent injunction against enforcement of the most recent version of the ordinance, and the Supreme Court unanimously affirmed. Justice Stevens began by acknowledging that signs are a "form of expression" protected by the Free Speech Clause. Signs, however, "pose distinctive problems that are subject to municipalities' police powers." Unlike oral speech, signs pose a variety of problems that "legitimately call for regulation." Following a review of relevant cases, Stevens suggested that there are two "analytically distinct" grounds for challenging municipal regulation of sign. One is that the regulation "restricts too little" because its exemptions discriminate on the basis of the signs' content. An impermissibly underinclusive regulation may either attempt to give one side of a "debatable public question an advantage," or place government in a position to "select the permissible subjects for public debate." The Court took Ladue's word that the exemptions in its ordinance were free of "impermissible content or viewpoint discrimination." Stevens then proceeded to the second ground on which regulations might be attacked—that they "simply prohibit too much protected speech." He compared Ladue's ordinance to the one struck down in *Linmark Associates, Inc. v. Willingboro* (431 U.S. 85: 1977). There, the Court held that a municipality's interest in maintaining a "stable, racially integrated neighborhood" was insufficient to support a prohibition of residential "for sale" signs. Ladue argued that the ordinance was intended to minimize "visual clutter" associated with signs. Ladue's interest was "concededly valid, but no more compelling than the interests at stake in *Linmark*." Further, while the *Linmark* ordinance applied only to a form of commercial speech, the Ladue ordinance covered "even such absolutely pivotal speech as a sign protesting an imminent government decision to go to war." The impact of Ladue's ordinance on free communication was seen as "manifestly greater" than in *Linmark*. The ordinance left residents of Ladue with virtually no way to display any sign on their property. Indeed, Stevens suggested that Ladue has "almost completely foreclosed a venerable means of communication that is unique and important." Signs that "react to a local happening or express a view on a controversial issue both reflect and animate change in the life of a community." The Court also was unpersuaded that Ladue's ordinance was nothing more than a "time, place or manner" regulation that left residents with sufficient alternate means to express themselves. Displaying a sign from one's own residence, said Stevens, "often carries a message quite distinct from placing the same sign somewhere else, or conveying the same text or picture by other means." The location of signs provides information about the identity of the speaker, an "important component of many attempts to persuade." While government may need to "mediate among various competing uses, including expressive ones," for public streets and facilities, its "need to regulate temperate speech from the home is surely much less pressing."

Journalist's Privilege

***Branzburg v. Hayes*, 408 U.S. 665, 33 L. Ed. 2d 626, 92 S. Ct. 2646 (1972)** Held that newspersons must disclose sources of information to a grand jury. *Branzburg* rejected the argument of newspersons that they possess a privileged relationship with their sources. After having published reports about drug use and manufacture, Hayes was subpoenaed to appear before a state grand jury and identify those persons he had seen using and making illegal narcotics. Hayes refused to testify and was cited for contempt. Through Justice White, a 5–4 majority of the Supreme Court opined that the First Amendment "does not invalidate every incidental burdening of the press that may result from the enforcement of civil or criminal statutes of general applicability." In balancing the interests of protecting the criminal process and the news gathering function of the press, the former must prevail. The consequential but uncertain burden is not sufficient to treat newspersons differently than any other citizens. They must respond to relevant questions put to them in the course of a valid grand jury investigation or criminal trial. The burden in *Branzburg* was not prior restraint, a tax, a penalty on content, or a compulsion to publish. The Court suggested, however, that the impact of its holding would be limited. "Only where news sources themselves are implicated in crime or possess information relevant to the grand jury's task need they or the reporter be concerned about grand jury subpoenas. Nothing before us indicates that a large number or percentage of all confidential news sources fall into either category." Finally, the Court argued that abuse or harassment of the press would be subject to judicial scrutiny and possible intervention. Justice Stewart issued a dissent in which Justices

Brennan and Marshall concurred. He said the Court had undermined the historic independence of the press by attempting to annex the journalistic profession as an investigative arm of the government. Justice Stewart argued that freedom of the press requires the ability to gather news which, in turn, is often contingent on a confidential relationship of reporter and source. The dissenters would have required the state to show (1) that probable cause exists to believe a newsperson has relevant information; (2) that the information cannot be obtained from any other source; and (3) that the state has a compelling interest in the information. Justice Douglas also dissented. He said that forcing a reporter before a grand jury has "two retarding effects upon the ear and pen of the press." One is that fear of exposure will cause dissidents to communicate less openly to reporters. The other is that concerns about accountability will cause editors and critics to write with more restrained pens. Douglas suggested more generally that the press has a "preferred position in our constitutional scheme." The position of the press is not designed to enhance profit or set newspeople apart as a favored class. It is intended to "bring fulfillment to the public's right to know." *See also* EDITORIAL PRIVILEGE, p. 405; FREE PRESS CLAUSE, p. 415; NEWSPERSON'S PRIVILEGE, p. 436.

Significance　　　*Branzburg* said that even an unconditional freedom to publish would be of limited value if information gathering was unprotected. To protect that function, several states have adopted shield laws designed to protect the confidentiality of sources. No such legislation exists at the federal level, although *Branzburg* did prompt introduction of such proposals. The Burger Court also has rejected other claims of the press regarding its rights in the gathering of information. In *Saxbe v. Washington Post Co.* (417 U.S. 843: 1974), the Court upheld federal prison regulations which prohibited press interviews with designated or particular inmates. The Court said the Constitution does not impose upon government the "affirmative duty to make available to journalists sources of information not available to members of the public generally." Four years later, in *Houchins v. KQED, Inc.* (438 U.S. 1: 1978), the Court upheld a refusal to allow media access to a county jail which had been the site of a prisoner's suicide and other alleged violent incidents, as well as charges of inhumane conditions. The majority saw the case as one involving a "special privilege of access" such as that denied in *Saxbe.* This is "a right which is not essential to guarantee the freedom to communicate or publish." The Court also refused to defer to editorial privilege in the libel case of *Herbert v. Lando* (441 U.S. 153: 1979). Herbert was a retired Army officer with extended service in Vietnam. He received widespread media attention when he accused his superior officers of covering up reports of atrocities and other war crimes. Some three years after Herbert's disclosures, the Columbia Broadcasting System broadcast a report on Herbert and his charges on the television program "60 Minutes." Lando produced and edited the program. He also published an article on Herbert in the *Atlantic Monthly*. Herbert's suit alleged that the "program and article falsely and maliciously portrayed him as a liar and a person who had made war crime charges to explain his relief from command." In attempting to develop proofs for his case, Herbert tried to obtain the testimony of Lando before trial, but Lando refused claiming the First Amendment protected against "inquiry into the state of mind of those who edit, produce, or publish, and into the editorial process." The Supreme Court found against Lando. The Court held that the First Amendment does not restrict the sources from which a plaintiff can obtain evidence. Indeed, "it is essential to proving liability that plaintiffs focus on the conduct and state of mind of the defendants." If demonstration of liability is potentially possible, "the thoughts and editorial processes of the alleged defamer would be open to examination." Such examination includes being able to inquire directly from the defendants whether they knew or had reason to suspect that their damaging publication was in error. The editorial privilege sought by Lando would constitute substantial interference with the ability of a defamation plaintiff to establish the ingredients of malice. The Court ruled in *Cohen v. Cowles Media Co.* (501 U.S. 663: 1991) that the news media is not protected from damage suits if the promise of confidentiality is breached. Cohen was closely associated with a gubernatorial campaign in Minnesota. He offered to render certain information about the opposing candidate for lieutenant governor, but only if the media promised not to disclose him as the source. The promise was given, and the information was exchanged. Over the objection of the reporters who had promised confidentiality, the editorial staff of two newspapers decided to reveal Cohen's name. It was their editorial judgment that readers were entitled to know the source and his interest in the outcome of the gubernatorial election. Cohen subsequently lost his job. He brought suit in state court alleging, among other things, breach of contract. The Minnesota Supreme Court ruled that the First Amendment prevented enforcement of such civil claims against the newspapers. The U.S. Supreme Court disagreed in a 5–4 decision. The newspapers relied on previous decisions holding that states could not "punish" publication of lawfully obtained information. The Court, however, did not see that line of cases as governing here. Rather, the Court drew upon those decisions rejecting special privilege for the press. Justice White stated for the majority that it is "beyond dispute" that a newspaper has "no special immunity from the application of general laws." Generally applicable laws such as Minnesota's do not offend the First Amendment "simply because their enforcement against the press has incidental effects on its ability to gather and report the news." Because the law does not target or single out the press, but is applicable to all Minnesotans, the First Amendment does not preclude application to the press. Further, the Court rejected the argument that the law punished publication of truthful information. The Minnesota law that provided for compensatory damages did not inflict a form of punishment. Rather, it was intended to "simply require those making promises to keep them."

Public Decency

Barnes v. Glen Theatre, Inc. 501 U.S. 560, 115 L. Ed. 2d 504, 111 S. Ct. 2456 (1991) Rejected the argument that the First Amendment precludes a state from enforcing a public decency law to prohibit nude dancing. The parties had agreed that the nude performances were not obscene. As a result, the five-justice majority used symbolic expression standards to resolve the constitutional question. A regulation can only withstand First Amendment scrutiny if it furthers a substantial governmental interest. That interest must be unrelated to the suppression of expression. Further, the regulation may only incidentally affect expression and is to be only as extensive as is required to further the substantial interest. Chief Justice Rehnquist noted the state's "traditional interest in protecting societal order and morality." This interest was seen as both substantial and not directed at expression. Indecency statutes, said Rehnquist, "reflect moral disapproval of people appearing in the nude among strangers in public places." While nude dancing is expressive conduct within the "outer perimeters" of the First Amendment, it is only "marginally so." In Rehnquist's view, the state was not attempting to regulate nudity because of any erotic message, but because the nudity was public. It is the public nudity that is the targeted "evil the state seeks to prevent, whether or not it is combined with expressive activity." Justices O'Connor and Kennedy joined Rehnquist's plurality opinion while Justices Scalia and Souter issued concurring opinions. Scalia saw the indecency law as a general law not specifically directed at expression. As a result, the law was "not subject to First Amendment scrutiny at all." Souter deferred to the state's substantial interest in "combatting the secondary effects of adult entertainment establishments." Justice White issued a dissent joined by Justices Blackmun, Marshall, and Stevens. He saw the regulation as aimed at the message communicated by nude dancing. It is only because such performances "may generate emotions and feelings of eroticism and sensuality among the spectators that the state seeks to regulate such expressive activity." Generating thoughts and emotions is the essence of communication." The nudity component of nude dancing cannot, said White, "be neatly pigeon-holed as conduct independent of any expression component of the dance." White suggested the indecency law in this case should receive the "most exacting scrutiny" as the flag-burning cases. In the dissenters' view, those cases should have controlled the outcome in this case. That nude dancing "may not be high art, to say the least, and may not appeal to the Court is hardly an excuse for distorting and ignoring settled doctrine." *See also* OBSCENITY, p. 437; *YOUNG v. AMERICAN MINI THEATRES, INC.* (427 U.S. 50: 1976), p. 136.

Significance   *Glen Theatre* represents a number of recent cases that have raised questions about local regulation of "adult" entertainment. The Court has generally supported local regulation provided expression is not completely prohibited and a compelling interest can be demonstrated. In *Young v. American Mini Theatres, Inc.* (427 U.S. 50: 1976), for example, the Court upheld zoning ordinances that regulated the location of adult theaters. Identified as a sufficient interest justifying the regulation was the preservation of the character of the city's neighborhoods and the quality of urban life more generally. Meeting the conditions of the compelling interest criterion is not always easy, however. In *Erznoznick v. Jacksonville* (422 U.S. 205: 1975), the Court struck down an ordinance that prohibited the exhibitions of films containing nudity if the screen could be seen from a public street. The Court cited the limited privacy interest of persons on the street, but it also stressed the overly broad sweep of the ordinance. In *Schad v. Borough of Mount Ephraim* (452 U.S. 61: 1981), the Court invalidated a zoning ordinance that banned live entertainment in a borough establishment. Convictions under the ordinance had been secured against an adult bookstore operator for having live nude dancers perform in the establishment. The borough argued that permitting such entertainment would conflict with its plan to create a commercial area catering only to the immediate needs of residents. The Court considered such justification "patently insufficient." The ordinance prohibited a "wide range of expression" that has long been held to be within the protection of the First and Fourteenth Amendments. Ten years after *Young*, the Court once again reviewed a local attempt to regulate the location of adult theaters in *City of Renton v. Playtime Theatres, Inc.* (475 U.S. 41: 1986). Using the same rationale stated in *Young*, the Court upheld a municipality's authority to require dispersal of such establishments. Since the municipal ordinance did not bar adult theaters entirely, it was reviewed as a "time, place, and manner" regulation. Such regulations are acceptable so long as they serve a substantial interest and do not unreasonably limit avenues of communication. Speaking for the Court, Justice Rehnquist said that the First Amendment requires only that a local unit refrain from denying individuals a "reasonable opportunity to open and operate an adult theater within the city." The regulation of indecency approach used in *Glen Theatre* differed from those in *Young* and *Renton* because it was not directly aimed at expression.

ASSEMBLY AND PROTEST
Enjoining Assembly

Carroll v. President and Commissioners of Princess Anne, 393 U.S. 175, 21 L. Ed. 2d 325, 89 S. Ct. 347 (1968)   Struck down an ex parte injunction prohibiting a rally of a militant white supremacist organization. *Carroll* speaks to the manner by which court restraining orders may be sought to enjoin persons from demonstrating in some way. Such injunctions are frequently, but not always, used in situations where permits or licenses to march or demonstrate have been denied. Carroll, a member of a white supremacist organization known as the National States Rights Party, participated in a rally at which aggressively and militantly racist and anti-Semitic speeches were made. At the conclusion of the speeches, it was announced that the rally would be resumed the next night. Local government officials obtained a restraining order in the meantime in an ex parte proceeding. The injunction restrained Carroll and others from holding public meetings for 10 days. The Supreme Court struck down the order in a unanimous judgment. The Court's primary objection was to the ex parte procedure. The order was issued "without notice to petitioners and without any effort, however informal, to invite or permit their participation in the proceedings." The Court recognized that ex parte orders may be appropriate in some situations, "but there is no place within the area of basic freedoms guaranteed by the First Amendment for such orders." Absence of an adversary proceeding deprives a trial court of the facts necessary to make a judgment. There is "insufficient assurance of the balanced analysis and careful conclusions which are essential in the area of First Amendment adjudication." The same absence of information makes it more difficult to construct an order in the narrowest and least stifling terms. *See also* ADDERLEY *v.* FLORIDA (385 U.S. 39: 1966), p. 142; ASSEMBLY, RIGHT TO, p. 385.

Significance   *Carroll v. President and Commissioners of Princess Anne* established procedural guidelines through which court orders might be obtained against demonstrators. The permit-injunction approach had often been used against civil-rights demonstrators. In *Walker v. Birmingham* (388 U.S. 307: 1967), the Court upheld an injunction issued following denial of a parade permit. Walker, Martin Luther King, Jr., and others involved in the proposed parade disobeyed the injunction without seeking appellate review of either the injunction or the permit denial which precipitated the court order. A five-justice majority found the potentially persuasive objections to the Birmingham permit system to be subordinate to the failure of the demonstrators to obey the court order. The dissenters in *Walker* would have voided the injunction on the grounds that the permit system was unconstitutionally discriminatory. Permits are satisfactory as long as they are confined to reasonable time, place, and manner limitations. Permit or license requirements which are not content neutral or which allow too much discretion to permit-granting officials are unacceptable to the Court. A more recent injunction episode involved attempts by the Village of Skokie, Illinois, to prevent an assembly of the National Socialist Party of America, a self-proclaimed Nazi organization. More than half of Skokie's residents are Jewish and a sizeable number were survivors of German concentration camps. Prior to the assembly, an injunction was secured from a state court enjoining the National Socialist Party from a uniformed march, display of swastikas, and distribution of materials which might "promote hatred against persons of the Jewish faith or ancestry." The Illinois Supreme Court refused to stay the injunction. The U. S. Supreme Court, in *National Socialist Party v. Skokie* (432 U.S. 43: 1977), reversed because the denial of the stay at the state level deprived the Party of its right to demonstrate for the period until an appellate review could occur. The period was estimated to be a year or more. The Court said that if a "State seeks to impose a restraint of this kind, it must provide strict procedural safeguards including appellate review. Absent such review, the State must instead allow the stay." The Party never assembled in Skokie, choosing instead to hold a rally in a Chicago park.

The Court dealt with a different kind of permit requirement in *Forsyth County v. The Nationalist Movement* (120 L. Ed. 2d 101: 1992). In 1987, Forsyth County, Georgia, was the site of a number of civil-rights demonstrations as well as counterdemonstrations. In response, Forsyth County adopted a permit ordinance that imposed a fee as a condition for obtaining permission to use public property for expressive activity. The county administrator had authority to set the amount of the fee up to a maximum of $1,000 for each day the public properties were used. The Supreme Court found the ordinance unconstitutional. The central objection was that the ordinance gave the local government, in the person of the county administrator, "unbridled discretion" and created the possibility that assessments might be influenced by the content of the expression. Justice Blackmun said, "Speech cannot be financially burdened, any more than it can be punished or banned, simply because it might offend a hostile mob."

The public forum concept was the critical consideration in *International Society for Krishna Consciousness, Inc. v. Lee* (120 L. Ed. 2d 541: 1992). Members of Krishna Consciousness are required by their faith to go to public places and engage in activities including literature distribution and solicitation of donations. The Port Authority of New York and New Jersey operates the three major airports in and near New York City. The Port Authority permitted the Krishnas to engage in various activities in the common areas of the airport grounds, but prohibited the same conduct in those airport locations that had been leased to private airlines. Much of the terminal space fell into the latter category. The Krishnas sought to extend their access to airport grounds and challenged the restrictions on First Amendment grounds. The Supreme Court agreed that the Krishnas were engaged in activities generally protected by the First Amendment, but upheld the ban on solicitations for money on a 6–3 vote. At the same time, the restriction on distribution of literature was held to be unconstitutional by a vote of 5–4. The Court's rulings hinged on whether the air terminals were public forums historically dedicated to expressive activities. If so, the terminals could only be regulated to serve a "compelling" governmental interest. The "tradition of airport activity," said Chief Justice Rehnquist, "does not demonstrate that airports have historically been available for speech activity." Rather, the six-justice majority saw airline terminals as intended to serve airline passengers and personnel and not the public at large. The ban on direct solicitation (begging) was found to be a reasonable way to avoid excessive congestion and disruption to passengers as they moved through the terminals. The members of the Court who would have overturned the regulation of solicitation—Justices Souter, Blackmun, and Stevens—saw the airport as a public forum where solicitation should be protected conduct. Justices O'Connor and Kennedy joined the dissenters on the solicitation question to strike down the restriction on literature distribution. They felt the regulation could not satisfy even the reasonableness standard applied to a nonpublic forum. One additional practice raising questions of assembly and expression has been protest on the premises of clinics performing abortions. This issue is examined in the entry of *Bray v. Alexandria Women's Health Clinic* (122 L. Ed. 2d 34: 1993), located in Chapter 6 of this supplement.

ASSOCIATION

Electoral Process

Burson v. Freeman, **504 U.S. __, 119 L. Ed. 2d 5, 112 S. Ct. 1846 (1992)**
Permitted a state to ban political activities, including the distribution of political campaign materials, within 100 feet of a polling place on election

day. Upon examination of the history of election regulations, the Court found a "wide-spread and time-tested consensus that some restricted zone is necessary to serve the States' compelling interest in preventing voter intimidation and election fraud." The regulation had been challenged as both over- and underinclusive. The Court concluded the law was neither. Less inclusive regulations reach only the "most blatant and specific attempts to impede elections." The underinclusive argument focused on the content-based character of the restriction. It regulated political expression only around polling places. Justice Blackmun said that failure to regulate all speech does not "render the statute fatally underinclusive." The Court found no evidence that political candidates "have used other forms of solicitation or exit polling to commit such electoral abuses [as voter intimidation or fraud]." Blackmun focused on the secret ballot as an integral effort to curb electoral abuses. The only way to preserve the secrecy of the ballot, he argued, "is to limit access to the area around the voter." Justice Stevens, joined by O'Connor and Souter, dissented. They saw the law as a restriction of speech based on its content. As such, the law "somewhat perversely disfavors speech that normally is accorded greater protection than the kinds of speech that the statute does not regulate." Creation of campaign free zones may protect orderly access to the polls, but at the same time prevent last-minute campaigning. It was the dissenters' view that this regulation unnecessarily "hindered" the latter. *See also* ASSOCIATION, RIGHT OF, p. 386.

Significance   As a rule, the Supreme Court is suspect of regulations that might burden participation in elections. At the same time, states needs to protect the integrity of the electoral process. Thus, the Court may uphold restrictions designed to insulate the voting place from campaigning activities. A different kind of electoral regulation was before the Court in *Burdick v. Takushi* (119 L. Ed. 2d 245: 1992). Here the Court ruled that a state ban on write-in voting imposed only a "very limited burden" on the right to vote. Citing several different ways party or independent candidates may appear on Hawaii's primary ballot, The Court concluded that the restriction on write-in voting did not unreasonably "interfere with the right of voters to associate and have candidates of their choice placed on the ballot." The Court also rejected the contention that a voter is entitled both to cast and have counted a "protest vote." The function of the election process, said Justice White, is to "'winnow out and finally reject all but the chosen,'" not to provide means of giving vent to 'short-range political goals, pique, or personal quarrels.'" Justices Kennedy, Blackmun, and Stevens saw the ban on write-in voting as preventing voters dissatisfied with choices available to them "from participating in Hawaiian elections in a meaningful manner."

2. The Fourth Amendment

Warrantless Arrest

Riverside County v. McLaughlin, **500 U.S. 44, 114 L. Ed. 2d 49, 111 S. Ct. 1661 (1991)** Defined how promptly persons arrested without a warrant must appear before a judicial officer. *Gerstein v. Pugh* (420 U.S. 103: 1975) required that persons arrested without warrants have "prompt" judicial determinations of whether probable cause existed. Riverside County incorporated probable cause determinations into its arraignment procedure. Under county policy, arraignments are to take place without unnecessary delay, but within two days of arrest exclusive of weekends and holidays. The Court, speaking through Justice O'Connor, said *Gerstein* had established a "practical compromise" between the interests of arrested persons and the "realities" of law enforcement. *Gerstein* allowed local jurisdiction some latitude in procedures used to make probable cause determinations. Riverside County was free under *Gerstein* to combine probable cause determinations with arraignments. The Court recognized that some delays are "inevitable." For that reason, it is reasonable to postpone probable cause hearings in some situations as police "cope with the everyday problems of processing suspects through an overly burdened criminal justice system." At the same time, said O'Connor, "flexibility has its limits; *Gerstein* is not a blank check." The Court concluded that probable cause hearings held within 48 hours of arrest will, "as a general matter, comply with the promptness requirement of *Gerstein*." *Gerstein* violations may still occur within the first 48 hours, but the burden of demonstrating unreasonable delay rests with the arrested party. After 48 hours, the "calculus changes." The burden then shifts to the government to demonstrate the existence of a "bona fide emergency" or other extraordinary circumstance. "Delay in a case beyond 48 hours in order to consolidate pre-trial proceedings," said O'Connor, "will not qualify as an extraordinary circumstance." Nor will intervening weekends or holidays provide the basis for permissible delay. Using this standard, the Riverside County policy did not comply with the *Gerstein* promptness requirement. Justices Scalia, Marshall, Blackmun, and Stevens felt the Fourth Amendment required that a probable cause hearing occur "immediately upon completion of the administrative steps incident to arrest." Justice Scalia said that 24 hours should define the outer limit of reasonable delay. *See also* EXIGENT CIRCUMSTANCE, p. 410.

Significance   The arrest situation has often given rise to difficult Fourth Amendment questions. This has been especially true of warrantless arrests. *California v. Hodari D.* (499 U.S. 621: 1991) examined the issue of when custody begins and how custody status affects the seizure of evidence. The Court ruled that a fleeing suspect has not been "seized" and does not yet come within the reach of Fourth Amendment. As a result, any evidence discarded prior to actual seizure is admissible in court regardless of the degree of suspicion the police had for instigating a chase. A group of youths including Hodari D. were standing on a street corner. They fled upon sighting a police car approaching. While the police car was unmarked, the officer who gave chase on foot was wearing a jacket that clearly identified him as a police officer. The officer did not chase Hodari directly, but rather circled around the block which eventually placed him in front of Hodari as he ran up an adjacent street. Hodari had been watching behind him as he ran and was almost face-to-face with the officer before seeing him. Upon facing the officer, Hodari turned and set off in the opposite direction. As he fled, he discarded a small rock. The officer gave chase and subsequently tackled Hodari. The discarded article turned out to be crack cocaine. The cocaine was introduced as evidence in the juvenile proceeding against Hodari. A California appellate court ruled the evidence should have been suppressed under terms of the Fourth Amendment since Hodari had been "seized" from the time of his face-to-face confrontation with the officer. In the appellate court's view, the officer did not have cause to seize Hodari. The cocaine was thus the fruit of an illegal seizure. In a 7–2 decision, the Supreme Court reversed. The Court resolved this issue by using the common law concept of arrest. An arrest occurs when a person is restrained by application of physical force, or a person submits to the "assertion of authority" by an officer. Neither occurred in this case. Even if the officer's pursuit could be considered a "show of authority," Hodari did not comply. As a result, Hodari was not seized until he was physically restrained. Street pursuits inevitably place the public at "some risk." In the Court's view, police orders to stop will seldom be without basis. The few unlawful orders that do occur, however, would not be deterred by application of the exclusionary rule to those where the orders are disobeyed. The dissenters, Justices Stevens and Marshall, felt the decision was focused not on the reasonableness of police conduct, but rather on the response of the suspect. The "character of a citizen's response," he said, "should not govern the constitutionality of the officer's conduct." Stevens concluded that the ruling would prompt unlawful displays of force that will "frighten countless innocent persons into surrendering whatever privacy rights they have."

   Powell v. Nevada (128 L. Ed. 2d 1: 1994) considered retroactive application of *McLaughlin*. Kitrich Powell was arrested for felony child abuse on 3 November 1989. Although the arresting officer prepared a sworn declaration that same day, a magistrate did not find cause to hold Powell for a preliminary hearing until four days later (on 7 November). After receiving *Miranda* warnings, Powell made prejudicial statements which were later used at his murder trial. Powell was subsequently found guilty and sentenced to death. His appeal focused on the elapsed time between his arrest and judicial determination of whether cause existed for that arrest. Under *McLaughlin,* delay of more than 48 hours is presumptively unreasonable under the Fourth Amendment. The Nevada Supreme Court ruled that *McLaughlin* was inapplicable because it had been decided after Powell's case had commenced. The Supreme Court disagreed. The Court held that *McLaughlin* applies to all cases, including Powell's, which were not final at the time *McLaughlin* was decided. While it was clear that there was a *McLaughlin* violation in this case, *McLaughlin* did not specify the relief to which Powell was entitled as a result of the violation. The Court remanded the case to the Nevada Supreme Court to allow it to consider the appropriate remedy for a delay in determining probable cause.

In *United States v. Alvarez-Machain* (119 L. Ed. 2d 441: 1992), the Court ruled that agents of the United States may ignore the terms of extradition agreements and forcibly bring a criminal suspect from a foreign country to the United States to stand trial. Alvarez-Machain, a Mexican citizen and a physician, was sought by the United States for his alleged involvement in the kidnapping and murder of a Drug Enforcement Administration (DEA) agent. Under terms of a 1980 agreement with Mexico, the United States could have requested extradition. Because Alvarez-Machain was a Mexican citizen, Mexico could have chosen either to extradite him or undertake its own prosecution of him. No extradition request was made, however. Instead, Alvarez-Machain was seized in Mexico by Mexican bounty hunters, taken to El Paso, Texas, and delivered to DEA authorities. Alvarez-Machain contended that having an extradition agreement would make no sense "if either nation were free to resort to forcible kidnapping to gain the presence of an individual for prosecution in a manner not contemplated by the treaty." Chief Justice Rehnquist spoke for the six-justice majority in saying, "We do not read the treaty in such a fashion." Rather, Rehnquist said that the treaty "does not purport to specify the only way in which one country may gain custody of a national of the other country for the purposes of prosecution." Viewing the terms of the treaty literally, Rehnquist said the agreement "says nothing about the obligations of the United States and Mexico to refrain from forcible abductions..." and should not be read as though such limitations are contained implicitly.

Automobile Searches

United States v. Ross, 456 U.S. 798, 72 L. Ed. 2d 572, 102 S. Ct. 2157 (1982) Permitted the warrantless search of a container found in a lawfully stopped automobile. The ruling was that as long as probable cause exists, police authority to perform a warrantless search is coextensive with a magistrate's authority to issue a warrant. Following a tip, police officers found a car in a location specified by the informant. The informant was known to the police and previously had provided reliable information. The driver of the car, Ross, matched the informant's description. The informant had said that drugs were contained in the trunk of the car. On stopping the car and opening the trunk, the police found a closed paper bag. It was opened and heroin was discovered. A zippered pouch containing cash was subsequently found as well. Ross sought to have the evidence suppressed, but he was unsuccessful and convicted. The court of appeals agreed with Ross, holding that the bag and pouch could not be opened in the absence of a warrant. The Supreme Court reversed the court of appeals in a 6–3 decision. The opinion of the Court was delivered by Justice Stevens. He traced the history of the automobile warrant exception and reiterated the impracticability of having to secure a warrant where transportation of contraband was involved. He said that relief from securing a warrant does not diminish the probable cause requirement, however. The only warrantless automobile search permissible is one "supported by probable cause." The probable cause determination must be based on objective facts that could justify the issuance of a warrant by a magistrate. The mere "subjective good faith" of a police officer is insufficient to constitute probable cause. Once the probable cause requirement has been met, the practical consequences of the automobile warrant exception would be largely nullified if the scope of the search did not include containers and packages found inside the vehicle. A warranted search of any premises extends to the entire area in which the object of the search may be found. This rule applies equally to all containers and carries over to the warrantless search of an automobile. Stevens noted that the protection of the Fourth Amendment "varies in different settings." A container that is a person's possession at the time of arrest may be searched "even without any specific suspicion concerning its contents." The privacy interests of an individual must give way to the finding of probable cause. Stevens concluded by saying the scope of a warrantless automobile search is not defined by the nature of the container. It is defined by "the object of the search and the places in which there is probable cause to believe that it may be found." Justices White, Brennan, and Marshall dissented. Marshall said the decision repeals the Fourth Amendment warrant requirement. The value of a probable cause determination by a neutral and detached magistrate is lost by permitting police officers to make the same judgment. Marshall saw the ruling as "flatly inconsistent" with established principles concerning the scope of the automobile warrant exception. *See also CHAMBERS v. MARONEY* (399 U.S. 42: 1970), p. 182; *SOUTH DAKOTA v. OPPERMAN* (428 U.S. 364: 1978), p. 185; *UNITED STATES v. ROBINSON* (414 U.S. 218: 1973), p. 183.

Significance   In *Ross,* the Court allowed the warrantless search of containers found in automobiles. The case constitutes a significant change in Court policy in this sensitive area. Prior to *Ross,* the Court had held that containers found in cars were protected unless their contents were in plain view, a rule derived from several cases having to do with the expectations of privacy attaching to luggage. In *United States v. Chadwick* (433 U.S. 1: 1977), the Court refused to permit the warrantless search of a secured footlocker taken from an automobile trunk. It said the locked container conveyed a privacy expectation that required warrant protection. In *Arkansas v. Sanders* (442 U.S. 753: 1979), the Court rejected the automobile exception as the basis for a warrantless search of anything, including a suitcase, found in the course of the examination of an automobile. Two years later, in *Robbins v. California* (453 U.S. 420: 1981), the Court held that a closed container found during a lawful automobile search was constitutionally protected to the same extent as are closed items of luggage found anywhere else. *Ross* distinguished *Chadwick* and overruled *Robbins.* The Court maintained that the *Chadwick* decision did not rest on the automobile exception because the footlocker itself "was the suspected locus of the contraband." But not all movable containers are subject to warrantless search after seizure even if they come in contact with an automobile. Thus, *Ross* retained *Chadwick. Robbins,* on the other hand, involved cause to search a whole automobile, not just a footlocker. The *Robbins* prohibition on the search of a closed container found in the execution of the lawful search of an automobile was rejected by *Ross.* So long as probable cause exists to search an automobile, the expectation of privacy does not extend to closed containers which might be capable of concealing the object of the search. In *United States v. Johns* (469 U.S. 478: 1985), the Court extended *Ross* to warrantless searches of packages occurring three days after the packages were seized. Given the fact that authorities could have opened the containers at the time of the seizure under the *Ross* rule, the Court found no requirement that the containers be examined immediately.

California v. Acevedo (500 U.S. 565: 1991) gave the Court the opportunity to reconsider the intersection of *Sanders* and *Ross.* Acevedo was seen leaving an apartment carrying a paper bag the size of marijuana packages the police knew to be in the apartment. Acevedo placed the bag in the trunk of his car and was stopped by police as he began to drive away. A search of the trunk revealed a bag containing marijuana. A California appellate court held the case to be controlled by *Sanders* rather than *Ross* because while police had probable cause to believe the bag contained marijuana, there was no probable cause to believe the car itself otherwise contained contraband. The Supreme Court granted certiorari to reconsider whether a warrant was required for the police to open the bag "simply because they lack probable cause to search the entire car." *Sanders* required a warrant for such a search. But *Sanders,* said Justice Blackmun for a six-justice majority, did not set out a "clear and unequivocal guideline." To the contrary, *Sanders* not only "failed to protect privacy interests effectively," but it also "confused courts and police officers and impeded effective law enforcement." Cases such as *Sanders* have established, Blackmun continued, a "curious line between the search of an automobile that coincidentally turns up a container and the search of a container that coincidentally turns up in an automobile." The protections of the Fourth Amendment "must not turn on such coincidences." The Court concluded it was better to adopt a clear rule for automobile searches generally and eliminate the warrant requirement established for closed containers in *Sanders.* The new ruling allows police to search an automobile and containers within it "where they have probable cause to believe contraband or evidence is contained." Justice Stevens, in dissent, noted that the police are required to have a warrant to open containers like luggage that people may carry on the street. He felt it "anomalous" that the requirement does not apply when a person puts the same container into a privately owned automobile.

Florida v. Jimeno (500 U.S. 248: 1991) involved the added element of consent. Police followed Jimeno after overhearing him arrange what seemed to be a narcotics transaction. His car was stopped by police for failure to stop at a traffic light. The officer who stopped the car told Jimeno that he had reason to believe there were drugs in the car. The officer asked Jimeno for permission to search the vehicle. Jimeno consented. Cocaine was eventually discovered in a closed paper bag found on the floor of the vehicle. The cocaine was suppressed at trial because Jimeno's consent to have his car searched was ruled not to include consent to search the paper bag. The Supreme Court ruled that Jimeno's consent to search his car implicitly extended to closed containers found in the course of the vehicle search provided the container might reasonably hold the object of the search. Chief Justice Rehnquist said that the "touchstone" of the Fourth Amendment is reasonableness. The basis for assessing the scope of a suspect's consent is "objective reasonableness—what would the typical reasonable person have understood by the exchange between the officer and the suspect." Rehnquist said the terms of the search authorization in this case were "simple." The officer conveyed the belief that drugs were in the car.

Jimeno was aware of that suspicion, but did not place any explicit limitation on the scope of the search. Under these circumstances, the Court thought it was "objectively reasonable for the police to conclude that the general consent to search the respondent's [Jimeno's] car included consent to search containers within that car which might bear drugs."

Stop and Frisk

Terry v. Ohio, **392 U.S. 1, 20 L. Ed. 2d 889, 88 S. Ct. 1868 (1968)**
Examined the practice of stop and frisk and established basic guidelines for a limited warrantless search conducted on persons behaving in a suspicious manner. A police officer of 39 years of service observed two men, later joined by a third, acting "suspiciously." Specifically, the officer felt the men were "casing" a particular store. The officer approached the men, identified himself as a police officer, and requested identification. Upon receiving an unsatisfactory response to his request, the officer frisked the men. Terry was found to have a gun in his possession, and was subsequently charged and convicted for carrying a concealed weapon. The Supreme Court upheld the validity of the stop and frisk practice, with only Justice Douglas dissenting. It was admitted in *Terry* that the officer did not have "probable cause" to search Terry. Indeed, this is why *Terry* is important in recent Fourth Amendment cases: the majority distinguished between a frisk and a full search. The Court concluded that the officer was entitled to conduct a cursory search for weapons. Such a search is "protective," and while it constitutes an "intrusion upon the sanctity of the person," it is briefer and more limited than a full search. The frisk was justified by the need to discover weapons which might be used to harm the officer or others. Thus, where the officer "observes unusual conduct which leads him reasonably to conclude in light of his experience that criminal activity may be afoot," where he identifies himself as a police officer, and where "nothing in the initial stages of the encounter serves to dispel his reasonable fear for his own or others' safety," he is entitled to conduct a cursory search. Justice Douglas argued that probable cause had not been satisfied with respect to the weapons charge, i.e., the officer had no basis to believe Terry was carrying a weapon, thus the search was invalid. *See also* STOP AND FRISK, p. 455.

Significance   *Terry v. Ohio* provided law enforcement authorities with the capability of executing preventive actions. Not only did *Terry* allow police to stop a person in situations deemed to be "suspicious," but *Terry* authorized a limited weapons patdown. Controlling in *Terry* was observed behavior which would justify or give cause for making the stop. Given cause to stop, the officer was entitled to conduct at least a cursory search.

Terry does not allow a full search unless the cursory search yields a weapon that leads to an actual custodial arrest. In *Sibron v. New York* (392 U.S. 40: 1968), a case decided with *Terry*, the Court disallowed a stop and frisk that netted a package of narcotics because the searching officer could not demonstrate cause for the stop. There was no reason to infer that Sibron was armed at the time of the stop or presented a danger to the officer. The Court felt the search of Sibron was a search for evidence, not for weapons. A similar absence of suspicion led the Court to strike down the "stop and identify" practice in *Brown v. Texas* (443 U.S. 47: 1979).

Several other cases provide examples of insufficient cause. In *United States v. Brignoni-Ponce* (422 U.S. 873: 1975), the Court held that vehicle stops to search for illegal aliens were impermissible unless specific cause could be shown. Random stops of vehicles simply on the basis of observed substantial trafficking in aliens was inadequate. More recently the Court held in *Delaware v. Prouse* (440 U.S. 648: 1979) that police could not randomly stop automobiles to check license and registration without some focused suspicion of a violation. To stop a driver, an officer must have cause comparable to the cause required to stop a person on foot. At the same time the Court upheld a search under a stop and identify ordinance later held to be unconstitutional. The Supreme Court upheld the use of so-called sobriety checklanes against Fourth Amendment challenge in *Michigan Department of State Police v. Sitz,* (496 U.S. 444: 1990). Law enforcement officers briefly stop all drivers at such checkpoints in an attempt to detect signs of intoxication. Every state utilizes some kind of checkpoint method in an effort to combat drunk driving. Chief Justice Rehnquist, speaking for a six-justice majority, said such stops are "seizures within the meaning of the Fourth Amendment." The question in *Sitz* was "whether such seizures are reasonable." The question was resolved by weighing the state's interest in preventing drunk driving against the intrusion on drivers as individuals. The Court began by characterizing the scope of the problem. "No one can seriously dispute the magnitude of the drunk driving problem or the state's interest in eradicating it." Rehnquist referred to both media accounts of "alcohol-related death and mutilation," and the statistical data which show an annual death toll in excess of 25,000. At the same time, the "intrusion on motorists stopped briefly at sobriety checkpoints is slight." The Court said that these stops were similar to highway stops to detect illegal aliens. Such stops as these do not involve "standardless and unconstrained discretion" on the part of law enforcement officers. Empirical data showed that operation of the checkpoints produces arrests for alcohol impairment. While the check lanes may not be the best means available to enforcement of drunk driving laws, the approach "can reasonably be said to advance" the state interest in preventing alcohol-impaired driving. Justices Brennan, Marshall, and Stevens dissented. They felt the Fourth Amendment precluded any stop without "some level of individualized suspicion." The Burger Court expanded upon *Terry* in *Adams v. Williams* (407 U.S. 143: 1972) when it permitted a frisk based upon an informant's tip as opposed to an officer's own observations. In *Pennsylvania v. Mimms* (434 U.S. 106: 1977), the Court held that an officer could order a lawfully detained driver out of his automobile. Once out, the *Terry* standard must still be met. The Court concluded that considerations of an officer's safety justified having a driver leave a car, and that if cause exists to proceed with a frisk, a patdown is permissible. *Terry* and the cases that build upon it authorize substantial latitude for a cursory weapons search if observed or reported behavior can focus sufficient suspicion. Subsequent cases further define the scope of *Terry*.

In *United States v. Place* (462 U.S. 696: 1983), the Court held that suspicious luggage may be seized at an airport and subjected to a sniff test by a narcotics detection dog. In this case the permissible limits of a *Terry* stop were exceeded, however, when the luggage was kept for 90 minutes, the suspect was not informed of where the luggage would be taken, and detention officers failed to specify how the luggage might be returned. *Terry* was also extended in *Michigan v. Long* (463 U.S. 1032: 1983), when the Court allowed a protective search of the passenger compartment of a stopped car. The majority ruled that "*Terry* need not be read as restricting the preventative search to the person of the detained suspect." Search of the passenger compartment of a car is permissible as long as the police "possess an articulable and objectively reasonable belief that the suspect is potentially dangerous." Contraband discovered in the course of such a protective search is admissible evidence.

The Court used the reasonable suspicion standard of *Terry* to uphold searches by school officials in *New Jersey v. T. L. O.* (469 U.S. 325: 1985). The Court held that searching a student is justified if there are "reasonable grounds for suspecting" the search will yield evidence that laws or school rules are being violated. Such searches are permissible if they are related to the objectives of the search and are not excessively intrusive, given the age and sex of the student and the nature of the infraction. The Court recognized that searches are a "severe violation" of the student's privacy. It therefore urged school officials to limit their conduct "according to the dictates of reason." But the Court said society must recognize that drug use and crime are "major social problems," and that searches are justified as a means of maintaining school discipline. Although it noted that constitutional protections did apply in this case, the Court permitted the search based on the existence of reasonable suspicion. Further evolution of *Terry* occurred in *United States v. Sharpe* (470 U.S. 675: 1985), where the Court upheld short-term, i.e., twenty minute, investigative detention where reasonable suspicion exists. In *Hayes v. Florida* (470 U.S. 811: 1985), however, the Court said that police officers may not take a suspect to police headquarters for finger-printing in the absence of probable cause, a warrant, or the person's consent. The Court left the door open for a brief detention for field administration of fingerprinting when reasonable suspicion exists. It said such detention "is not necessarily impermissible." A vagueness criterion has been incorporated into this analysis as well. In *Kolender v. Lawson* (461 U.S. 352: 1983), the Court struck down a California law requiring persons who "loiter or wander on the streets" to provide "credible and reliable" identification, and to "account for their presence" when requested. The majority ruled that the statute was vague and that it vested virtually complete discretion in police officers to determine if the enactment requirements had been satisfied. While stop and frisk remains a valuable law enforcement practice, *Brown v. Texas, supra,* firmly established that reasonable suspicion must exist for such a stop to occur. *Terry* permitted a cursory weapons patdown of a person police suspect may be armed. The question in *Minnesota v. Dickerson* (124 L. Ed. 2d 334: 1993) was whether police may seize articles other than weapons detected during the weapons frisk. A unanimous Court ruled that such seizures are constitutional so long as the officer stays within the limits established by *Terry.* Timothy Dickerson was observed leaving a building known to be used for drug trafficking. In addition, his behavior was felt to be "suspicious" to officers who observed him. He was subsequently stopped and subjected to a weapons frisk. No weapons were found, but the officer touched a small lump in Dickerson's pocket. Believing the lump to be crack co-caine, the officer reached into the pocket and seized a small bag of cocaine. Dickerson unsuccessfully sought to suppress the cocaine and was convicted of possession. The Court saw discoveries of contraband by touch as analogous to plain view discoveries. Justice White said that if a police officer lawfully pats down a suspect and "feels an object whose contour or mass makes its identity immediately apparent, there has been no invasion of the suspect's privacy beyond that already authorized by the officer's search for weapons." If the object discovered by touch is indeed contra-band, its warrantless seizure is "justified by the same practical considera-tions that inhere in the plain view context." White noted that Terry itself demonstrates that "touch is capable of revealing the nature of an object with sufficient reliability to suppress a seizure." Even if it were true, White continued, that the "sense of touch is generally less reliable than the sense of sight, that only suggests that officers will less often be able to justify seizures of unseen contraband." Like detection of contraband by sight, discoveries by touch must meet the Fourth Amendment requirement that an officer has probable cause to believe an item is contraband before seizing it. Satisfying this requirement "ensures against excessively specu-lative seizures."

Consent Searches

Schneckloth v. Bustamonte, **412 U.S. 218, 36 L. Ed. 2d 854, 93 S. Ct. 2041 (1973)** Explored what is involved in determining the voluntariness of consenting to a search. A police officer stopped an automobile occupied by six persons including Bustamonte. After requesting identification and establishing that the car was owned by the brother of one of the occupants, the officer asked if he could search the interior of the car. The owner's brother agreed. When the officer asked whether the trunk opened, the owner's brother took the car keys and opened the trunk. Several stolen checks were found in the trunk and were subsequently entered into evidence at Bustamonte's trial. The Supreme Court upheld the use of the evidence. The key to the case was a determination of whether consent had been voluntarily given. A six-justice majority said "two competing concerns must be accommodated in determining the meaning of a 'voluntary' consent—the legitimate need for such searches and the equally important requirement of assuring the absence of coercion." Such problems cannot be "resolved by any infallible touchstone." The Court stressed the "totality of circumstances" in making judgments in these kinds of cases and concluded that consent had been voluntarily given in *Schneckloth.* The majority rejected the argument that consent must be evaluated in the same way as a waiver of rights pertaining to a fair trial. The majority opted not to require that individuals know of their right to refuse consent in order to establish a voluntary consent. The dissenters, Justices Douglas, Brennan, and Marshall, argued that before consent could be obtained, a person must be informed of his or her right to refuse consent. *See also* CONSENT SEARCH, p. 398; EXIGENT CIRCUMSTANCE, p. 410; *UNITED STATES v. MATLOCK* (415 U.S. 164: 1974), p. 193.

Significance In *Schneckloth,* the Court refused to require that persons be informed that they need not consent to searches. *Schneckloth* effectively distinguishes between search and self-incrimination situations, holding that an individual need be apprised of legal options only in the instance of self-incrimination. While the *Schneckloth* decision still requires that the prosecution bear the burden of proof in showing that a consent was voluntarily obtained, *Schneckloth* excludes knowledge of the right to withhold consent as an absolute element of showing voluntary consent. A number of states use the more demanding standard that all persons must be informed that they may opt not to consent to a search. Presuming a consent has been voluntarily obtained, there remains the question of how much the consent allows authorities to search. Consent may be limited to specific places to be searched or specific items for which to be searched.

If it cannot be shown that a suspect has voluntarily consented to an unlimited search, the search ought to be carefully limited. Consent may also be withdrawn, and searches continued after consent is revoked must be otherwise defensible. Even a suspect's consent may be insufficient to uphold a search. The Court held in *Florida v. Royer* (460 U.S. 491: 1983) that if a suspect is detained beyond the permissible bounds of an investigative stop, his consent to a search of his suitcases becomes "tainted by the illegal detention." The voluntariness standard also says the person consenting to a search must actually possess the capacity to consent. (*See United States v. Matlock*, 415 U.S. 164: 1974).

Finally, a Rehnquist Court decision further illustrates the direction of recent consent search rulings. Law enforcement officers often board interstate buses laid over at a stop and seek the consent of passengers to submit to searches of their luggage. The action is known as "working the buses," and it is a fairly common drug interdiction tactic. The Court upheld the practice in *Florida v. Bostick* (501 U.S. 429: 1991). Permission was sought to search Bostick's luggage even though there was no reason to suspect Bostick was carrying drugs. Bostick consented to a search which yielded cocaine. The Florida Supreme Court ruled that "working the buses" was categorically unconstitutional because a reasonable person would not have felt free to leave the bus to avoid the request for permission to search. Six members of the U.S. Supreme Court, however, did not see the practice as unlawful in every situation. A "consensual encounter," said Justice O'Connor for the majority, does not "trigger Fourth Amendment scrutiny." Merely asking a passenger to consent does not constitute a "seizure." Even without particularized suspicion, police may generally ask questions of individual passengers and request consent to search. The request becomes improper if it conveys that compliance is not optional. Consent that is the product of any kind of intimidation is "not consent at all." The appropriate test is whether, considering all the circumstances, a passenger would feel free to refuse the request to search. The Court rejected Bostick's argument that because the encounter occurred on a bus, he was less "free to leave." It was this "free to leave" test that governed the thinking of the Florida Supreme Court. O'Connor said the focus on freedom to leave was misplaced. The fact Bostick did not feel free to leave was largely because of his decision to take the bus in the first place. When someone is seated on a bus and has no wish to leave, inquiry into whether or not he should leave is "not an accurate measure of the coercive effect of the encounter." Rather, said O'Connor, the crucial test is whether, on the basis of all the circumstances surrounding the encounter, the police conduct "would have communicated to a reasonable person that he was not at liberty to ignore the police presence and go about his business."

Since the Florida courts did not apply this standard, the case was remanded. Dissenting Justices Marshall, Blackmun, and Stevens saw these "dragnet-style sweeps" as highly coercive. Consent is obtained, Marshall observed, because few passengers are willing to leave the bus and risk being "stranded in unfamiliar locations."

Prisoners' Rights

Wilson v. Seiter, **501 U.S. 294, 115 L. Ed. 2d 271, 111 S. Ct. 2321 (1991)**
Held that a showing of intent is required to win a suit based on the Cruel and Unusual Punishment Clause of the Eighth Amendment. Justice Scalia wrote for a five-justice majority saying the Eighth Amendment bars only cruel and unusual punishments. If the pain or discontent alleged by the prisoners was not "formally meted out as punishment" by statute or the sentencing judge, "some mental element must be attributed to the inflicting officer before it can qualify." The Court then addressed the standard to be used in determining state of mind. Conduct must be "wanton," Scalia said, but wantonness does not have a "fixed meaning." Rather, it must be determined "with due regard for differences in the kind of conduct against which an Eighth Amendment objection is lodged." The Court concluded that wantonness of conduct depends on the "constraints facing the official" as opposed to effect upon the prisoner. In situations such as responding to a prison disturbance, actions of prison officials are balanced against "competing institutional concerns." Wanton conduct would be more difficult to demonstrate in a disturbance situation than in one where officials failed to adequately attend to medical needs. Unlike the emergency situation, the state would have no interest against which providing medical care might "clash." In the emergency situation, a finding of wantonness would require a showing of malicious and sadistic action designed to cause harm. That standard, though, was seen as too demanding for cases involving challenges of ongoing conditions. In the nonemergency case, wantonness is demonstrated by a showing of "deliberate inattendance" by prison officials. Justices White, Marshall, Blackmun, and Stevens dissented. They preferred to focus exclusively on effects of actions or inactions on prisoners. They saw intent as not very "meaningful" in prison condition cases. Poor conditions, in their view, might too easily be attributed to factors such as insufficient funding rather than "deliberate indifference" on the part of prison officials. *See also BLOCK v. RUTHERFORD* (468 U.S. 576: 1984), p. 93 (Supplement 2).

Significance   The Court has typically afforded authorities substantial latitude in administering detention facilities. Until recently, these cases often have focused on Fourth Amendment issues. For example, the Court upheld unscheduled searches of prisoners' cells in *Block v. Rutherford* (468 U.S. 576: 1984), and random searches of prisoners themselves in *Hudson v. Palmer* (468 U.S. 517: 1984). The Court similarly has been deferential to prison authorities when inmate claims are based on the Cruel and Unusual Punishment Clause of the Eighth Amendment. In *Bell v. Wolfish* (441 U.S. 520: 1979), for example, the Court allowed "double bunking" of prisoners—assigning two persons to cells originally designed for single occupancy. Long-term double-celling was subsequently upheld in *Rhodes v. Chapman* (452 U.S. 337: 1981). Other Eighth Amendment cases involving prison practices and conditions have followed. The question in *Hudson v. McMillian* (503 U.S. 1: 1992) was whether Eighth Amendment protection extended to excessive physical force situations where the injuries sustained by the prisoner are not serious. In reviewing the dismissal of Hudson's suit, the court of appeals had ruled that an excessive force claim requires a showing, among other things, of "significant injury." The Supreme Court reversed. The "core judicial inquiry," said Justice O'Connor, is whether force is applied in a "good-faith effort to maintain or restore discipline, or maliciously and sadistically to cause harm." The extent of injury suffered by the defendant was seen by the Court as but one of several factors relevant to determining whether force was used in a wanton or unjustified manner. Such a determination is also based on whether force was necessary at all, the relationship of a perceived need for force, the amount of force actually used, whether the threat to which the prison officials responded was "reasonably perceived," and what, if any, effort was made to "temper the severity of a forceful response." Thus it was the Court's judgment that absence of serious injury is "relevant to the Eighth Amendment inquiry, but does not end it." The Court also rejected the argument that serious injury constitutes a threshold condition for satisfying the "objective component" of the Eighth Amendment. Such claims, said O'Connor, are "contextual and responsive to 'contemporary standards of decency.'" When the context is excessive force and malicious and sadistic use of force by prison officials, "contemporary standards of decency always are violated" even if "significant injury" is not evident. If this were not so, the Eighth Amendment "would permit any physical punishment, no matter how diabolic or inhuman, inflicting less than some arbitrary quantity of injury." Justices Thomas and Scalia dissented saying that the use of force that causes only "insignificant harm" to a prisoner may be "immoral, it may be tortious, it may be criminal, and it may be even be remediable under other provisions of the Federal Constitution, but it is not 'cruel and unusual punishment.'"

The question in *Helling v. McKinney* (125 L. Ed. 2d 22: 1993) was whether the Eighth Amendment prohibition on cruel and unusual punishment applies to future health threats that may come from confinement with a heavy smoker. In a 7–2 decision, the Court ruled that the Eighth Amendment can reach such future health risks and remanded the case for assessment of McKinney's claims. Justice White said that contemporary standards of decency "require no less" than for the treatment of a prisoner and the conditions of his confinement be subject to Eighth Amendment scrutiny. An Eighth Amendment violation requires a showing of "deliberate indifference" by prison officials to the health needs of an inmate. The Court rejected Nevada's contention that the Amendment does not protect against prison conditions that "merely threaten to cause health problems in the future." We have "great difficulty agreeing that prison authorities may not be indifferent to an inmate's current health problems," said White, "but may ignore a condition of confinement that is sure or very likely to cause serious illness and needless suffering the next week or month or year." The Court saw the situations as similar to one where an inmate could successfully complain about "demonstrably unsafe drinking water without waiting for an attack of dysentery." The Court saw nothing "novel" about applying the Eighth Amendment against future harm. It would be "odd," White said, "to deny an injunction to inmates who plainly proved an unsafe, life-threatening condition in their prison on the ground that nothing yet had happened to them." The Court then remanded the case in order to give McKinney an opportunity to develop his Eighth Amendment claim. White then discussed some of the evidentiary requirements McKinney must meet. He must show that it is contrary to contemporary standards of decency for anyone to be exposed to environmental tobacco smoke (ETS) and that the prison authorities were "deliberately indifferent" to his complaints. Further, McKinney must show that he was exposed to "unreasonably high level of ETS." Review of this objective factor must include the fact that he had been transferred to another detention facility and that he is no longer the cellmate of a heavy smoker. Besides any statistical inquiry into the potential health risk caused by ETS exposure, McKinney would need to demonstrate that the health risk he had claimed is "not one that today's society chooses to tolerate." Relevant to this subjective factor of deliberate indifference by prison officials are the current attitudes and conduct that may have "changed considerably" since the case was initiated. Justice Thomas, in dissent, was most concerned about the expansion of the Eighth Amendment "beyond all bounds of history and precedent." The word *punishment* in the Eighth Amendment refers to the penalty imposed upon conviction of criminal charges. The word "does not encompass a prisoner's injuries that bear no relation to his sentence."

Finally, the Supreme Court held in *Farmer v. Brennan* (128 L. Ed. 2d 811: 1994) that prison authorities can be held responsible for failing to protect a prisoner from physical harm at the hands of other prisoners. Dee Farmer, a transsexual, is a male who considers himself a female and looks like a female. When he was transferred to a federal maximum security facility in Terre Haute, Indiana, he had undergone treatment to change his sex, but had not yet had a "sex change" operation. He was placed in the general population of males at the facility, and within two weeks he was beaten and raped by an inmate. The question was whether prison officials can be held liable if they knew or should have known that Farmer would be in danger when placed in the male population of a maximum security prison. The district court dismissed Farmer's suit, but the U.S. Supreme Court unanimously reversed. Justice Souter began by saying that the Constitution neither "mandate[s] comfortable prisons" nor "permit[s] inhumane ones," but it does place restraints on prison officials. The difficult task of defining the criteria against prison officials' conduct is to be examined. Two requirements have emerged. The first is that the conduct of prison officials leads to "serious" harm. Second, the officials must have a "sufficiently culpable state of mind," that they showed a "deliberate indifference" to an inmate's welfare. This case focused on the test for deliberate indifference. Farmer sought to have the Court fashion an objective test with deliberate indifference defined similarly to the civil concept of "recklessness." The Court did not do so. Instead, it said that a prison official cannot be found liable under the Eighth Amendment for denying a prisoner "humane conditions of confinement" unless the official "knows of and disregards an excessive risk to inmate health or safety." The official must be aware of the facts upon which an inference of serious harm is based and aware that he or she must draw the same inference of danger. The Eighth Amendment, said Souter, "does not outlaw cruel and unusual 'conditions'; it outlaws cruel and unusual 'punishments.'" An official's failure to alleviate a risk that should have been perceived but was not "cannot under our cases be condemned as the infliction of punishment." At the same time, an Eighth Amendment claimant "need not show that a prison official acted or failed to act believing that harm actually would befall an inmate." It is enough, Souter continued, that the official acted or failed to act "despite his knowledge of a substantial risk of serious harm." Whether a prison official actually had the required knowledge of substantial risk is a "question of fact subject to demonstration in the usual ways, including inference from circumstantial evidence." Prison officials charged with deliberate indifference might show in response that they were unaware of underlying facts indicating substantial danger, or that they were aware of the underlying facts, but concluded that any risk to the inmate was insubstantial or nonexistent. Prison officials also might free themselves from liability if they can show they "responded reasonably to the risk, even if the harm ultimately was not averted."

3. The Fifth Amendment

Double Jeopardy: Sameness

Grady v. Corbin, 495 U.S. 508, 109 L. Ed. 2d 548, 110 S. Ct. 2084 (1990)
Examined the pivotal double jeopardy issue of sameness. Corbin was
responsible for an automobile accident in which a person died. Corbin
was ticketed at the scene for drunk driving and driving on the wrong side
of the road. Shortly thereafter, Corbin pleaded guilty to those charges.
The prosecution failed to inform the trial court that the accident had
resulted in a fatality before the court accepted Corbin's plea and imposed
sentence. Two months later, Corbin was indicted on several charges
stemming from the accident including negligent homicide and third-
degree reckless assault. Under the test established in *Blockberger v. United
States* (284 U.S. 299: 1932), the indictments covered charges that were not
the same as those to which Corbin had earlier pleaded. The Supreme
Court said that a subsequent prosecution must do more than "merely
survive" *Blockberger* standards, however. The state had admitted in this case
that it would attempt to establish the essential elements of the homicide
and assault charges on the basis of Corbin's conduct that had led to the
earlier convictions. The Court ruled that the state is precluded from
establishing an "essential element" of a crime on the basis of the same
conduct for which a defendant has been convicted. The Court made it
clear this was not a "same evidence" test. Rather, the "critical inquiry is
what conduct the State will prove, not the evidence the State will use to
prove that conduct." Subsequent prosecutions for homicide and assault
could have been pursued in this case if they did not rely on proving the
conduct for which Corbin had already been convicted. The Court also
pointed out that with "adequate preparation and foresight" on the part
of the prosecution, the traffic offenses and the charges from the indictment could have been pursued in a single proceeding thus "avoiding this
double jeopardy question." *See also ASHE v. SWENSON* (397 U.S. 436: 1970),
p. 213; DOUBLE JEOPARDY, p. 403.

Significance   The sameness issue found in *Grady* has been before the
Rehnquist Court several times. Under the "sameness" test established in
Blockberger, two offenses are not the same if they contain at least one
different element. The Court ruled in *Dowling v. United States* (493 U.S.

342: 1990), however, that the double jeopardy prohibition did not prevent the admission of evidence relating to another alleged crime for which a defendant had been acquitted. Dowling was prosecuted in federal court for bank robbery. The prosecution sought to introduce evidence that Dowling had been involved in other crimes. Specifically, the prosecution attempted to obtain testimony from a woman into whose home Dowling allegedly had broken. In both the break-in and the robbery, the perpetrator had worn a ski mask and carried a small hand gun. The woman had unmasked Dowling during the break-in and was able to identify him. Notwithstanding that identification, Dowling had been acquitted on charges associated with that break-in. The prosecution for the bank robbery wished to have the woman describe Dowling to strengthen identification of him as the bank robber. The woman could also identify a second man from the break-in. This same man had been seen outside the bank in what was believed to be the intended getaway car, and the prosecution wished to reinforce the link between Dowling and the second man. As the woman concluded her testimony, the jury was informed that Dowling had been acquitted on the charge involving the witness. The jury was also instructed of the limited purpose for which the testimony was introduced. The Supreme Court ruled that neither the doctrine of collateral estoppel nor considerations of due process precluded her testimony. In this case, the prior acquittal did not "determine the ultimate fact issue" in the bank robbery because the prosecution was not required to prove that Dowling had entered the witness's home. The Court was also of the view that the judge's limiting jury instruction kept the testimony from being "fundamentally unfair" because the jury could assess the truthfulness and significance of the witness's testimony. The Court ruled in *United States v. Felix* (118 L. Ed. 2d 25: 1992) that *Grady* did not preclude prosecution for substantive offenses even if some of the evidence used by the government was based on offenses for which the defendant was previously convicted. "Mere overlap" in proof between two prosecutions, said Chief Justice Rehnquist, "does not establish a double jeopardy violation." *Grady* "disclaimed any intention" of adopting a "same evidence" test. It is thus an "extravagant reading" of *Grady* to prevent the government from using as evidence in one prosecution acts of misconduct that might have been included in an earlier prosecution. Similarly, the Court held that prosecution for conspiracy is permissible even when the government relies on some of the overt acts of which the defendant has been previously convicted. Long before *Grady*, the Court established the rule that a "substantive crime, and a conspiracy to commit that crime, are not the 'same offense' for double jeopardy purposes." The Court said in *Grady* that in addition to meeting the *Blockburger* test, a subsequent prosecution also must satisfy a "same conduct" test. The *Grady* rule says that a second prosecution is not permitted if the conduct needed to prove the second charge is conduct for which the person has already been prosecuted. *Grady* was dissettling for this reason. Two members of the five-justice *Grady* majority, Justices Brennan and Marshall, then left the Court.

The consolidated cases of *United States v. Dixon* and *United States v. Foster* (125 L. Ed. 2d 556: 1993) gave the Supreme Court an opportunity to re-examine the *Grady* "sameness" test. The Court used *Dixon/Foster* to overrule the *Grady* standard. Both Dixon and Foster were convicted of criminal contempt. The double jeopardy question in both was whether the contempt convictions barred subsequent prosecutions on the offenses upon which the contempt was based. Alvin Dixon was arrested for second degree murder. He was later released on bond on the condition that he commit no further crimes. While still awaiting trial on the original charge, Dixon was arrested for possession of cocaine with intent to distribute. He was subsequently found in contempt of court for violating the conditions of his pre-trial release. He was sentenced to a term in jail on the contempt conviction. The District of Columbia Court of Appeals ruled that prosecution for the substantive drug offense was barred by the Double Jeopardy Clause under *Blockburger*. The court of appeals found that there were no elements of the drug charge different from the elements constituting the criminal contempt. The Supreme Court agreed. Since the subsequent prosecution of Dixon failed *Blockburger*, it was unnecessary to use *Grady*. The *Foster* case, on the other hand, provided the Supreme Court with the opportunity to reconsider *Grady's* "same conduct" test. Michael Foster's ex-wife obtained a protective order from a District of Columbia court requiring that he not molest, assault, or threaten physical abuse to his former wife or to her mother. Foster violated the order a number of times, and he was found in contempt of the protective order. He was subsequently indicted on charges of simple assault (one count), assault with intent to kill (one count), and threatening to injure (three counts). The court of appeals dismissed the indictment on all five counts, based on *Grady*. The Supreme Court agreed (6–3) that prosecution for simple assault was barred under *Blockburger*. In a 5–4 ruling, however, the Court held that prosecution of Foster could occur on the remaining four counts even though these prosecutions would have been barred under the "same conduct" test of *Grady*. Justice Scalia, an outspoken dissenter in *Grady*, delivered the opinion of the Court. Unlike *Blockburger*, the "same conduct" rule announced in *Grady* is "wholly inconsistent" with earlier Supreme Court decisions and with the "clear common-law understanding of double jeopardy." In Scalia's view, there is simply "no authority except *Grady*" for the proposition that the Double Jeopardy Clause has different meanings in the successive prosecution and successive punishment contexts. That is because, Scalia continued, it is "embarrassing to assert that the single term *same offence* (the words of the Fifth Amendment at issue here) has two different meanings—that what *is* the same offense is yet *not* the same offense." Not only was it "wrong in principle," Scalia suggested that *Grady* "has already proved unstable in application." He pointed to the conspiracy exception recognized in *Felix*. *Dixon/Foster* was "yet another situation" in which a pre-*Grady* understanding would have allowed a second trial only to be barred by the "same conduct" test. Scalia thought it time to acknowledge what is "compellingly clear"—that the *Grady* decision "was a mistake." Chief Justice Rehnquist and Justices O'Connor and Thomas were of the view that "as a general matter, double jeopardy does not bar a subsequent prosecution based on conduct for which a defendant has been held in criminal contempt." Because the crime of contempt has different elements from any substantive criminal charge, they would have permitted the prosecution of Dixon on the drug charge and the prosecution of Foster on the simple assault indictment because they are separate offenses under the *Blockburger* test. Justices White, Souter, Blackmun, and Stevens believed that all of Foster's counts were barred from prosecution without relying on *Grady*.

The Court turned to the multiple punishments question in *Montana Department of Revenue of Montana v. Kurth Ranch* (128 L. Ed. 2d 767: 1994). The Court ruled that states could not levy a drug tax upon persons who have been subjected to criminal penalties for the same conduct. The Montana Dangerous Drug Tax Act provides that anyone who stores or possesses marijuana (or other specified controlled substances) can be taxed at 10 percent of the drug's market value or $100 per ounce of marijuana, whichever is greater. The act further provides that the tax could be "collected only after any state or federal fines or forfeitures have been satisfied." Six members of the Richard Kurth family were charged with various drug offenses following a raid on the family farm during which federal officers seized a variety of contraband including 2155 live marijuana plants. The local prosecutor also filed a civil action seeking forfeiture of cash and equipment confiscated from the Kurth ranch. An officer participating in the raid completed a tax assessment form totalling $865,000 (at $100 an ounce of seized marijuana). The Kurths filed for bankruptcy and challenged the constitutionality of the tax on double jeopardy grounds. The Supreme Court ruled for the Kurths in a 5–4 decision. As a general proposition, said Justice Stevens, the "unlawfulness of an activity does not prevent its taxation." The Court had no doubt that Montana could collect its marijuana possession tax had it not previously punished the taxpayer for the same offense. The issue in this case, however, was whether the tax has punitive characteristics that bring it under the constraints of the Double Jeopardy Clause. Previous decisions, Stevens said, suggest that a tax should not be invalidated simply because "its enforcement might be oppressive or because the legislature's motive is suspect." Nonetheless, the penalizing features of a tax can cause it to lose its character of a tax and become a "mere penalty with the characteristics of regulation and punishment." Legislative labeling does not control whether a tax is immune from double jeopardy scrutiny. At some point, an exaction labeled as a tax approaches punishment, and the Court's task is to determine whether the tax under review crosses that line. Neither a high rate of taxation nor an obvious deterrent purpose automatically makes a tax a form of punishment. Here, however, these factors are "consistent with a punitive character." Stevens pointed to an assessment against marijuana that was more than eight times the market value. That Montana intended the tax to deter people from possessing marijuana is "beyond question." Even these features of the Montana law were not wholly dispositive. Other unusual features, however, "set the Montana statute apart from most taxes." First, the tax is conditioned on the commission of a crime. This condition, said Stevens, is "significant of penal and prohibitory intent" rather than of the raising of revenue. Second, the tax also is exacted only after the taxpayer has been arrested for the "precise conduct that gives rise to tax obligation in the first place." People arrested for possession of marijuana in Montana "constitute the entire class of taxpayers subject to the Montana tax." Stevens distinguished taxes imposed on illegal activities from "mixed motive" taxes such as those imposed on cigarettes. The justifications for so-called "mixed motive" taxes do not apply when the taxed activity is completely prohibited, however. In such instances, the need to raise revenue would be "equally well served" by simply increasing the fine imposed on conviction. Third, the Montana tax is purportedly a form of property tax—a tax on the possession and storage of controlled substances. At the time the tax is imposed, the property is likely to have been confiscated by the state and destroyed. A tax on the possession of goods that no longer exist or that could not have been lawfully possessed also reflect the punitive character of the Montana tax. Taken as a whole, Stevens concluded, the Montana drug tax is a "concoction of anomalies, too far removed in crucial respects from a standard tax assessment to escape characterization as punishment for the purpose of double jeopardy analysis." Chief Justice Rehnquist, joined by Justices O'Connor and Scalia, dissented. They saw the ruling as substantially departing from existing double jeopardy doctrine. It was also the view of the dissenters' that the Montana tax had a nonpenal purpose of raising revenue as well as a legitimate deterrence purpose. Because the tax did not have a punitive purpose, it could not be regarded as a second punishment.

Grand Jury

Costello v. United States, **350 U.S. 359, 100 L. Ed. 397, 76 S. Ct. 406 (1956)** Examined whether grand juries must utilize the same procedural and evidentiary rules as are required for jury trials. Costello, an organized crime figure, was indicted by a grand jury for tax evasion. He claimed that the grand jury indictments had been based on hearsay evidence and should be dismissed. Costello was subsequently convicted. A unanimous Court upheld the conviction based on the challenged indictments. The Court held that no constitutional provision "prescribes the kind of evidence upon which grand juries must act." The work of grand juries was intended not to be "hampered by rigid procedural or evidentiary rules." Citing the history out of which the English grand jury system evolved, the Court noted that grand jurors could "act on their own knowledge and were free to make their presentments or indictments on such information as they deemed satisfactory." The Court noted the excessive delays which would be produced by challenges to indictments on grounds of evidence inadequacy. It would mean that a defendant could "insist on a kind of preliminary trial to determine competency and adequacy of the evidence before the grand jury." Such is not required by the Fifth Amendment. The Court concluded its opinion by reiterating that a preliminary trial "would run counter to the whole history of the grand jury institution, in which laymen conduct their inquiries unfettered by technical rules." *See also* BRANZBURG *v.* HAYES (408 U.S. 665: 1972), p. 125; GRAND JURY, p. 418.

Significance　　*Costello* graphically demonstrated the broad operating latitude the Supreme Court typically has extended to grand juries. *Costello* reflects the categorical distinction between the charging process and processes designed to adjudicate guilt. Without question, the grand jury can operate more informally. Procedural and evidentiary rules were referred to as possible "impediments" to the charging role of grand juries. Although decided in 1953, the position of *Costello* remains virtually unaltered, and the consequences of the case are apparent in at least three ways. First, *Costello* underscored the investigative function of grand juries and the Court's view that grand juries must be exposed to the widest range of information in performing the accusatorial function. All other interests are generally subordinate to this end. Second, because of the primacy of the investigatory role, *Costello* enhances the influence of the prosecutor in guiding the operations of a grand jury. The greater the level of informality allowed in grand jury proceedings, the greater the discretion which can be utilized by the prosecutor in selecting witnesses and other evidence for grand jury consideration. Third, *Costello's* emphasis on informality raises certain questions regarding protection of witnesses' rights, specifically the right against self-incrimination and the right of assistance of counsel.

Other problems have been noted related to the use of immunity and the threat of the contempt power. The latter can be seen in *Branzburg v. Hayes* (408 U.S. 665: 1972), where a reporter was compelled to disclose information to a grand jury or be subjected to penalties for contempt. In *United States v. Washington* (431 U.S. 181: 1977), the Court considered the question of whether a grand jury witness must be specifically warned that he may be indicted by that grand jury. Further, must he be explicitly informed that if he is indicted, his testimony may be used against him at his trial? Washington was not warned of either possibility, but the Supreme Court held 7–2 that his grand jury statements were admissible at his trial. The majority concluded that the Fifth Amendment does not "preclude a witness from testifying voluntarily in matters which may incriminate him." Unless compulsion can be shown, the Fifth Amendment does not automatically apply because testimony has an incriminating effect. Once Washington had been warned generally that he could remain silent and that statements he made could be used against him, that advice "eliminated any possible compulsion to self-incrimination which may otherwise exist."

The Burger Court rendered several additional decisions involving grand jury practices. In *United States v. Mandujano* (425 U.S. 564: 1976), a person was indicted by a grand jury for making false statements to the grand jury. The defendant attempted to have the grand jury testimony suppressed on the ground that he had not received complete *Miranda* warnings prior to his appearance. A unanimous Court concluded that the testimony need not be suppressed. The Court stressed two themes in *Mandujano*. First, the *Miranda* decision "did not perceive judicial inquiries and custodial interrogation as equivalents." The grand jury setting is so "wholly different from custodial police interrogation" that to apply *Miranda* to grand juries is an "extravagant expansion never remotely contemplated by the Court in *Miranda*." Second, the Court deferred to the broadest view of the grand jury's investigative function. The Court spoke of witnesses being "legally bound to give testimony" and having an "absolute duty to answer all questions." While the privilege against self-incrimination can be asserted, the Court clearly did not wish to interfere with the grand jury's capacity to conduct a complete inquiry. In *United States v. Calandra* (414 U.S. 338: 1974), the Court refused to extend the exclusionary rule to grand jury proceedings. Once again the Court spoke of the need to maintain broad investigative powers for grand juries. Extending the exclusionary rule would "seriously impede" grand jury inquiries and "unduly interfere with the effective and expeditious discharge of the grand jury's duties." The policy preferences reflected in

Washington prevailed because the grand jury function is clearly distinct from guilt adjudication at the trial stage. Since the grand jury is designed to investigate and accuse, the Court decided it can best perform that function by using the widest range of evidence available. That evidence may properly come before a grand jury through procedures which are substantially less formal and protective than those found at the trial stage. This same view was recently reflected in the Rehnquist Court's ruling in *United States v. Williams* (118 L. Ed. 2d 352: 1992). In *Williams*, a five-justice majority held that federal district courts do not have the authority to dismiss indictments in cases where prosecutors withhold evidence favorable to the accused. Such authority, said Justice Scalia, would "neither preserve nor enhance the traditional functioning of the institution that the Fifth Amendment demands." Rather, to require prosecutors to present exculpatory as well as inculpatory evidence would alter the grand jury's historical role, transforming it from an accusatory to an adjudicatory body." Further, given the grand jury's "operational separateness" from the court constituting it, the Supreme Court's view was that district courts could not invoke the "judicial supervisory power as a basis for prescribing modes of grand jury procedure."

Custodial Interrogation

Edwards v. Arizona, **451 U.S. 477, 68 L. Ed. 2d 378, 101 S. Ct. 1880 (1981)**
Ruled that police cannot reinitiate questioning following a defendant's request to have an attorney present. Edwards was arrested on a murder warrant and informed of his rights under *Miranda.* At a point early in his interrogation, Edwards determined that he wanted to consult with an attorney. The questioning stopped at that point. The next morning, other offficers came to the jail and asked to talk with Edwards. He indicated that he did not wish to see the officers. He was told by the detention officer, however, that he "had" to talk with them. Once again Edwards was advised of his rights. After listening to part of a tape in which an accomplice implicated him in the crime, Edwards incriminated himself. The Supreme Court unanimously reversed his conviction. *Miranda* requires that waivers of the right to counsel are not only voluntary, but also "constitute a knowing and intelligent relinquishment or abandonment of a known right or privilege." While an arrestee may validly waive *Miranda* protections, such waivers ought to be carefully scrutinized to insure they are knowing. Even more rigorous safeguards are necessary when an accused asks for counsel. The Court held that a valid waiver of the right to counsel cannot be established by showing only that the accused "responded to further police-initiated custodial interrogation" even after advising the person of his or her rights. In other words, if the right to assistance of counsel is asserted, only defendant-initiated communication

with police may occur. *See also* MIRANDA *v.* ARIZONA (384 U.S. 436: 1966), p. 219; SELF-INCRIMINATION CLAUSE, p. 448.

Significance   Police-initiated conversations that produce incriminating statements have been a particularly problematic aspect of *Miranda*. The reasoning in *Edwards* was applied in *Michigan v. Jackson* (475 U.S. 625: 1986). Following his arraignment on a murder charge, Jackson requested that counsel be appointed. Before he could meet with his lawyer, officers administered *Miranda* warnings to Jackson and interrogated him. The interrogation yielded a confession. The Court said that when the officers initiated the interview after the defendant requested counsel "at arraignment or similar proceeding," any subsequent waiver of the right to counsel for that police-initiated interrogation is invalid. *Arizona v. Roberson* (486 U.S. 675: 1988) raised the issue of whether the *Edwards* rule reaches separate investigations of wholly independent offenses. Roberson was arrested for burglary and advised of his rights. He indicated that he wished to consult counsel before responding to any questions. Three days later, while Roberson was still detained and awaiting contact with a lawyer, a different officer, who was unaware that Roberson had requested counsel, again advised Roberson of his rights and began questioning him about another burglary. The interrogation on the second offense produced an incriminating statement. The Supreme Court held that *Edwards* extended to such situations. The *Edwards* rule, said the Court, "benefits the accused and the State alike." It protects the suspect against "inherently compelling pressures of custodial interrogation" by "creating a presumption" that a waiver of counsel is defective. At the same time, the rule provides "clear and unequivocal" guidelines for conducting custodial interrogations. Given these benefits, the Court saw no reason to create an exception to *Edwards* for the interrogation relating to a separate offense. The "eagerness" of officers to question a suspect is comparable for the officers engaged in separate investigations and those involved in a single inquiry. If the suspect is unable to "cope with" custodial interrogation, additional questioning without counsel will "exacerbate whatever compulsion to speak" the suspect may feel. Simply giving "fresh sets" of warnings will "not necessarily reassure" a suspect who is yet to receive requested counsel. Neither did the Court regard the second officer's ignorance of the earlier request for counsel to be relevant. The *Edwards* rule "focuses on the state of mind of the suspect, not the police." Moreover, the officer could have discovered that Roberson had requested counsel simply by examining the arresting officer's report. The Court clarified the *Edwards* rule in *Minnick v. Mississippi* (498 U.S. 146: 1990). Minnick's interrogation was terminated when he requested counsel. Minnick subsequently met with counsel. Interrogation was later resumed at police initiative in absence of Minnick's lawyer, and Minnick confessed to capital murder. The issue in this case was whether the protection afforded by *Edwards* is satisfied once a person meets with counsel. The Court said *Edwards* requires more. It requires that once counsel is requested, interrogation may not resume in absence of counsel "whether or not the accused has consulted with his attorney." Consultation itself, said the Court, does not protect the suspect from "persistent attempts by officers to persuade him to waive his rights, or from the coercive pressures that accompany custody and that may increase as custody is prolonged."

The Court examined the distinctions between the right to counsel based on the Sixth Amendment and the Fifth Amendment right to counsel attached to custodial interrogation in *McNeil v. Wisconsin* (501 U.S. 171: 1991). McNeil was arrested on an armed robbery warrant. He was read his *Miranda* rights and declined to respond to police attempts to question him. He did not request an attorney immediately, but was represented by appointed counsel at his arraignment. While he was detained on the armed robbery charge, McNeil was questioned about other crimes. He was given his *Miranda* warnings on the second set of crimes, and he signed the appropriate waiver forms prior to making incriminating statements. McNeil unsuccessfully sought to have the statements suppressed by the trial court. The Wisconsin Supreme Court ruled that McNeil's request for representation at his arraignment on the armed robbery charge did not invoke the Fifth Amendment right to counsel as derived through *Miranda*. The Supreme Court agreed in a 6–3 decision. The Court's position was that McNeil had invoked only his Sixth Amendment right to counsel. The Sixth Amendment right, said Justice Scalia, is "offense-specific," and cannot be invoked for "all future prosecutions." As distinct from the Fifth Amendment right, the right to counsel based on the Sixth Amendment "does not attach until a prosecution is commenced." This occurs when adversary judicial criminal proceedings are begun—whether by way of "formal charge, preliminary hearing, indictment, information, or arraignment." The Court rejected McNeil's argument to combine coverage of the two rights because they protect distinct interests. The purpose of the Sixth Amendment guarantee is to protect the "unaided layman at critical confrontations with his 'expert adversary,' the government." This protection is designed to come after the adverse positions of the government and the defendants have "solidified with respect to a particular alleged crime." The Fifth Amendment right as guaranteed by *Miranda* is designed to protect "quite a different interest: the suspect's desire to deal with the police only through counsel." Justices Stevens, Marshall, and Blackmun saw the offense-specific limitation on the attorney-client relationship as one that "could only generate confusion" in a theoretical sense. Symbolically, Stevens said, the decision is "ominous because it reflects a preference for an inquisitorial system that regards the defense lawyer as an impediment rather than a servant to the cause of justice."

Stansbury v. California (128 L. Ed. 2d 293: 1994) considered the question of when a person is in custody and thus entitled to *Miranda* warnings prior to interrogation. Robert Stansbury was asked to accompany police to a police facility for questioning as a possible witness in the investigation of the death of a 10-year-old girl. Because Stansbury was not considered a suspect initially, he was not given *Miranda* warnings. Suspicion of Stansbury's involvement in the murder was triggered by some of his disclosures during the interview. At the point police began to consider Stansbury a suspect, the interview was stopped and Stansbury was advised on his rights. The state trial court did not suppress the statements made by Stansbury prior to his being advised on the ground that he was not in custody until the point at which suspicion, absent at the outset of the interview, was actually aroused. The U.S. Supreme Court unanimously reversed, holding that an officer's "subjective and undisclosed view" concerning whether the person under interrogation is a suspect is "irrelevant" to the assessment of whether the person is in custody. The Court said it was well established that the initial determination of custody depends on the "objective circumstances of the interrogation," and not on the "subjective views harbored by either the interrogating officers or the person being questioned." The officer's undisclosed view that a person being questioned is a suspect "does not bear upon the question whether the individual is in custody for purposes of *Miranda*." Unless communicated or otherwise manifested to the person being questioned, an officer's "evolving but unarticulated suspicions do not affect the objective circumstances of an interrogation or interview, and thus cannot affect the *Miranda* custody inquiry." An officer's beliefs are relevant only to the extent that they "would affect how a reasonable person in the position of the individual being questioned would gauge the breadth of his or her 'freedom of action.'" Even a clear statement from an officer that a person is a suspect is not, in itself, dispositive of the custody issue, as some suspects remain free to leave prior to the police decision to arrest. The impact of an officer's level of suspicion is bound to the facts and circumstances of the particular case. An officer's views concerning the nature of an interrogation, or beliefs concerning the potential culpability of an individual being questioned, may be "among many factors" that bear upon the assessment whether that individual was in custody, but only if the officer's views or beliefs were "somehow manifested to the individual under interrogation and would have affected how a reasonable person in that position would perceive his or her freedom to leave.

A confession made by a person within six hours of arrest is, by federal statute [18 USCS Section 3501(c)], admissible in a federal prosecution even if there is delay in presenting the person to a federal magistrate. *United States v. Alvarez-Sanchez* (128 L. Ed. 2d 319: 1994) considered when the clock begins to run in a situation where the defendant is in custody on state criminal charges. State authorities found counterfeit currency while executing a warrant to search a residence for evidence relating to state drug charges. Alvarez-Sanchez was arrested and booked on the state charges on a Friday evening. He remained in custody over the weekend. On Monday morning, local officials informed the Secret Service about the counterfeit currency. Shortly after, Secret Service agents took possession of the currency and began to interview Alvarez-Sanchez. *Miranda* was administered to him before the interview. Alvarez-Sanchez admitted to the agents that he knew the currency was counterfeit, and was arrested. Congestion in the federal magistrate's docket prevented presentment until the following morning. Alvarez-Sanchez sought to suppress the statement made during the interview because of the delay between his arrest on state charges and his presentment on the federal charge. The Supreme Court unanimously reversed, ruling that the statement was admissible. The Court's resolution of this case hinged on whether terms of Section 3501(c) were triggered at all. Alvarez-Sanchez argued that he was under arrest for Section 3501(c) purposes during the interview at the Sheriff's Department and that his incriminating statements to Secret Service agents constituted a confession governed by Section 3501(c). Because the statute applies to persons in custody of "any" law enforcement agency or officer, Alvarez-Sanchez argued that the six-hour time period begins whenever a person is arrested by local, state, or federal officers. It was the Court's judgment that dispositive weight could not be placed on the broad reference to "any" law enforcement agency or officer in isolation. The terms of the statute can apply only when there is some delay in presentment. There can be no "delay" in bringing a person before a federal magistrate until, at a minimum, there is "some obligation to bring the person before such a judicial officer in the first place." A duty to present a person to a federal magistrate, Thomas continued, "does not arise until the person has been arrested for a *federal* offense." Thus, if a person is arrested for a federal offense by "any" law enforcement official—federal, state, or local—that person is under arrest for purposes of Section 3501(c). In this case, Alvarez-Sanchez was under arrest on state narcotics charges at the time he made his inculpatory statement to the federal agents. The terms of Section 3501(c) did not come into play until he was arrested by agents on the federal charge after he had made the statement. As a result, nothing in Section 3501(c) authorized suppression of the statement. The state's failure to arraign or prosecute did not affect the Court's conclusion.

Davis v. United States (129 L. Ed. 2d 362: 1994) examined the issue of whether *Miranda* requires cessation of all police questioning when a suspect's request for counsel is ambiguous. Robert Davis, a member of the U.S. Navy, was questioned by Naval Investigation Service agents in connection with the death of a sailor. He was advised of his rights under *Miranda* and waived them prior to commencing the interview. About 90 minutes into the interview, he said "Maybe I should talk to a lawyer." When the investigators asked him if he was requesting a lawyer, Davis indicated he was not. The interview continued following a short break and a readministration of the *Miranda* warnings. About an hour after the interview resumed, Davis formally requested as lawyer. At his military trial, Davis unsuccessfully sought to suppress statements made prior to his unambiguous request for counsel. The Supreme Court unanimously affirmed the conviction, although four of the justices did not join Justice O'Connor's opinion of the Court. Under *Edwards,* a subject who requests counsel is not to be questioned further until counsel has been made available, or the suspect reinitiates a conversation. *Edwards* provides a "second layer of prophylaxis" for *Miranda,* and is designed to prevent police from "badgering" a subject into waiving previously asserted *Miranda* protections. If, however, a suspect makes "ambiguous or equivocal" reference to counsel that a "reasonable officer in light of the circumstances would have understood only that the suspect might be invoking the right to counsel," cessation of questioning is not required. To commence the *Edwards* rule, counsel must be requested "unambiguously." That is, the suspect must state his desire to have counsel present "sufficiently clearly" that a reasonable officer would understand the statement to be an actual request for an attorney. If a statement is not sufficiently clear, *Edwards* does not require that officers stop questioning. A rule that would require cessation of questioning where counsel was unclearly discussed, said O'Connor, would transform *Miranda* protections into "wholly irrational obstacles to legitimate police investigative activity"; it would "needlessly" keep police from interviewing a suspect in the absence of counsel "even if the suspect did not wish to have a lawyer present." O'Connor characterized *Edwards* as providing a "bright line" that can be applied in the "real world" of investigation without unduly hampering information gathering. To require questioning to end if a suspect makes a statement that might be a request for an attorney, this "clarity and ease of application would be lost." Accordingly, the Court chose not to adopt a rule requiring officers to ask "clarifying questions" under these circumstances. Justice Souter, joined by Justices Blackmun, Stevens, and

Ginsburg, concurred in the judgment to affirm Davis's conviction. They would have preferred a rule prohibiting further interrogation until it could be determined whether an unambiguous statement might be an actual request for counsel. Justice Souter said that the *Miranda* protections are designed to assure that an individual's right to "choose between speech and silence remains unfettered throughout the interrogation process." In their view, requiring clarifying questions before proceeding further would have better served the objectives of *Miranda*.

Self-Incrimination: Harmless Error

Arizona v. Fulminante, 499 U.S. 279, 113 L. Ed. 2d 302, 111 S. Ct. 1246 (1991)   Extended harmless error analysis to coerced confession situations. Fulminante was suspected of killing his stepdaughter in Arizona, although charges were not brought against him. He subsequently left Arizona for New Jersey, where he was arrested on an unrelated federal charge. He was sentenced to a short term in a federal facility in New York. Rumored at the institution to be a child killer, Fulminante was subjected to abusive treatment by some of the inmates. Fulminante then met another inmate who offered to protect him from the other inmates in exchange for truth about the killing of the stepdaughter. Fulminante confessed to the murder. Unbeknown to Fulminante, the inmate to whom he confessed was an FBI informant. Fulminante unsuccessfully sought to suppress the confession at trial, and he was convicted. The Arizona Supreme Court found the confession coerced, however, and reversed his conviction. In a 5–4 ruling, the U.S. Supreme Court held that the harmless error analysis applies to the admissibility of coerced confessions. Chief Justice Rehnquist wrote for the five-justice majority. He started with the harmless error standards set forth in *Chapman v. California* (386 U.S. 18: 1967). *Chapman* had held that harmless error analysis could not be for coerced confessions, trial before a biased judge, and absence of defense counsel. The majority viewed the *Chapman* discussion of coerced confession as an "historical reference" rather than as the adoption of a firm rule. More crucially, Rehnquist saw use of an involuntary confession as a "classic trial error," something "markedly different" from the two other constitutional violations referred to in *Chapman*. The latter are "structural defects in the constitution of the trial mechanism." Such defects affect the "framework within which the trial proceeds, rather than simply an error in the trial process itself." These are defects that cannot be subjected to harmless error standards. In contrast, the admission of involuntary statements is a trial error "similar in both degree and kind" to erroneous admission of other kinds of evidence. Introduction of an involuntary confession is the kind of trial error, said Rehnquist, that can be "quantitatively assessed in the context of other evidence presented." When reviewing a case in which an involuntary statement is admitted, the appellate court is to review the remaining evidence to determine whether use of the statement was harmless beyond a reasonable doubt. Rehnquist acknowledged that the involuntary confession may have a "more dramatic effect" on a trial than other kinds of trial error. In such cases, the error is clearly not harmless. That eventuality, however, is not a reason for "eschewing the harmless error test entirely." Using harmless error analysis, the Supreme Court agreed with the Arizona Supreme Court that Fulminante's confession was indeed coerced under the "totality of circumstances" standard. Furthermore, its admission at his trial was not harmless. The Supreme Court affirmed the Arizona court's ruling that a new trial on the murder charge was required. Justice White spoke for Justices Marshall, Blackmun, and Stevens in dissent. They felt *Chapman* precluded harmless error analysis in coerced confession situations. They felt the majority had departed from a "vast body" of precedent to arrive at its conclusion. To permit use of coerced confessions, said White, is "inconsistent" with the proposition that we do not use an "inquisitorial system of criminal justice." White also characterized the distinction between trial errors and structural defects as a "meaningless dichotomy." *See also* SELF-INCRIMINATION CLAUSE, p. 448.

Significance   Constitutional error in a criminal case does not automatically require reversal of a conviction. Some error made during a criminal trial may not be serious enough to affect the outcome of the trial. In other words, this kind of error is regarded as nonprejudicial to the rights of the defendant. Harmless error analysis can be applied to a number of procedural errors. *Chapman* identified three categories of errors which could not be subjected to harmless error analysis, however. These categories are absence of defense counsel, trial before a biased judge, and use of a coerced confession which required reversal of convictions. In *Fulminante*, the Supreme Court removed use of a coerced confession from that list. The harmless error concept is an analytic device used by appellate courts as they review actions of lower courts. In order for an appellate court to preserve a conviction, it must be convinced beyond a reasonable doubt that the mistake was harmless. The *Fulminante* ruling leaves only two kinds of error outside the reach of harmless error analysis. By enlarging the scope of harmless error, *Fulminante* reduces to some degree the probability of a successful appeal by those convicted at trial.

4. The Sixth Amendment

Confrontation

Coy v. Iowa, 487 U.S. 1012, 101 L. Ed. 2d 857, 108 S. Ct. 2798 (1988)
Examined the issue of whether placing a screen between the defendant
charged with child molestation and the child victims violated the Confrontation Clause. Under provisions of a state law, a screen was used while
the victims testified, which blocked Coy from their view although he was
able to both see and hear them. The trial court rejected Coy's contention
that the procedure violated his right to confront witnesses against him.
Coy was convicted and was unsuccessful on appeal within the state courts.
The Supreme Court struck down the procedure in a 6–2 decision. The
Court said that it "never doubted" that the confrontation protection
"guarantees the defendant a face-to-face meeting" with witnesses. The
protection has been essential to fairness "over the centuries" because a
witness may "feel quite differently" when he testifies looking at the person
whom he harmed "distorting or mistaking the facts." The face-to-face
confrontation, like the right to cross-examine, "ensures the integrity of
the fact-finding process." The state, said the Court, cannot deny the
"profound effect" the presence of the defendant may have on a witness
since it is the "same phenomenon used to establish the potential trauma
that allegedly justified the extraordinary procedure" used in this case.
That face-to-face presence "may unfortunately upset the truthful rape
victim or abused child," the Court said, but it may also "undo the false
accuser, or reveal the child to be coached by a malevolent adult." Constitutional protections simply "have costs," the Court observed. The Court
then turned to the matter of whether the confrontation right was violated
here, and its conclusion was that it had. The state argued that the
confrontation interest was "outweighed by the necessity of protecting
victims of sexual abuse." The state claimed that such necessity was established by the statute which created a "legislatively imposed presumption
of trauma." The Court ruled that this was not enough. "Something more"
than the "generalized finding" underlying the law is required when an
exception to a constitutional protection is not "firmly rooted in our
jurisprudence." The Court said the exception created by the law "could
hardly be viewed as firmly rooted." Since the state made no "individual
findings" that the witnesses in this case "needed special protection," the

judgment in this case could not be "sustained by any conceivable exception." *See also* CONFRONTATION CLAUSE, p. 397; *POINTER v. TEXAS* (380 U.S. 400: 1965), p. 247.

Significance   As reflected in *Coy*, maintenance of the right to confront may exact a high price. This has been especially true in cases where children are the victims of criminal conduct. Another example is *Pennsylvania v. Ritchie* (480 U.S. 39: 1987). Ritchie was prosecuted for several sex offenses against his minor daughter. He sought to obtain records on the daughter from a state child welfare agency in hope of finding information helpful to his defense. The agency refused to comply with a subpoena, citing a state statute intended to protect the confidentiality of such records. The trial judge refused to order disclosure. The Supreme Court did not agree that there was a confrontation violation, but ruled that Ritchie had a Due Process Clause right to have the records of the child welfare agency submitted to the trial court for review by the judge. The Court found the state's interest in protecting the records to be considerable, but the interest of ensuring Ritchie a fair trial was also substantial. In *Kentucky v. Stincer* (482 U.S. 730: 1987), the Court ruled that a defendant charged with child molestation is not entitled to attend a pre-trial hearing on the competency of child witnesses to testify. Stincer argued that the competency hearing was a stage of trial and was therefore subject to the requirements of the Confrontation Clause. The Court replied that since the functional purpose of the clause was to promote reliability by ensuring an opportunity for cross-examination, a more useful inquiry was whether exclusion of Stincer interfered with that opportunity. The Court saw no such interference. Once witness competency was determined, the witnesses were subject to full and complete cross-examination in the presence of the defendant. The Court found no indication that Stincer's presence at the competency proceeding "would have been useful in ensuring a more reliable determination as to whether the witnesses were competent to testify."

Coy established that physical courtroom confrontation is an irreducible minimum of the confrontation protection. Exceptions would be considered only in furtherance of important public policy. *Maryland v. Craig* (497 U.S. 836: 1990) clarified this matter by holding that states could protect child abuse victims by allowing them to testify on closed-circuit television. Justice O'Connor said for a five-justice majority that neither *Coy* nor any other previous ruling established that a defendant has an "absolute right to a face-to-face meeting" with witnesses. While the Confrontation Clause "reflects a preference for face-to-face confrontation at trial,…we cannot say that such confrontation is an indispensable element of the Sixth Amendment guarantee." The "central concern" of the clause is to "insure the reliability of evidence...by subjecting it to rigorous testing in the context of an adversary proceeding." Maryland's procedure of using closed-circuit television does prevent the child witness from seeing the defendant, but it "preserves all the other elements of the confrontation right." The presence of these other elements "adequately insures that the testimony is both reliable and subject to rigorous adversarial testing in a manner functionally equivalent to that accorded live, in-person testimony." The "critical inquiry" in *Craig* was whether use of the television procedure is needed to further an important state interest. The Court concluded that protection of minor victims of sex crimes from "further trauma and embarrassment is a compelling one." Further, the Court determined that the interest in the "physical and psychological well-being of child abuse victims may be sufficiently important to outweigh, at least in some cases, a defendant's right to face his or her accusers in court." Justice Scalia dissented, seeing the confrontation protection as absolute. He said the Court had "no authority" to "speculate" that where confrontation "causes significant emotional distress in a child witness," it might "disserve" the "truth-seeking goal" of the clause. For "good or bad," said Scalia, the "Sixth Amendment requires confrontation, and we are not at liberty to ignore it."

In *Idaho v. Wright* (497 U.S. 805: 1990), the Court said that states may not utilize hearsay exceptions that permit doctors or other adults to testify about their conversations with abuse victims. At issue in this case was the testimony of a pediatrician who represented statements made to him by a three-year-old girl. The Court concluded that the statements could not be admitted because they "lacked the particularized guarantees of trustworthiness necessary to satisfy the requirement of the Confrontation Clause...." *White v. Illinois* (502 U.S. 346: 1992) examined the extent to which the Confrontation Clause precludes hearsay evidence in child abuse cases. White was convicted on several charges including aggravated criminal sexual assault. The victim was the four-year-old daughter of a former girlfriend. The prosecution twice attempted to use the victim as a witness, but she experienced "emotional difficulty on being brought to the courtroom" and left in both instances without testifying. The trial court was not asked to make a finding that the victim was unavailable to testify. Instead, the victim's statements about what happened were conveyed by five witnesses with whom she had talked within four hours of the incident. Over White's objection, the trial court found three of the witnesses qualified for the spontaneous declaration hearsay exception, while the other two qualified for the medical examination exception. White challenged his conviction on confrontation grounds, asserting that the prosecution was required to show the declarant unavailable to testify before introducing hearsay testimony under *Ohio v. Roberts* (448 U.S. 56:

1980). More recent cases have held that *Roberts* must be confined to its own facts. So understood, said Rehnquist, *Roberts* "stands for the proposition that unavailability analysis is a part of the Confrontation Clause inquiry only when the challenged out-of-court statements were made in the course of a prior judicial proceeding." *Roberts* aside, Rehnquist reiterated the evidentiary rationale for allowing hearsay testimony that represents spontaneous declarations and statements made while receiving medical care. The contexts in which such statements occur provide "substantial guarantees of their trustworthiness." Those same factors that contribute to the statements' reliability "cannot be recaptured even by later in-court testimony." The restrictions that generally apply to hearsay reflect a preference for in-court testimony because it permits the opportunity for cross-examination. On the other hand, "where proferred hearsay has sufficient guarantees of reliability to come within a firmly rooted exception to the hearsay rule, the Confrontation Clause is satisfied." To exclude such probative statements "under the strictures of the Confrontation Clause would be the height of wrong-headedness, given that the Confrontation Clause has as a basic purpose the promotion of the 'integrity of the fact-finding process.'" Finally, White contended that hearsay testimony offered by a child should be permitted only on a showing that it is necessary to protect the physical and psychological well-being of the child. The Court saw no basis for "importing the necessity requirement" applied to in-court procedures into the "much different context" of out-of-court declarations admitted under established exceptions to the hearsay rule.

State "rape-shield" laws designed to protect victim witnesses in sexual assault prosecutions present yet another confrontation question. These laws make it difficult for rape defendants to introduce evidence of the victim's past sexual conduct. The Michigan rape-shield law allows a defendant to show that he had a past sexual relationship with the victim. In order to introduce evidence of that relationship, however, the defendant must notify the court and prosecution of his intent to do so within ten days of the arraignment. If such notice is given by the deadline, a closed hearing is held to determine whether the evidence is relevant and not unduly prejudicial to the victim. The Court reviewed Michigan's rape-shield law in *Michigan v. Lucas* (500 U.S. 145: 1991). Lucas sought to establish a prior sexual involvement with the victim, but he failed to meet the ten-day deadline. As a result, the trial court excluded the evidence. In a 7–2 decision, the Supreme Court ruled that exclusion of evidence on procedural grounds does not violate the Confrontation Clause in every instance. Rather, the right to confront may, in appropriate situations, "bow to accommodate other legitimate interests in the criminal trial process." Michigan's law, said Justice O'Connor, represents a "valid legislative determination that rape victims deserve heightened protection against surprise, harassment, and unnecessary invasions of privacy." The Court determined that there are circumstances when the interests served by the notice requirement may preclude evidence of a previous sexual relationship between the defendant and the victim. The Michigan court's adoption of a per se rule disallowing exclusion of such evidence was too "rigid" an interpretation of what the Confrontation Clause requires. Justices Stevens and Marshall disagreed. In their view, suppression of the evidence for failure to meet procedural requirements was excessively punitive. *Williamson v. United States* (129 L. Ed. 2d 476: 1994) examined the declaration-against-penal-interest exception to hearsay rules. Hearsay testimony is generally inadmissible because the accused has no opportunity to cross-examine or confront the absent adverse witness. As a result, the evidence may be unreliable. Under Federal Rule of Evidence 804(b)(3), statements that open a speaker to possible prosecution qualify for a hearsay rule exception because the speaker probably would not have made the statement if he or she did not believe it to be truthful. Reginald Harris was stopped on a Georgia highway, and authorities found cocaine in his car. During the questioning that followed his arrest, Harris admitted that he received and transported cocaine. Harris also named Williamson as the owner of the cocaine, but refused to testify at Williamson's trial. The District Court ruled that under 804(b)(3) that a Drug Enforcement Administration agent could testify as to Harris' custodial statements which, in addition to admitting his own guilt, implicated Williamson. Williamson was convicted and his conviction was affirmed by the court of appeals. A unanimous Supreme Court vacated the judgment. Justice O'Connor reviewed the rationale for the exception, but suggested that although a person makes a "broadly self-inculpatory confession, [that] does not make more credible the confession's non–self-inculpatory parts." Indeed, O'Connor observed that one of the most effective ways to lie is to "mix falsehood with truth, especially truth that seems particularly persuasive because of its self-inculpatory nature." When part of the confession is actually self-exculpatory, the proposition on which the exception is founded "becomes even less applicable." Self-exculpatory statements are "exactly the ones," said O'Connor, which people are "most likely to make even when they are false; and mere proximity to other, self-inculpatory statements does not increase the plausibility of the self-exculpatory statements." While self-inculpatory statements are generally more reliable, reliability does not extend to statements collateral to the self-inculpatory statement. The Court concluded that there was no reason to treat such collateral statements any differently than other hearsay statements that are excluded. It was the Court's conclusion in this case that the trial court admitted too much of what Harris said.

Some of his confession was admissible under Rule 804(b)(3), but the portions that implicated Williamson "did little to subject Harris himself to criminal liability," and thus were inadmissible under 804(b)(3).

Defendant Competency

Riggins v. Nevada, **504 U.S. __, 118 L. Ed. 2d 479, 112 S. Ct. 1810 (1992)** Held that a state cannot require a defendant asserting an insanity defense to take antipsychotic medication during his trial unless there exists "overriding justification." Speaking for a seven-justice majority, Justice O'Connor said that medicating the defendant might impair his defense. Under terms of *Washington v. Harper* (494 U.S. 210: 1990), Riggins had a due process interest in avoiding involuntary administration of the medication. Once Riggins asserted that interest, Nevada was obligated to show the medication to be "medically appropriate," and despite less intrusive alternatives, "essential for the sake of Riggins' own safety or the safety of others." In this case, however, the trial court permitted Riggins to be medicated without a determination of need or a review of possible alternatives. Riggins further had contended that his trial rights had been violated because he was kept from effectively advancing an insanity defense. While O'Connor did not directly embrace this contention, she did say that the trial court's error "may well have impaired the constitutionally protected trial rights Riggins invokes." It was "clearly possible," said O'Connor, that medicating Riggins could have impacted not only on Riggins's "outward appearance, but also the content of his testimony on direct and cross examination, his ability to follow the proceedings, or the substance of his communication with counsel." Justice Thomas, joined by Scalia, dissented. They were of the view that Riggins's "inability to introduce evidence of his mental condition as he desired did not render his trial fundamentally unfair." *See also* COMPULSORY PROCESS, p. 497.

Significance   In another ruling dealing with a defendant's mental state, the Court held in *Medina v. California* (120 L. Ed. 2d 353: 1992) that states may require criminal defendants to carry the burden of proof in determining competency to stand trial. Justice Kennedy said for the majority that historical practice is "probative of whether a procedural rule can be characterized as fundamental." Lack of "settled tradition" on this issue reflects the absence of any fundamental due process principle. Kennedy went on to suggest that expanding constitutional rights of the accused "under the open-ended rubric of the due process clause invites undue interference with both considered legislative judgments and the careful balance that the Constitution strikes between liberty and order." A restrained interpretive approach to due process on criminal rights issues requires judges to give state procedural practices "substantial deference." Justices Blackmun and Stevens dissented, expressing strong reservations about the trial and conviction of a person "about whom the evidence of competency is so equivocal and unclear."

The issue in *Taylor v. Illinois* (480 U.S. 400: 1988) was whether the Compulsory Process Clause permitted the defense to use surprise witnesses. Prior to Taylor's trial, prosecution filed a discovery motion to obtain a list of defense witnesses. Taylor's response, as well as an amended answer, failed to list a particular witness. After the trial had begun, defense attorney sought to orally amend the discovery answer to include the previously undisclosed witness, indicating that he had been unable to locate the witness earlier, thus he had not included his name on the list. Subsequently, the witness disclosed, among other things, that defense counsel had come to his home prior to the trial. The trial judge refused to allow the witness to testify on the grounds that the defense attorney had violated discovery rules. The Supreme Court ruled that disallowing the testimony of the undisclosed witness as a sanction for the discovery violation did not abridge the defendant's compulsory process rights. The Court described these rights as affording the defendant the fundamental right to present witnesses in his defense. While noting that violations of the right may occur by imposition of discovery sanctions which preclude testimony by the witness, the right is not an "absolute bar to preclusion," in part because there is a "significant difference" between the right to compulsory process and other Sixth Amendment rights. Most Sixth Amendment protections "arise automatically" when the criminal process begins whereas the compulsory process protection depends on defendant's initiative. The "very nature" of the right requires that its "effective use be preceded by deliberate planning and affirmative conduct." The adversary process "could not function effectively" without adherence to rules of procedure that govern "orderly presentation of facts and arguments."

The Due Process Clause was interpreted in 1970 to require the prosecution to demonstrate a criminal defendant's guilt "beyond a reasonable doubt." A number of states have attempted to refine through jury instructions the meaning of the "reasonable doubt" concept. *Victor v. Nebraska* (and the consolidated case *Sandoval v. California*) (127 L. Ed. 2d 583: 1994) provided the Supreme Court with the opportunity to examine the approach used by two states. The Court reversed a capital murder conviction in *Cage v. Louisiana* (498 U.S. 39: 1990) because jurors could have interpreted the reasonable doubt instruction to allow a finding of guilt based on a level of proof less than required by the Due Process Clause. The instruction given in *Cage* characterized reasonable doubt as "substantial doubt" requiring "not an absolute or mathematical certainty, but a moral certainty." It was the Supreme Court's judgment in *Cage* that the instruction represented reasonable doubt, actual substantial doubt, and moral certainty as virtually equivalent. As a result, the state's burden of proof was effectively lowered. The jury instruction used in the trials of Victor and Sandoval, respectively, also defined reasonable doubt in terms of moral certainty. Victor and Sandoval claimed their respective instructions suffered from the same deficiency as the instructions struck down in *Cage*. The Supreme Court, however, affirmed both convictions. Victor's primary argument was that equating reasonable doubt with a substantial doubt "overstated the degree of doubt necessary for acquittal." The Court was concerned that the jury would interpret the term "substantial doubt" in parallel with a preceding reference to "grave uncertainty." The Victor instruction, however, distinguished between a substantial doubt and "fanciful conjecture," a distinction not present in the *Cage* instruction. Considering Victor's instruction as a whole, the overall "context" makes it clear that "substantial" is used in the sense of "existence rather than magnitude of the doubt...." As a result, the Court did not think it was likely that the jury would have interpreted the instruction to indicate that "the doubt must be anything other than a reasonable one." O'Connor said that while the Court does not "countenance" the use of the term "moral certainty," the inclusion of that phrase did not render the instruction given in Victor's case constitutionally deficient. The instruction given in Sandoval's case has its genesis in a charge developed in the mid–nineteenth century. In particular, Sandoval objected to the use of the terms "moral evidence" and "moral certainty" in the instruction. The Court observed that the phrase "moral evidence" is not a "mainstay of the modern lexicon," but concluded after consulting several contemporary dictionaries that the phrase did not mean "anything different today than it did in the 19th century." It was the Court's view that the instruction defined the phrase. The jurors were told that "everything relating to human affairs, and depending on moral evidence is open to some possible or imaginary doubt...." Moral evidence, in this sentence, "can only mean empirical evidence offered to prove such matters—the proof introduced at trial." The Court was "somewhat more concerned" that the phrase "moral certainty" had lost its historical meaning, and that a modern jury would understand it to allow conviction on proof that does not meet the reasonable doubt standard. Again, the Court considered the definition from contemporary dictionaries. While the Court was willing to accept Sandoval's premise that the phrase "moral certainty, standing alone," might not be recognized by modern jurors as synonymous with "proof beyond a reasonable doubt," it was the Court's judgment that the California instruction was not necessarily unconstitutional as a result. Although the term "moral certainty" might be "ambiguous in the abstract," the remainder of the instruction the Sandoval jury received "lends content to the phrase." In the *Cage* instruction, the jurors simply were told that they had to be "morally certain of the defendant's guilt...." There was nothing else to lend meaning to the phrase. This was not true in Sandoval's case. Sandoval's jury was told that a reasonable doubt is "that state of the case which, after the entire comparison and consideration of all the evidence, leaves the minds of the jurors in that condition that they cannot say they feel an abiding conviction, to a moral certainty, of the truth of the charge." The instruction thus explicitly told the jurors that their conclusion had to be based on the evidence in the case. As a result, there is "no reasonable likelihood that the jury would have understood moral certainty to be disassociated from the evidence in the case." While the Court was unanimously of the view that Sandoval's jury did not understand the words *moral certainty* to suggest a standard of proof lower than due process requires, O'Connor indicated that the Court was generally dissatisfied with continued use of the phrase. Indeed, O'Connor said that the Court does not "condone use of the phrase." As suggested by definitions contained in contemporary dictionaries, the meaning of the phrase has changed over time, and it may "continue to do so to the point that it conflicts with the [due process] standard."

Speedy Trial

Barker v. Wingo, 407 U.S. 514, 33 L. Ed. 2d 101, 92 S. Ct. 2182 (1972)
Established criteria by which claims of denial of speedy trial may be evaluated. *Klopfer v. North Carolina* (386 U.S. 213: 1967) had already decided that the speedy trial provisions of the Sixth Amendment applied to the states. Defendant Barker was charged with murder and had a trial date set. Between the original trial date October 21, 1958 and October, 1963, Barker's trial was continued seventeen times. Barker did not object to the first eleven continuances because he was on pre-trial release through most of the period. When eventually tried, Barker was convicted and sentenced to life. The Supreme Court unanimously upheld Barker's conviction. Before fashioning a speedy trial test in the case, Justice Powell considered the unique character of the speedy trial protection. He called it "generically different" from other constitutional protections because there is a "societal interest in providing a speedy trial which exists separate from, and at times in opposition to, the interests of the accused." The speedy trial concept is also "amorphous" and "vague"—more so than other rights of the accused. Writing for the Court, Justice Powell rejected specific timetables and the "on demand" approach as inflexible. Instead he devised a "balancing test" for evaluating speedy trial claims. The test contained four elements and "compels courts to approach speedy trial

cases on an ad hoc basis." The four factors identified are: (1) length of delay, (2) reasons offered by the government (prosecution) to justify the delay, (3) the defendant's assertion of his or her right to a speedy trial, and (4) prejudice to the defendant in terms of pre-trial incarceration, anxiety, and impairment of the defense itself. Applying these criteria to *Barker,* the Court concluded that despite the lengthy delay, Barker's defense was not prejudiced. He was on release throughout most of the period, and he failed seriously to assert the right to a speedy trial. *See also* SPEEDY TRIAL, p. 452.

Significance Barker v. Wingo provides a uniquely two-edged protection in relation to a speedy trial. The defendant must be protected from lengthy pre-trial detention and diminution of the capacity to offer a defense, but the prosecutor's case must be similarly protected from erosion by delay. *Barker* established several criteria for assessing when a speedy trial has not occurred. In fashioning the four criteria listed above, the Court rejected both the fixed time and "demand-waiver" approaches. Instead, the Court opted for a balancing test which is compatible with the Burger Court's general preference for examining the "totality of the circumstances." Several other cases speak to the matter of when the speedy trial protection begins, i.e., when the clock starts to run. *United States v. Marion* (404 U.S. 307: 1971) examined a three-year delay between a criminal act and the filing of charges. The Court concluded that the speedy trial guarantee does not apply "until the putative defendant in some way becomes an 'accused.'" *United States v. Lovasco* (431 U.S. 783: 1977) also considered preindictment delay. In *Lovasco,* the prosecution had a chargeable case within a month of the crime but did not seek indictment for an additional 17 months. The delay was attributed to an inability to finish the investigation of the case against Lovasco as well as several others. Compounding the situation was the fact that the defendant lost the testimony of two witnesses who died during the 18-month delay. Nonetheless, the Court found for the prosecution and refused to find an investigative delay prior to indictment a fatal defect. The Court refused to require prosecutors to charge as soon as evidence might be minimally sufficient. The Court did recognize that "reckless" preindictment delay or delay aimed at gaining an advantage did constitute a denial of due process. In *United States v. MacDonald* (456 U.S. 1: 1982), a murder case which drew national attention, the Court found that the time between dismissed charges brought within the military system of justice and the subsequent filing of civilian charges is not subject to speedy trial protection. The Court reiterated *MacDonald* in *United States v. Loud Hawk* (474 U.S. 302: 1986), saying that the time when persons are free of all restrictions on their liberty is not to be included in the computation of delay. It is only the "actual restraints imposed by arrest and holding to answer a criminal charge that engages the protection of the Speedy Trial Clause." The Court also said in *Loud Hawk* that delay attributable to any interlocutory appeal must be weighed within the *Barker* test, but it does not necessarily weigh effectively toward the person invoking the Speedy Trial Clause. Thus the burden of demonstrating violation of the speedy trial protection clearly rests with the defense, and cases such as *Marion, Lovasco,* and *MacDonald* reflect the Court's preference for limiting the stages or time periods to which the speedy trial protection applies. In the meantime Congress has legislated a speedy trial time period for federal courts. An accused must be brought to trial within 70 days of his or her first court appearance to answer criminal charges. That time period can be tolled for various reasons, usually consistent with defense requests. Some states also have enacted speedy trial legislation, frequently allowing six months from the time of arraignment. The balancing test of *Barker* still applies, however. Indeed, the Rehnquist Court extended the scope of *Barker* by identifying a fair trial dimension in the case of *Doggett v. United States* (120 L. Ed. 2d 520: 1992). Doggett had been indicted on federal drug charges, but left the country before he could be arrested. He subsequently reentered the country and lived openly using his own name until his arrest more than eight years after his indictment. The Court ruled 5–4 that Doggett's speedy trial right had been violated. The Court focused on the fourth *Barker* criterion, prejudiced suffered by the defendant as a consequence of the delay. Doggett failed to demonstrate that the delay had weakened his ability to raise specific defenses. The Court said, however, that "consideration of prejudice is not limited to the specifically demonstrable." Rather, it generally must be recognized that excessive delay "presumptively compromises the reliability of a trial in ways that neither party can prove or, for that matter, identify." Such presumptive prejudice is "part of the mix of relevant facts, and its importance increases with the length of delay." On this basis, the majority concluded that the negligent delay between Doggett's indictment and arrest "presumptively prejudiced his ability to prepare an adequate defense."

Jury Trial

Williams v. Florida, 399 U.S. 78, 26 L. Ed. 2d 446, 90 S. Ct. 1893 (1970)
Considered whether a jury of less than 12 persons satisfied the constitutional requirement of *Duncan v. Louisiana* (391 U.S. 145: 1968) that no state could deny trial by jury in a criminal case. The Court found that Florida's trial of Williams with a jury of six persons met the requirement. Justice White concentrated on three principles in the majority opinion.

First, while the jury is deeply rooted in our legal history, he found nothing from historical evidence to suggest the framers intended that exactly twelve persons should always serve on a jury, or that the number twelve was an "indispensable component" of the Sixth Amendment. Second, juries should be large enough to promote group deliberation, free from "outside attempts at intimidation." The Court found nothing to lead it to believe that this goal was "in any meaningful sense less likely to be achieved when the jury numbers six than when it numbers twelve." Third, juries must "provide a fair possibility for obtaining a representative cross section of the community." The Court found the difference between twelve and six to be "negligible" in this regard. As long as selection processes prevent arbitrary or discriminatory exclusions, the Court felt "the concern that the cross section will be significantly diminished if the jury is decreased in size from twelve to six seems an unrealistic one." Justice Marshall dissented, arguing that the Fourteenth Amendment required a twelve-member jury in cases where a defendant such as Williams could be sent to prison for the remainder of his life upon conviction. Justice Blackman did not participate in the decision. *See also* APODACA *v.* OREGON (406 U.S. 404: 1972), p. 257; JURY, p. 431; SIXTH AMENDMENT, p. 241.

Significance   *Williams* represented an unexpected departure from English common law tradition. The tradition clearly acknowledged a jury of 12 persons. When *Duncan* established the fundamental character of the jury trial at the state level, it was presumed that state juries would have 12 jurors, as do federal juries. The rationale offered by the Court in *Williams* for smaller juries has been subjected to serious criticism, particularly as it relates to the deliberative and representational aspects of twelve- versus six-person juries. The Court subsequently did establish that six was the constitutionally acceptable minimum. In *Ballew v. Georgia* (435 U.S. 223: 1978), the Court considered a conviction by a five-member jury in a state obscenity case. A unanimous Court, including all five members who had voted in the *Williams* majority eight years earlier, found a five-member jury to be constitutionally defective. The Court's opinion used as its rationale the reasons offered by critics of the *Williams* decision. The Court found that "effective group deliberation" and the ability adequately to represent a cross-section of the community was seriously threatened by a five-member jury. Critics say the difference between six and five appears to be entirely arbitrary. The *Williams* decision provided the states with considerable latitude in utilizing juries in criminal cases. Jury trials are guaranteed to any defendant charged with a "serious" offense. *Blanton v. City of North Las Vegas* (489 U.S. 538: 1989) considered whether the right to a jury trial extends to a first-offense driving-while-intoxicated charge where the maximum detention is six months. The Court ruled unanimously that the penalty faced by first-offense defendants was not sufficiently severe to constitute a "serious" offense for jury trial purposes. The "most relevant criterion" for determining the seriousness of an offense is the "maximum authorized penalty fixed by the legislature." When an offense carries a maximum of less than six months, it is "presumed to be petty" unless it can be shown by the defendant that additional penalties, when viewed "in conjunction with the maximum authorized period of incarceration, are so severe that they clearly reflect a legislative determination that the offense in question is a 'serious' one." Applying this standard to Blanton's first-offense driving-while-intoxicated charge, the Court saw no evidence that the state legislature saw the offense as "serious."

The Rehnquist Court has expanded the number of issues subject to harmless error review over the past several terms. This approach creates at least the possibility that errors committed before or during a trial can be regarded as harmless when it is clear that a conviction was not affected by the error. The question in *Sullivan v. Louisiana* (124 L. Ed. 2d 182: 1993) was whether a questionable jury instruction on reasonable doubt could be subjected to harmless error. It was the unanimous judgment of the Supreme Court that it could not. Justice Scalia suggested for the Court that harmless error review, under terms established in *Chapman v. California* (386 U.S. 18: 1967), was "illogical" in this case. The entire premise of harmless error review—demonstration of guilt beyond a doubt notwithstanding the error—does not exist in this situation. The jury never convicted the accused on the basis of the guilt beyond a reasonable doubt standard. The question of whether the "same verdict of guilty beyond a reasonable doubt would have been rendered absent the constitutional error is utterly meaningless." In the Court's view, there was nothing, "no object...upon which harmless error scrutiny can operate." The essential connection to a beyond a reasonable doubt factual finding cannot be established where the erroneous jury instruction consists of a "misdescription of the burden of proof, which vitiates *all* the jury's findings." An appellate court can only engage in "pure speculation—its view of what a reasonable jury would have done." When a reviewing court does that, the "wrong entity judges the defendant guilty." The guarantee of a jury decision is a "'basic protection' whose precise effects are unmeasurable, but without which a criminal trial cannot reliably serve its function." Denying an accused the right to a jury verdict of guilt beyond a reasonable doubt thus constitutes a "structural error," a type of error for which harmless error review is inappropriate.

The Insanity Defense Reform Act of 1984 (IDRA) provides for a verdict of not guilty by reason of insanity (NGI) in federal criminal cases. Terry Shannon sought to offer a defense of insanity in response to federal firearm charges. At trial, Shannon requested a jury instruction that if he was found NGI, he would be placed in a mental facility where he would remain until it could be demonstrated that he was no longer a threat to himself or others. The trial court refused to give this instruction, and the jury subsequently found Shannon guilty. The court of appeals agreed that Shannon was not entitled to an instruction describing the consequences of a NGI verdict. The Supreme Court affirmed in a *Shannon v. United States* (129 L. Ed. 2d 459: 1994). The Court rejected Shannon's general contention that an instruction on consequences of a verdict is required. When a jury has no sentencing function, it is "well established" that it should be admonished to reach its verdict without regard to what sentence might be imposed. Information about the consequences of a decision is, thus, "irrelevant to the jury's task." Furthermore, providing a jury with such information "invites them to ponder matters that are not within their province, distracts them from their fact-finding responsibilities, and creates a strong possibility of confusion." The Court also found no support to Shannon's contention that IDRA requires such an instruction in the instance of the NGI verdict. Even if some jurors mistakenly believe that defendants found NGI will be released from custody immediately, the jurors were instructed that the issue of punishment ought not enter their consideration. Although it may "take effort on a juror's part to ignore the potential consequences of the verdict, the effort required in a case in which an NGI defense is raised is no different from that required in many other situations." Justice Thomas also suggested that the Court was not convinced that the instruction Shannon sought would be effective. Under IDRA, a post-NGI verdict hearing must be held within 40 days to determine whether the defendant should be released or hospitalized. Instead of encouraging a juror to return an NGI verdict as Shannon predicts, Thomas said a juror might vote to convict in order to eliminate the possibility that a dangerous defendant could be released after 40 days or less. Whether such an instruction would work to Shannon's advantage or not was seen, however, as "beside the point." The Court's central concern is that the "inevitable result of such an instruction would be to draw the jury's attention toward the very thing—the possible consequences of its verdict—it should ignore."

Jury Selection

Batson v. Kentucky, **476 U.S. 79, 90 L. Ed. 2d 69, 106 S. Ct. 1712 (1986)**
Held that the Equal Protection Clause precludes racially discriminatory use of peremptory challenges of potential jurors by prosecutors. During Batson's burglary trial, the prosecutor used his peremptory challenges to remove all four black persons from the venire. Batson was subsequently

convicted by an all-white jury. The Kentucky Supreme Court affirmed the conviction based on *Swain v. Alabama* (380 U.S. 202: 1965). The Supreme Court used the *Batson* case to reexamine the element of *Swain* dealing with the burden of evidence a defendant must demonstrate in support of any claim of discriminatory use of peremptory challenges. In a 7–2 decision, the Court shifted much of the burden previously resting with the defendant to the prosecution. As established in previous cases, the Court reaffirmed that exclusion of blacks from jury service was an evil the Fourteenth Amendment was designed to cure. Purposeful racial discrimination violates a defendant's right to equal protection because it denies him the protection that trial by jury is intended to secure. A defendant is entitled to a venire of jurors who are indifferently chosen. Beyond its impact on defendants, the Court observed that such discrimination unlawfully denies persons an opportunity to participate in jury service and "undermines public confidence in the fairness of our system of justice." The targeted component of the selection process in this case was the peremptory challenge. Prosecutors are generally entitled to strike jurors for "any reason at all," although challenge exclusively on racial grounds is forbidden. Under *Swain,* a defendant was required to demonstrate an ongoing pattern of discrimination in order to set aside a conviction. The Court in *Batson* viewed this requirement as a "crippling burden of proof," and one which left prosecutorial strikes "largely immune from constitutional scrutiny." Accordingly, the Court concluded that a defendant may establish a *prima facie* case of intentional discrimination based exclusively on a prosecutor's use of the peremptory challenges at the defendant's trial. Once a defendant establishes such a *prima facie* case, the burden shifts to the state to offer a neutral explanation for challenging black jurors. The explanation need not rise to the level justifying exercise of a challenge for cause. The Court reiterated its recognition that the peremptory challenge "occupies an important position in our trial procedures." At the same time, the practice has been used as a means of discrimination. By requiring trial courts to be sensitive to discriminatory use of the procedure, *Batson* "enforces the mandate of equal protection and furthers the ends of justice." Justice Marshall would have gone further. Citing in a concurring opinion "common and flagrant" abuses of the peremptory challenge, he urged elimination of this step from the jury selection process. Chief Justice Burger and Justice Rehnquist dissented, voicing a preference for the evidentiary standard established in *Swain. See also* JURY, p. 431; *RISTAINO v. ROSS* (424 U.S. 589: 1976), p. 254.

Significance   *Batson* had its origin in *Norris v. Alabama* (294 U.S. 587: 1935). The *Norris* case, an appeal growing out of the notorious Scottsboro trial, prohibited systematic exclusion of persons from jury service on the basis of race. *Norris* allowed discriminatory practice to be inferred from statistics demonstrating inequity of access. Thirty years later, the Court dealt with the use of peremptory strikes against claims of purposeful discrimination in *Swain*. *Swain* was brought to the Supreme Court because more subtle methods of discrimination had been designed since *Norris* to minimize the involvement of blacks and others in jury service. The Court's decision in *Swain* did not abandon the basic thrust of *Norris* in terms of systematic exclusion, but it made the burden of proving discriminatory practice much more difficult. Though less compelling facts than were present in *Swain* have prevailed in establishing a *prima facie* case of discrimination in more recent cases, there remains no specific expectation that general population ratios will be reflected in specific juries, as held in *Castaneda v. Partida* (430 U.S. 482: 1977). Cases such as *Taylor v. Louisiana* (419 U.S. 522: 1975) and *Duren v. Missouri* (439 U.S. 357: 1979) rejected certain state selection methods on the grounds that they systematically excluded women from jury service. But the Court has continued generally to defer to the states in the establishment and administration of techniques designed to draw juries and assure that they are representative crosssections of the community. In *Batson*, however, the Court for the first time imposed restraints on the way prosecutors may use their peremptory challenges. In doing so it substantially modified *Swain*. Where systematic racial exclusion can be shown, convictions must be reversed. The rule extends to intentional discrimination in the selection of grand jurors as well. Such discrimination is a "grave constitutional trespass" and wholly within the power of the state to prevent.

The Court has since examined a number of unanswered questions from *Batson*. *Powers v. Ohio* (499 U.S. 400: 1991) focused on the race of the defendant claiming a *Batson* violation. The prosecution used peremptory challenges to remove seven black jurors from Powers' jury. Powers, a white murder defendant, unsuccessfully asserted a *Batson* objection at trial. On appeal, Powers contended that his own race was irrelevant to an attempt to file a *Batson*-based objection to the discriminatory use of peremptory challenges. Ohio countered that *Batson* should be confined to the circumstances of that case, and that the race of the objecting defendant is a relevant precondition for a *Batson* challenge. The Court rejected both state arguments. *Batson* was designed, said Justice Kennedy, to serve "multiple ends, only one of which was to protect individual defendants from discrimination in the selection of jurors." *Batson* recognized as well that discriminatory use of peremptory challenges harms the excluded juror and the community at large. Racial exclusion directly violates the "overriding command" of the Equal Protection Clause, as race is unrelated to a person's fitness to serve as a juror and cannot be used as a "proxy for determining juror bias or competence." Another aspect of *Batson* was examined in *Hernandez v. New York* (500 U.S. 352: 1991). In

Hernandez, the prosecutor used some of his peremptory challenges to remove the only Latino prospective jurors. Hernandez raised a *Batson* objection, but before the trial court ruled on whether a *prima facie* case existed, the prosecutor offered an explanation for their removal. Both of the removed jurors were bilinguals, and it was the prosecutor's impression that when he asked them whether they would accept the court translator as the final word on witness testimony, both "looked away" and hesitatingly said they "would try." Hernandez's *Batson* claim was denied, and he was subsequently convicted. The Supreme Court ruled that the exclusion of the Latino jurors was race-neutral and affirmed Hernandez's conviction in a 6–3 ruling, but split on the reasons supporting the outcome. Justice Kennedy attempted to keep the ruling narrow saying the exclusion of persons because they are bilingual may be neither "wise" nor constitutional in all cases. Kennedy considered discriminatory effect a relevant measure of impermissible conduct, but a constitutional violation requires a showing of intent in addition. Language is an unacceptable basis of exclusion of Hispanics as such. A general pattern of exclusion on the basis of language might constitute a pretext for unlawful discrimination. Kennedy, however, was satisfied with the trial court finding that the basis for the prosecutor's peremptory strikes in this case were the "specific responses and demeanor" of the jurors and not the fact they were Hispanic or bilingual. As emphasis that this ruling should not be read as encouraging exclusion of prospective jurors on the basis of language, Kennedy said that it would be a "harsh paradox" that one might become sufficiently proficient in English to participate as a juror only to be excluded "because he knows a second language as well." Justices O'Connor and Scalia agreed the exclusions were race neutral, but were reluctant to acknowledge the relevance of disparate impact in assessing language-based exclusions.

The Court extended the *Batson* rule to civil juries in *Edmonson v. Leesville Concrete Co.* (500 U.S. 614: 1991). The six-justice majority spoke through Justice Kennedy, who said that racial discrimination in selecting a jury for a civil proceeding "harms the excluded juror no less than discrimination in a criminal trial." While conduct of private parties is often beyond the reach of the Constitution, Kennedy drew upon the concept of state action as the foundation for the ruling. State action exists when private parties make "extensive use of state procedures with the overt, significant assistance of state officials." Without government participation, the peremptory challenge system, as well as the jury trial system of which it is a part, "simply could not exist." By enforcing discriminatory use of peremptory challenges, the courts have not only become party to the discrimination, but has "elected to place its power, property, and prestige" behind any discrimination. The peremptory challenge, said Kennedy, is used in selecting an "entity that is a quintessential governmental body, having no attributes of a private actor." The Court further extended the reach of *Batson* and the reasoning of *Edmonson* in *Georgia v. McCollum* (120 L. Ed. 2d 33: 1992), holding that, like the prosecution, criminal defendants cannot exclude prospective jurors on the basis of race. Extension of *Batson* in this way, said Justice Blackmun, is designed to "remedy the harm done to the dignity of persons and the integrity of the courts" by race-based discrimination. Whether at the initiative of the state or of the defense, if a court allows exclusion of jurors because of group bias, it becomes a "willing participant in the scheme that could only undermine the very foundation of our system of justice—our citizens' confidence in it." It was the Court's conclusion that racial exclusion of jurors by the defendant constituted state action. The jury system performs "critical governmental functions," functions that are both "unique and constitutionally compelled" in a criminal case. Whether exclusion of jurors results from actions of the prosecution or the defense, the "perception and the reality in a criminal trial will be that the court has excused jurors based on race, an outcome that will be attributed to the State." Finally, the Court considered whether the interests served by *Batson* need give way to the rights of criminal defendants. Blackmun said that it was important to remember that peremptory challenges "are not constitutionally protected fundamental rights." Rather, they are "but one state-created means to the constitutional end of an impartial jury and a fair trial." Blackmun also distinguished between a peremptory challenge "to discriminate invidiously against jurors on account of race and exercising a peremptory challenge to remove an individual juror who harbors racial prejudice."

The Court, he said, has "firmly rejected" the view that "assumptions of partiality based on race provide a legitimate basis for disqualifying a person as an impartial juror." Justice Thomas concurred that the *Edmonson* rationale needed to reach criminal defendants. At the same time, however, he expressed reservations about the Court's "continuing attempts" to regulate peremptory challenges. He suggested that black criminal defendants "will rue the day that this Court ventured down this road that inexorably will lead to the elimination of peremptory strikes." While jurors might be protected, Thomas said, the decision "leaves defendants with less means of protecting themselves." Unless prejudice is admitted during voir dire, defendants must allow jurors to sit and "run the risk that racial animus will affect the verdict." In his view, the Court effectively "exalted the right of citizens to sit on juries over the rights of the criminal defendant," even though it is the latter who faces possible conviction and punishment. Justices O'Connor and Scalia issued separate dissents. Both pointed to an absence of state action. Scalia indicated that he thought *Edmonson* had been "wrongly decided," and that this decision amounted to a "reduction to the terminally absurd: A criminal defendant, in the process of defending himself against the state, is held to be acting on behalf of the state...." O'Connor also felt the Court's decision did not advance nondiscriminatory criminal justice. She suggested, to the contrary, that use of peremptory challenges may help overcome racial bias, for there is "substantial reason to believe that the distorting influence of race is minimized on a racially mixed jury."

The Court extended the *Batson* ruling to gender in *J.E.B. v. Alabama ex rel. T.B.* (128 L. Ed. 2d 89: 1994). T. B. was a defendant in a paternity action. The state used 9 of its 10 peremptory challenges to remove male jurors. As a consequence, the case was tried by an all female jury. The jury concluded that T. B. was the child's father. The Alabama appellate courts ruled that the *Batson* rule did not extend to gender-based discrimination. In a 6–3 decision, the Supreme Court reversed. Justice Blackmun delivered the opinion of the Court. Discrimination in jury selection, "whether based on race or on gender," causes harm to litigants, the community, and the individual jurors who are "wrongfully excluded from participation in the judicial process." The Court found virtually no support for the conclusion that gender alone is an accurate predictor of juror's attitudes, and refused to "condone the same stereotypes that justified the wholesale exclusion of women from juries and the ballot box." The state, Blackmun said, "seems to assume that gross generalizations that would be deemed impermissible if made on the basis of race are somehow permissible when made on the basis of gender." Since *Batson*, Blackmun continued, we have "reaffirmed repeatedly our commitment to jury selection procedures that are fair and nondiscriminatory." In this case, the Court reaffirmed what, "by now, should be axiomatic: Intentional discrimination by state actors violates the Equal Protection Clause, particularly where, as here, the discrimination serves to ratify and perpetuate invidious, archaic and overbroad stereotypes about the relative abilities of men and women." Like race, gender is an "unconstitutional proxy for juror competence and impartiality."

Justice O'Connor concurred that the Equal Protection Clause precludes exclusion from jury service on the basis of gender. In her view, the "blow against gender discrimination is not costless." She characterized *Batson* as "intrus[ive]" in the jury selection process, citing the "now routine" *Batson* "mini-hearings" in state and federal courts. She predicted that by further "constitutionalizing" jury selection procedures, the Court increases the number of cases in which jury selection, "once a sideshow, will become part of the main event." O'Connor was also concerned about the further erosion of the role of the peremptory challenge. She said it has been demonstrated in a number of studies, that "like race, gender matters." She pointed to findings that show female jurors are somewhat more likely to convict than male jurors in rape cases. She suggested that "one need not be sexist to share the intuition that in certain cases, a person's gender and resulting life experience will be relevant to his or her view of [a] case." Individuals are not expected to ignore as jurors what they know as men or women. O'Connor's concern was that this ruling "severely limits a litigant's ability to act on this intuition, for the import of our holding is that any correlation between a juror's gender and attitudes is irrelevant as a matter of constitutional law. But to say that gender makes no difference as a matter of law is not to say that gender makes no difference as a matter of fact."

Justice Scalia, joined by Chief Justice Rehnquist and Justice Thomas, dissented. Scalia called the Court's opinion an "inspiring demonstration of how thoroughly up-to-date and right-thinking we Justices are in matters pertaining to the sexes...and how sternly we disapprove the male chauvinist attitudes of our predecessors." The dissenters viewed the core of the Court's reasoning as being that peremptory challenges on the basis of any characteristic subject to heightened scrutiny are unconstitutional under the Equal Protection Clause. Such a conclusion can only be reached, said Scalia, "by focusing unrealistically upon individual exercises of the peremptory challenges and ignoring the totality of the practice." Since all groups are subject to the peremptory challenge, Scalia concluded, "it is hard to see how any group is denied equal protection...."

Lockhart v. McCree, 476 U.S. 162, 90 L. Ed. 2d 137, 106 S. Ct. 1758 (1986) Decreed that opponents of capital punishment may be excluded from juries in death penalty cases. McCree was tried for capital felony murder in a state proceeding. During the voir dire process, the judge removed for cause, prior to the guilt adjudication phase of a two-stage capital trial, all prospective jurors who indicated they could not impose the death penalty. A jury subsequently convicted McCree but rejected the death penalty at the sentencing stage. Instead it set punishment at life imprisonment without parole. McCree failed in his attempt for relief in the state courts and sought federal habeas corpus relief. He contended that the "death qualification" of the jurors remaining to determine his guilt or innocence deprived him of an impartial jury chosen from a representative crosssection of the community. The Supreme Court ruled against McCree in a 6–3 vote. Justice Rehnquist began the majority opinion by pointing out several flaws in the evidence used by the lower courts to find that the death qualification produces conviction-prone juries. Even if the proposition could be demonstrated, Rehnquist said, the Constitution does not preclude use of death-qualified juries in capital trials. The fair cross section requirement cannot be applied to limit use of either for cause or peremptory challenges or to require that petit juries (as distinct from jury panels or venires) reflect the composition of the community at large. Further, the essence of a fair cross section claim is the systematic exclusion of a distinctive group in the community. Groups defined solely in terms of shared attitudes that would substantially impair their functioning as jurors are not distinctive groups for fair cross section purposes. Exclusion here did not occur for reasons completely unrelated to the ability of members of the group to function as jurors. This differentiated the *Lockhart* case from those where exclusion of a distinctive group arbitrarily skewed the composition of a jury and denied defendants the benefit of community judgment. *See also* JURY, p. 431; *RISTAINO v. ROSS* (424 U.S. 589: 1976), p. 254.

Significance   *Lockhart v. McCree* is the most recent of a series of decisions dealing with the troublesome issue of juror impartiality in capital cases. In *Witherspoon v. Illinois* (391 U.S. 510: 1968), the Court found that a jury cannot be selected which is uncommonly willing to condemn a person to death. Yet the Court refused to announce a per se constitutional rule requiring the reversal of every jury selected in the Illinois fashion. The Court said simply that in this case the jury "fell woefully short of that impartiality to which petitioner was entitled under the Sixth and Four-teenth Amendments." Writing for the majority, Justice Stewart found it clear that imposing the death penalty by a "hanging jury" would deprive the defendant of his life without due process of law. *Witherspoon*, however, was decided before the states were required to use two-stage processes separately to adjudicate guilt and then consider sentence. Since 1976, opponents of the death penalty have typically been excluded from both stages. This produced several followup cases to *Witherspoon*. While the latter remains generally in effect, the modifications brought in later cases up through *Lockhart* stem from the bifurcation requirement.

In *Davis v. Georgia* (429 U.S. 122: 1976), Court voided the death sentence of a state prisoner whose sentence had been imposed by a jury from which one prospective juror had been excluded because of general reservations about the death penalty. In *Adams v. Texas* (448 U.S. 38: 1980), the Court considered whether a state could exclude from a jury those persons unable to swear under oath that the extant possibility of the death penalty would not affect their deliberations. With only Justice Rehnquist dissenting, the Court decided that *Witherspoon* required rever-sal of the oath process. While still allowing exclusion of people who cannot be impartial, the majority was not satisfied that irrevocable opposition could be inferred from failure to swear to the impossibility of imposing the death penalty. The *Witherspoon* test for exclusion established that jurors could be excluded for cause only if they make it unmistakably clear they would automatically vote against the death penalty without regard to evidence. The Court softened this standard in *Wainwright v. Witt* (469 U.S.

412: 1985), where it held that a better criterion was whether a prospective juror's views would prevent or substantially impair performance of the juror function. *Wainwright* modified the *Witherspoon* automatic judgment language to say that in order to exclude a juror for cause, a juror's bias need not be shown with unmistakable clarity. *Lockhart* clearly moved even further from *Witherspoon* in the direction of allowing a death qualification for prospective jurors. *Lockhart* permitted the prosecution to have removed any prospective juror who indicates he or she absolutely could not under any circumstances impose a death sentence. In *Morgan v. Illinois* (119 L. Ed. 2d 492: 1992), the Court ruled that criminal defendants have a comparable right to remove prospective jurors who would automatically impose the death sentence upon conviction of the defendant. Justice White said for a six-justice majority that a juror who will automatically rule for the death penalty "will fail in good faith to consider the evidence of aggravating and mitigating circumstances" as the jury instructions require. Because such a juror has already formed a judgment on sentence, presence or absence of either aggravating or mitigating circumstances is "entirely irrelevant." Accordingly, capital defendants must be permitted during voir dire to "ascertain whether his prospective jurors function under such misconception." Justices Scalia, Rehnquist, and Thomas disagreed with Justice White. Scalia argued that because the Sixth Amendment does not require jury participation in capital sentencing proceedings, the "subsidiary requirement that the requisite jury be impartial" is not necessary either.

Ristaino v. Ross, **424 U.S. 589, 47 L. Ed. 2d 258, 96 S. Ct. 1017 (1976)**
Considered the question of whether a defendant is constitutionally entitled to ask questions specifically directed toward racial prejudice during the voir dire examination of prospective jurors. The trial judge denied the defendant's motion to pose the question, and a black defendant was subsequently convicted in a state court of violent crimes against a white victim. The Supreme Court concurred in the trial judge's decision in a 6–2 vote. Justice Stevens did not participate. Justice Powell reasoned for the majority that the Constitution "does not always entitle a defendant to have questions posed during voir dire specifically directed to matters that conceivably might prejudice veniremen against him." Though circumstances might warrant specific questions about racial prejudice, these were matters to be handled through the exercise of "sound discretion" by the trial court, a function "particularly within the province of the trial judge." The mere fact that the victim and the defendant were of different races was not in itself something which was "likely to distort the trial."

Therefore the defendant was not entitled to voir dire questions pursuing race prejudice. Justices Brennan and Marshall dissented. *See also* JURY, p. 431.

Significance   *Ristaino v. Ross* is representative of the Burger Court's view of what kinds of questions a defendant is entitled to pursue during a voir dire examination. The voir dire process is a series of questions posed to prospective jurors to determine their impartiality. A prospective juror found to be partial on the basis of his or her responses is excused from service on a given jury "for cause." The supervision of voir dire rests with the trial judge. *Ristaino* decided that a trial judge's discretion has been properly exercised when a defendant is denied the opportunity to probe the racial prejudice of prospective jurors simply because the defendant and victim of the crime are of different races. *Ristaino* underscored the requirement that a defendant must demonstrate unusual circumstances such as the presence of a racial issue as an actual component of a particular case. A similar holding involving national origin was made in *Rosales-Lopez v. United States* (451 U.S. 182: 1981), in which a Mexican defendant, at trial for illegally bringing Mexican aliens into the country, wished to ask potential jurors about possible prejudice toward Mexicans. In *Ham v. South Carolina* (409 U.S. 524: 1973), the Court concluded that questions relating to racial prejudice were appropriate given the defendant's visibility in the civil rights movement in the locality of his trial. *Ristaino, Ham,* and *Rosales-Lopez* place the monitoring of the jury selection process, specifically the conduct of the voir dire examination, exclusively in the hands of the trial judge. This rule was modified for capital cases in *Turner v. Murray* (476 U.S. 28: 1986). The Court said a capital defendant accused of an interracial crime is entitled to have prospective jurors informed of the race of the victim and questioned on the issue of racial bias during voir dire. The Court believed the risk of racial prejudice infecting a capital sentencing proceeding is especially serious in light of the complete finality of the death sentence. The Court has also held that a juror's failure properly to answer a question during voir dire does not require retrial. In *McDonough Power Equipment, Inc. v. Greenwood* (464 U.S. 548: 1984), the Court said that unless a showing can be made that failure to disclose actually denied a party an impartial jury, the invalidation of a jury decision is not required. To mandate vacating the jury decision in such a circumstance "ill serves the important end of finality." It would be "to insist on something closer to perfection than our judicial system can be expected to give." *Mu'Min v. Virginia* (500 U.S. 415: 1991) considered the outer limits of the voir dire examination in cases where there is the possibility of prejudicial pre-trial publicity. Mu'Min was charged with murder in a case which received substantial publicity. His attorney sought to have prospective jurors individually examined and proposed 64 voir dire questions to probe the specific information to which members of the venire had been exposed. The trial court denied Mu'Min's motions and examined prospective jurors as a group and then in smaller groups of four. A jury was eventually empaneled, and Mu'Min was convicted. The Supreme Court affirmed the conviction in a 5–4 decision. Chief Justice Rehnquist said for the majority that trial courts have historically been accorded wide discretion in conducting voir dire. The voir dire must "cover the subject" of the pre-trial publicity, but need not do more. Rehnquist acknowledged that focused inquiries on the content of news reports might be revealing of a juror's "general outlook," and be helpful in making decisions about when to use peremptory challenges. At the same time, the Court was not convinced that such benefit should become the basis of a constitutional requirement. Constitutionally compelled questions must be more than merely "helpful" in assessing impartiality. The questions the Constitution requires are those which render a trial "fundamentally unfair" if they go unasked.

Pre-Trial Proceedings

Gannett Co. v. DePasquale, **443 U.S. 368, 61 L. Ed. 2d 608, 99 S. Ct. 2898 (1979)** Posed the question of whether the media could be denied access to a pre-trial suppression hearing. If the press is allowed to observe a judicial proceeding, it generally will be allowed to report what it observes. Since both the defense and prosecution agreed to close the proceeding at issue in *Gannett,* the case really asked whether the public has an independent right to an open pre-trial judicial hearing. In a 5–4 decision, the Court upheld the closed hearing. The majority reasoned that pre-trial suppression hearings as distinct from trials pose "special risks of unfairness." The objective of such hearings is to screen out unreliable or illegally obtained evidence. Pre-trial publicity about such evidence could "influence public opinion" and "inform potential jurors of inculpatory information wholly inadmissible at the actual trial." As for the public's independent right to access, the Court stressed two points. First, public interest in the application of the Sixth Amendment does not create "a constitutional right on the part of the public." The public interest is protected by the participants in the adversary process. Thus the public has no claim which could displace the defendant's desire to close the proceeding. Second, the common law tradition recognizes the difference between a pre-trial proceeding and the trial itself. "Pretrial proceedings, precisely because of [a] concern for a fair trial, were never characterized by the degree of openness as were actual trials." Justices Blackmun,

Brennan, Marshall, and White dissented. They concentrated on the benefits of open processes and what they considered to be unconstitutional limitations on the press. Justice Blackmun said that casting fair trial rights in terms of the accused is "not sufficient to permit the inference that the accused may compel a private proceeding simply by waiving that right." In addition, open proceedings are educative, allow police and prosecutorial performances to be scrutinized, and protect both the public and the defendant from partiality. The appearance of justice is important. "Secret hearings—though they are scrupulously fair in reality—are suspect by nature." *See also CHANDLER v. FLORIDA* (449 U.S. 560: 1981), p. 262; *NEBRASKA PRESS ASSOCIATION v. STUART* (427 U.S. 530: 1976), p. 259; *SHEPPARD v. MAXWELL* (384 U.S. 33: 1966), p. 258.

Significance   *Gannett Co. v. DePasquale* sidesteps the censorship question raised in *Nebraska Press Association v. Stuart* (427 U.S. 539: 1976). The press was not prohibited from publishing information it already possessed in the *Gannett* case. Rather than consider infringement of the First Amendment rights of a free press, *Gannett* focused on whether a defendant's interest in closing a pretrial hearing supersedes the public's interest in an open proceeding. The decision clearly raised the prospect of all judicial proceedings, even trials, being closed at the initiative of the defense. The Court refused to take that step in *Richmond Newspapers, Inc. v. Virginia* (448 U.S. 555: 1980). In *Richmond,* the Court would not permit closure of trial to the public and media, despite the defendant's request that this be done. With only Justice Rehnquist dissenting, the Court held that trials could not "summarily close courtroom doors" without interfering with First Amendment protections. Thus the potential for closure begun in *Gannett* was checked in *Richmond.* Remaining from *Gannett,* however, and reinforced by *Richmond,* is a great deference to trial judge discretion in dealing with closure. *Richmond* makes clear that closing trials is extreme, but if some overriding and demonstrable defendant interest can be shown, trials may indeed be closed to the public and the press. But what if a defendant wishes a pretrial proceeding to remain open? In *Waller v. Georgia* (467 U.S. 39: 1984), the Court held unanimously that the right to a public trial applies to a pretrial suppression hearing. The closure of such a hearing over the objections of a defendant can only occur if four criteria are met. First, the party wishing to close the proceeding must "advance an overriding interest that is likely to be prejudiced." Second, the closure must be "no broader than is necessary to protect that interest." Third, the trial court must consider "reasonable alternatives to closure." And finally, the trial court must make findings "adequate to support the closure."

The press is occasionally ordered not to disclose information about a pending criminal case in order to better protect against dissemination of prejudicial publicity. In *Gentile v. State Bar of Nevada* (501 U.S. 1030: 1991), the Court considered restrictions on an attorney's public comments about pending cases. Nevada Supreme Court Rule 177 prohibits a lawyer from making "extrajudicial comment" to the media that he or she knows or reasonably should know will have a "substantial likelihood of materially prejudicing" a pending proceeding. A subsection of the Rule lists the kinds of statements that would likely be prejudicial. The Rule also contains a "safe harbor" provision that indicates some kinds of statements that can be made "without fear of discipline notwithstanding other sections of the rule." Included in this subsection is language allowing a lawyer to state "without elaboration" the "general nature" of the defense. Gentile held a press conference after his client had been indicted. He referred to his client as a "scapegoat" on several occasions. He commented on his view of what the evidence would show at trial, but citing the Rule, Gentile refused to answer a number of questions that pressed for a more detailed response. Gentile's client was eventually acquitted. Immediately thereafter, the Disciplinary Board of the State Bar of Nevada found that Gentile had violated Rule 177. Gentile was reprimanded by the State Bar of Nevada, an action affirmed by the Nevada Supreme Court. Justices Kennedy, Marshall, Blackmun, Stevens, and O'Connor found Rule 177 to be unlawfully vague, however. In their view, the safe harbor language "misled [Gentile] into thinking he could give his press conference without fear of discipline." The Rule fails to give attorneys "fair notice" of the content that is to be avoided. Despite Gentile's study of the Rule and his "conscious effort at compliance," Gentile was unsuccessful at avoiding reprimand.

Assistance of Counsel

United States v. Monsanto, **491 U.S. 600, 105 L. Ed. 2d 512, 109 S. Ct. 2657 (1989)** Upheld forfeiture provisions under federal law, including seizure of those assets intended to secure privately retained defense counsel. Under provisions of the Racketeer Influenced and Corrupt Organization Act (RICO) and the Continuing Criminal Enterprise Act (CCE), the federal government may seize assets which are the proceeds of criminal activity. Congress expanded these forfeiture provisions in the Comprehensive Forfeiture Act of 1984, which focused on proceeds from organized crime activities and narcotics trafficking. The issues in *Monsanto* were whether forfeiture covers those assets intended to pay for defense counsel, and if so, whether such compelled forfeiture interferes with the defendant's Sixth Amendment right to counsel. When Monsanto was indicted for various crimes including RICO and CCE violations, the government obtained a restraining order freezing his assets as a preliminary step in the forfeiture process. Monsanto was unable to secure private counsel because attorneys feared forfeiture of their fees. Under "relation back" terms of the 1984 law, proceeds from criminal activity belong to the government from the time the crime is committed. In addition, the forfeiture applies not only to proceeds still in the hands of the defendant, but also to proceeds that have been paid to third parties subsequent to the crime. The trial judge appointed a publicly paid lawyer as Monsanto's counsel, recognizing that the restraining order had left him virtually indigent. The court of appeals heard the case *en banc* and ruled that attorneys' fees were exempt from forfeiture. The United States sought review. In a 5–4 decision, the Supreme Court ruled assets intended to cover attorneys' fees are not exempt from seizure, and that such seizure did not unconstitutionally interfere with the right to counsel. Justice White spoke for the Court, which saw the language in the Forfeiture Act as "plain and unambiguous." Congress could not have chosen "stronger words to express its intent that forfeiture be mandatory" under circumstances presented in these appeals. Neither does the statute contain any language which "even hints" that assets used for attorneys' fees are not included in seizable property. By enacting the Forfeiture Act, said White, Congress "decided to give force to the old adage that 'crime does not pay.'" There is no evidence, he continued, that Congress "intended to modify that nostrum to read, 'crime does not pay, except for attorney's fees.'" He noted that if the Court were mistaken as to congressional intent on this issue, "that body can amend this statute to otherwise provide." On the constitutional issue of assistance of counsel, the Court said that "nothing in [the Act] prevents a defendant from hiring the attorney of his choice," or "disqualifies any attorney from serving as a defendant's counsel." A defendant with nonforfeitable assets remains free to retain "any attorney of his choosing." There will be cases like these, however, where a defendant is unable to retain an attorney of choice. An "impecunious" defendant, said the Court, does not have the right to "choose their counsel." Neither do they have a "cognizable complaint" as long as they are "adequately represented by attorneys appointed by the court." Compulsory forfeiture of assets, even if such forfeiture renders a defendant unable to privately retain counsel, is not unconstitutional because defendants are not entitled to "spend another person's money for services rendered by an attorney." This proposition holds even if that money is the "only way that a defendant will be able to retain the attorney of his choice." Justices Blackmun, Brennan, Marshall, and Stevens dissented. They viewed the Sixth Amendment as a bar to congressional interference with the right to counsel. Justice Blackmun said that to consider attorneys' fees as part of forfeitable assets is "unseemly and unjust." The decision, said Blackmun, loses sight of the "distinct role of the right to counsel in protecting the integrity of the judicial process." Indeed, if Congress had set out to "undermine the adversarial system as we know it," it could not have "found a better engine of destruction" than to seize assets intended to pay for defense counsel. *See also* COUNSEL, ASSISTANCE OF, p. 399.

Significance   *Monsanto* was one of two asset seizure cases decided by the Court during the 1988 Term. The second case was *Caplin & Drysdale, Chartered v. United States* (491 U.S. 617: 1989). While the fact situation differed, the outcome was identical to *Monsanto*. Christopher Reckmeyer, a client of the law firm Caplin & Drysdale, was indicted for various narcotics offenses and a CCE violation. The defendant owed the law firm in excess of $26,000 in fees before the indictment, and had made a payment (with two $5,000 checks) on the day prior to his being indicted. Also on the day prior to the indictments, the government obtained a court order restraining Reckmeyer from transferring any assets relating to the indictment charges. When the law firm attempted to deposit Reckmeyer's checks, they were returned unpaid on the basis of the restraining order. Reckmeyer eventually pleaded guilty, was sentenced, and had virtually all his assets seized. Caplin & Drysdale filed a claim for the two $5000 checks returned unpaid at the outset, plus additional fees amounting to almost $200,000. As in *Monsanto,* the Court ruled that the assets intended to compensate private counsel were subject to forfeiture. The decision upheld forfeiture of assets even though such action deprived the defendant of the capacity to select private counsel himself.

Defendant's choice of counsel was also an issue in *Wheat v. United States* (486 U.S. 153: 1988). The Sixth Amendment generally entitles a defendant to select his or her counsel, but the right does not extend to a selection that creates a conflict of interest with the counsel's other clients. In *Wheat,* the Court reviewed a case in which the trial court, on motion by the prosecution, refused to allow a defendant to be represented by the attorney of his codefendants. Two days prior to his trial for participation in an extensive drug distribution conspiracy, Wheat sought to substitute the counsel of his two codefendants for his original attorney. Wheat and his codefendants were all willing to waive the right to conflict-free counsel. The trial court refused to allow the substitution on the grounds that the conflicts were "irreconcilable and unwaivable" because of the likelihood that Wheat would have to testify at the trial of the second codefendant while the third codefendant was likely to testify at Wheat's trial. The Supreme Court upheld the trial court's denial of the substitution of counsel. The Court noted that the Sixth Amendment right to choose one's own counsel is "circumscribed in several important respects." In cases where there is multiple representation, the trial court has a duty to take measures which are "appropriate to protect criminal defendants against counsel's conflicts of interest, including the issuance of separate representation orders." The Court examined the standard of competency that applies to a criminal defendant's decision to waive his right to counsel and plead guilty in *Godinez v. Moran* (125 L. Ed. 2d 321: 1993). The Court ruled in *Dusky v. United States* (362 U.S. 402: 1960) that an accused is competent to stand trial if he or she understands the proceedings against him or her, and whether he or she has the capacity "to consult with counsel and assist in the preparation of the defense." In a 7–2 decision, the Court ruled that if an accused is found competent to stand trial, he or she is also competent to discharge counsel and plead guilty to a serious crime, even capital murder. Justice Thomas said for the Court that the decision to plead guilty is a "profound one," but that decision is "no more complicated than the sum total of decisions that a defendant may be called upon to make during the course of a trial." Similarly, the Court did not see that the decision to waive the right to counsel "requires an appreciably higher level of mental functioning than the decision to waive any other constitutional right." The competence to waive right to counsel is not to be mistaken for the competence to represent oneself. Citing *Faretta v. California* (422 U.S. 806: 1975), Thomas said a defendant's ability to represent himself "has no bearing upon his competence to *choose* self-representation." Because a trial court must be satisfied that a defendant's waiver is both voluntary and knowing, there is in place a "heightened" standard for pleading guilty and waiving the right to counsel, but not a "heightened standard of *competence*." Thomas concluded by saying that while psychiatrists and scholars may find it "useful to classify the various kinds and degrees of competence," and while states are free to adopt more elaborate standards of competency than those set forth in *Dusky,* the "Due Process Clause does not impose these additional requirements." Justice Blackmun, joined by Justice Stevens, dissented. They felt a more rigorous standard was required for assessing a defendant's competency to waive counsel and represent himself. Blackmun said that a finding that a defendant is competent to stand trial "establishes only that he is capable of aiding his attorney in making the critical decisions required at trial or in plea negotiations." But, he continued, the "reliability or even relevance of such a finding vanishes when its basic premise—that counsel will be present—ceases to exist."

The Comprehensive Drug Abuse Prevention and Control Act of 1970 authorizes the federal government, among other things, to confiscate property acquired with the proceeds of drug crimes. The issue in *United States v. A Parcel of Land* (122 L. Ed. 2d 469: 1993) did not involve the right to counsel, but rather forfeiture of property belonging to someone other than the person involved in criminal conduct. One provision of the act says that title to a property vests with the government at the time any crime connected to the property is committed. The act also contains an "innocent owner" provision, however, that allows a person to establish that any criminal act was committed "without the knowledge or consent of the owner." Beth Ann Goodwin lived with Joseph Brenca for a period of six years. Brenca gave Goodwin money she used to purchase a house in which she lived with Brenca. Two years after Goodwin ended the relationship, the government seized the property on the grounds that the money Brenca had given her to buy the house came from his illicit sales of marijuana. A federal district court ruled that Goodwin had no standing to contest the forfeiture because she had received the purchase money as a gift; she was not the "bona fide purchaser." The district court also ruled that the innocent owner defense was available only to persons who owned the property prior to the criminal act(s) that prompted the forfeiture action. The Supreme Court overturned the trial court in a 6–3 decision, although there was no majority on the rationale. Justice Stevens pointed to language in the act establishing the innocent-owner exception, and noted that the term "owner" was used several times without qualification of the term. Such language, said Stevens, "is sufficiently unambiguous to foreclose any contention that it applies only to bona fide purchasers." It was the plurality view that Goodwin ought not be disqualified from claiming that she had no knowledge that the funds she had used to purchase the property were "proceeds traceable" to illegal drug transactions. The Court also rejected assertion of the relation back doctrine under these circumstances. Under this doctrine, title vests with the government at the time of a criminal act and no legal transfer of title can occur after that criminal act. The Court ruled that neither the act nor the common law rule "makes the Government an owner of property before forfeiture has been decreed." Justice Kennedy, joined by Chief Justice Rehnquist and Justice White, dissented. It was their view that Goodwin was not a bona fide owner. Rather, forfeiture is determined by the "title and ownership of the asset in the hands of the donor, not the donee." In this instance, the donor (Brenca) had more than knowledge of the criminal acts—"he performed them. Thus any defense based on his lack of knowledge is not a possibility."

5. The Eighth Amendment

HERRERA v. COLLINS (122 L. Ed. 2d 203:   Habeas Corpus Review   131
1993)
Graham v. Collins (122 L. Ed. 2d 260: 1993)
Brecht v. Abrahamson (123 L. Ed. 2d 353:
1993)
Withrow v. Williams (123 L. Ed. 2d 407:
1993)
McFarland v. Scott (129 L. Ed. 2d 666: 1994)

Excessive Imprisonment

Harmelin v. Michigan, 501 U.S. 957, 115 L. Ed. 2d 836, 111 S. Ct. 2680
(1991)   Held that a state may sentence someone to a life sentence
without the possibility of parole for the possession of substantial quantities
of illegal drugs. Harmelin had contended that the penalty was dispropor-
tionately heavy and, as a consequence, a violation of the Cruel and
Unusual Punishment Clause of the Eighth Amendment. Michigan is the
only state that provides for the life without parole sentence for possession
of more than 650 grams of cocaine. Five justices found no Eighth Amendment violation. These five justices were not in agreement, however, on
how far this ruling should extend. Chief Justice Rehnquist joined Justice
Scalia's opinion which said that the Eighth Amendment "contains no
proportionality guarantee." The Court had previously ruled in *Solem v.
Helm* (463 U.S. 277: 1983) that a state recidivist law which imposed a life
sentence without the possibility of parole for nonassaultive felonies was
cruel and unusual on proportionality grounds. Scalia and Rehnquist were
of the view that *Solem* was wrongly decided and should be overruled. *Solem*
had established three criteria by which sentence disproportion is to be
examined—inherent gravity of the offense, sentences imposed in the
same jurisdiction for the same offense, and sentences imposed in other
jurisdictions for the same crime. In Scalia's view, there are no "adequate
textual or historical standards" by which this can be done; there is no
"objective standard of gravity." Cross-jurisdictional comparisons were
further flawed because without a "constitutionally imposed uniformity
inimical to traditional notions of federalism, some states will always bear
the distinction of treating particularly offenders more severely than any
other state." Diversity of policy and means of implementing policy is,
continued Scalia, the "very *raison d'etre* of our federal system." The Eighth
Amendment is "not a ratchet, whereby a temporary consensus on leniency
for a particular crime fixes a permanent constitutional maximum, dis-
abling the States from giving effect to altered beliefs and responding to
changed social conditions." Scalia and Rehnquist also rejected Harmelin's contention that the Eighth Amendment contains a "required mitigation" doctrine that requires individualized sentencing in noncapital as
well as capital cases. In their view, mandatory sentencing is prohibited

105

only in death penalty situations. Justices Kennedy, O'Connor, and Souter did not find Harmelin's sentence to be excessive, but felt the Eighth Amendment does embrace a principle of proportionality which applies to both capital and noncapital cases. Kennedy spoke for the three and preferred to reinterpret *Solem* rather than abandon it. He began by saying that primary responsibility for prison terms "lies with the legislature," and courts should grant "substantial deference to the broad authority that legislatures necessarily possess in determining the types and limits of punishments for crimes." Kennedy said it was estimated that 650 grams of cocaine has a potential yield of 32,500 to 65,000 doses. Against those numbers, Kennedy characterized Harmelin's argument that his crime was nonviolent and victimless as "false to the point of absurdity." Harmelin's crime was seen as sufficiently severe that Michigan's legislature could rationally conclude the crime to be as "serious and violent as the crime of felony murder,...a crime for which no sentence would be disproportionate." Comparison of Harmelin's crime and his sentence did not, said Kennedy, "give rise to an inference of gross disproportionality." As a result, Kennedy did not feel it necessary to conduct further comparative review. Justices White, Marshall, Blackmun, and Stevens dissented. They objected to the mandatory approach which did not permit a tailoring of the sentence to the individual's "personal responsibility and moral guilt." Possession of drugs, even in the large quantity involved in this case, said White, "is not so serious an offense that it will always warrant, much less mandate, life imprisonment without the possibility of parole." The dissenters also saw Michigan's penalty as substantially more severe than other jurisdictions. White pointed out, for example, that possession of the same amount of cocaine in Alabama would subject a defendant to a mandatory minimum sentence of only five years in prison. *See also* CRUEL AND UNUSUAL PUNISHMENT, p. 401.

Significance   The disproportionality issue addressed in *Harmelin* has split the Court for more than a decade. In *Rummel v. Estelle* (445 U.S. 263: 1980), the Court assessed mandatory life sentences for repeat offenders. The Supreme Court decided that the criteria used to assess Georgia's choice of penalty for rape in *Coker v. Georgia* (433 U.S. 584: 1977) were not directly applicable in *Rummel*. The Court said great deference ought to be extended to legislative judgments where prison sentences are involved. While Texas had the most extreme habitual offender statute in the country, it differed in degree rather than in kind from other states. Short of differences in kind, the Eighth Amendment should not be used to invalidate judgments which are "peculiarly" matters for the legislature. Two years later in *Hutto v. Davis* (454 U.S. 370: 1982), the Court upheld the imposition of two consecutive 20-year prison terms and two $10,000 fines for the crime of possession and distribution of nine ounces of marijuana. Building on *Rummel*, the Court said there was no way to "make any constitutional distinction between a term of years and a shorter or longer term of years." While expressing some concern about the severity of the sentence received by prisoner Davis, the Court refrained from finding for him. To have done so would be "invariably a subjective decision," and courts should be "reluctant to review legislatively mandated terms of imprisonment." *Rummel* and *Davis* seemed to suggest that Eighth Amendment challenges of prison sentences would not be successful. Comity, notions of substituting federal judicial opinion for that of state legislatures, and a strict constructionist view of the Constitution help explain the Court's decisions in *Rummel* and *Davis*. *Harmelin* reflects the deference that is characteristic of the Court in cases involving criminal penalties. The decision also suggests that it is unlikely that the Court will extend the proportionality analysis to many prison sentences.

The Court considered whether the Excessive Fines Clause of the Eighth Amendment applies to property forfeitures in drugs cases in *Austin v. United States* (125 L. Ed. 2d 488: 1993). Federal law [21 U.S.C. §881(a)(4) and (a)(7)] permits civil forfeiture of any properties that are either used in or acquired with proceeds from illegal drug transactions. Richard Austin sold two grams of cocaine to an individual working with local police. The buyer had approached Austin at Austin's place of business. Austin left his shop, went to his trailer home which was located nearby, returned, and finally delivered the drugs to the buyer. Austin eventually pleaded guilty to one state count of possession of drugs with intent to distribute. Following his sentencing, a federal civil forfeiture proceeding was initiated. Austin's trailer home and place of business were both confiscated without trial on the grounds that these properties had been used in the drug transaction. Austin unsuccessfully argued before the Court of Appeals for the Eighth Circuit that the Excessive Fines Clause of the Eighth Amendment applied to civil forfeitures. A unanimous Supreme Court ruled in support of this argument, however, and remanded the case for consideration of whether the forfeiture ordered in Austin's case was excessive. Justice Blackmun said the general purpose of the Eighth Amendment (the Excessive Bail Clause excepted) was to "limit the government's power to punish." The Excessive Fines Clause more specifically limits the government's power to "extract payments, whether in cash or in kind, 'as *punishment* for some offense.'" The United States had argued that the civil forfeiture process is not limited by the Eighth Amendment. According to Justice Blackmun, however, the issue was not "whether forfeiture was civil or criminal, but rather whether it is punishment." Sanctions frequently serve more than one purpose. It is not necessary to "exclude the possibility that a forfeiture serves remedial purposes to conclude that it is subject to the limitations of the Excessive Fines Clause." All that must be shown is that the forfeiture "serv[es] in part to punish." The Court found the objective of punishment reflected in several ways—in the legislative history of Section 881, in Congress's choice of linking forfeiture directly to drug offenses, and in the inclusion of an "innocent owner defense." Despite arguments by the United States that Section 881 was remedial, the Court ruled that the government failed to show that the civil forfeiture process was exclusively so. A civil sanction that "cannot fairly be said *solely* to serve a remedial purpose, but rather can only be explained as also serving either retributive or deterrent purposes, is punishment, as we have come to understand the term." Austin asked the Court to fashion a "multi-factor" test for determining whether a forfeiture is "excessive." The Court refused. Instead, it noted that the court of appeals had "no occasion" to consider the factors that might apply since it had ruled such an inquiry was foreclosed. "Prudence," said Blackmun, "dictates that we allow the lower courts to consider that question in the first instance." Seizure of real estate that has been used to facilitate drug trafficking has become a central component of the war on drugs. James Good pleaded guilty to a drug charge in 1985 and was sentenced to a year of imprisonment and five years of probation. In 1989, the federal government began a civil forfeiture action against Good's property. A federal magistrate determined that there was probable cause to believe that the property was connected to Good's drug offense and issued a seizure warrant against the property. Good, who was living in Nicaragua at the time, was not notified that the forfeiture action had been commenced. Furthermore, there was no hearing on the issue of whether the property was forfeitable. A U.S. district court upheld the seizure, but was reversed by the U.S. Court of Appeals for the Ninth Circuit. The Supreme Court, in *United States v. Good Real Property* (126 L. Ed. 2d 490: 1994), affirmed the court of appeals in a 5–4 decision. The United States argued that because the civil forfeiture served a law enforcement purpose in this case, that it only need comply with the Fourth Amendment when seizing property. The Court disagreed. The seizure of property "implicates two explicit textual sources of constitutional protection," the Fourth Amendment and the Due Process Clause of the Fifth. The proper question in this case, said Kennedy, is not "which Amendment controls but whether either Amendment is violated." The Court agreed that the Fourth Amendment applies to civil seizures, but held that the "purpose and effect" of the government's action in this case went beyond the traditional meaning of search and seizure. The government did not seize the property to preserve evidence of criminal conduct, but rather to "assert ownership and control over the property itself." Legal action that can result in loss of property must comply with the Due Process Clause of the Fifth and Fourteenth Amendments. The Court said that the right to prior notice and a hearing is "central to the Constitution's command of due process." The purpose of this requirement is to protect an individual's use and possession of property from "arbitrary encroachment—to minimize substantively unfair or mistaken deprivations of property...." Prior decisions limited exceptions to the notice and hearing expectations to "extraordinary situations" where the government's interest is sufficiently great to justify such an exception. The Court utilized the three-part inquiry from *Mathews v. Eldridge* (424 U.S. 319: 1976) to determine whether civil forfeiture of property requires an exception from the notice and hearing requirements. Analysis under *Mathews* involves consideration of the private interest affected by the governmental action, the risk of erroneous deprivation of that interest as a result of the process used, and the asserted government interest. Using this test, the Court found Good's right to maintain control over his home without governmental interference of both "historic and continuing importance." Governmental seizure gives the government the right to prohibit sale, evict occupants, modify the property—to generally "supercede the owner in all rights pertaining to the use, possession, and enjoyment of the property." These interests are substantial. The Court then found that the practice of *ex parte* seizure created an "unacceptable risk of error." Although the intent of the drug forfeiture statute was not to deprive innocent owners of property, the *ex parte* approach "affords little or no protection to the innocent owner." Unless exigent circumstances exist, the Due Process Clause requires "notice and meaningful opportunity to be heard before seizing real property subject to civil forfeiture." Chief Justice Rehnquist, joined by Justices O'Connor and Scalia, dissented. It was their view that the *ex parte* process required by the Fourth Amendment was sufficient for property forfeitures and arrests alike.

Victim Impact Statements

Payne v. Tennessee, **501 U.S. 808, 115 L. Ed. 2d 720, 111 S. Ct. 2597 (1991)** Held that evidence reflecting the character of a victim and effects on the surviving family of a victim could be introduced at the sentencing stage of a murder trial. Chief Justice Rehnquist wrote for the six-justice majority saying that although adherence to prior decisions is the "preferred course," it is not an "inexorable command" in certain instances. Rehnquist noted that through a series of decisions the Court removed virtually all limits on the mitigating evidence a defendant can introduce. None of those cases ever said, however, that a defendant is entitled to consideration "wholly apart from the crime he committed." *Booth v. Maryland* (482 U.S. 496: 1987) "unfairly weighted the scales in a capital trial," said Rehnquist, by keeping the state from either offering a "glimpse of the life" the defendant chose to end or by characterizing the "loss to the victim's family and to society." States have the authority to devise new methods for dealing with capital cases. Victim impact evidence is "simply another form or method of informing the sentencing authority about the specific harm caused by the crime in question." The Court in *Booth* was "wrong in stating this kind of evidence leads to the arbitrary imposition of the death penalty." To the contrary, victim impact evidence generally serves "entirely legitimate" purposes. Justices Marshall, Blackmun, and Stevens dissented. *See also* CRUEL AND UNUSUAL PUNISHMENT, p. 401.

Significance   The Court ruled in *Booth v. Maryland* that use of victim impact statements (VIS) at the sentencing stage of a capital murder trial violated the Eighth Amendment. The VIS, required by state law, were based on interviews with the victim's family. They contained descriptions of the effects of the crime on the family, characterizations of the victim, and family opinions of the crime and the defendant. The Court said the information contained in the VIS may be "wholly unrelated to the blameworthiness" of the defendant. Rather, the VIS may cause the sentencing decision to turn on such factors as the degree to which the victim's family is willing and able to articulate its grief, or the relative worth of the victim's character. Use of family members' emotionally charged opinions could "serve no other purpose than to inflame the jury and divert it from deciding the case on the relevant evidence concerning the crime and the defendant." Similarly, the Court held in *South Carolina v. Gathers* (490 U.S. 805: 1989) that evidence about the character of the victim could not be used in the sentencing phase of a capital case when that evidence does not directly bear on the crime itself. Gathers was convicted of murder. At the end of his argument to the jury during the sentencing stage of Gathers's murder trial, the prosecutor read from some of the religious materials the victim was carrying at the time of the murder. The prosecutor characterized the victim based on inferences drawn from the fact he was carrying the religious materials and other items such as a voter registration card. The Court said that capital cases have "consistently recognized" that the death penalty be "tailored" to a defendant's "personal responsibility and moral guilt." Under the circumstances of this case, the Court said that the content of the various materials the victim happened to be carrying when he was attacked was "purely fortuitous," and could not "provide any information relevant to the defendant's moral culpability." *Booth* and *Gathers* were overruled by the Rehnquist Court in *Payne.*

Capital Punishment

Gregg v. Georgia, 428 U.S. 153, 49 L. Ed. 2d 859, 96 S. Ct. 2909 (1976) Examined whether the death penalty was a cruel and unusual punishment per se. Many state legislatures responded to *Furman v. Georgia* (408 U.S. 238: 1972) by revising their capital punishment statutes to structure sentencer discretion. In three 1976 cases, *Gregg, Proffitt v. Florida* (428 U.S. 242: 1976), and *Jurek v. Texas* (428 U.S. 262: 1976), the Supreme Court upheld statutes as revised by Georgia, Florida, and Texas, respectively. The Court said the death penalty included in the revised statutes "does not invariably violate the Constitution." Justice Potter Stewart, writing for the majority of seven, said that the Court may not "require the legislature to select the least severe penalty possible so long as the penalty selected is not cruelly inhumane or disproportionate." He found that since 35 state legislatures had provided for the death penalty after *Furman,* contemporary standards were not offended. He said retribution was a sufficient legislative objective to support the statutes; capital punishment was an "expression of society's moral outrage at particularly offensive conduct." The Court also considered whether death was an excessive penalty in itself, deciding in Justice Stewart's words that when life has been taken, death is not invariably "disproportionate." It is "an extreme sanction, suitable to the most extreme crimes." As for the statutory flaws alleged in *Furman,* Justice Stewart concluded that the state statute revisions adequately remedied the defects. Arbitrariness was eliminated through several procedural revisions: all the statutes contained bifurcated trial-sentence processes, the guilt discrimination stage was separated from the sentencing stage, and the statutes required appellate review and structured sentencer discretion through definition of aggravating and mitigating circumstances. A sentencer could not consider imposing death in the absence of aggravating circumstances. In summary, the Court's opinion was that sentencer discretion had been adequately structured in the state statutes. Justices Marshall and Brennan dissented. Both suggested that capital punishment was constitutionally offensive under any circumstances. Justice Marshall argued that a punishment may be excessive, and therefore cruel and unusual, even though there may be public support of it. He found the majority's ideas about retribution as the basis for punishment to be the "most disturbing" aspect of the *Gregg* decision. *See also* COKER v. GEORGIA (433 U.S. 584: 1977), p. 298; FURMAN v. GEORGIA (408 U.S. 238: 1972), p. 294; WOODSON v. NORTH CAROLINA (428 U.S. 280: 1976), p. 297.

111

Significance   *Gregg* clarified several central issues regarding capital punishment: (1) the Court held that death is a constitutionally permissible penalty for murder, given certain conditions, (2) *Gregg* acknowledged that retribution can serve as a sufficient basis for legislative decisions regarding penal policy, and (3) *Gregg* determined that structuring sentencer discretion through the definition of aggravating and mitigating circumstances remedied the problems cited in *Furman*. *Gregg* focused on the special character of the death penalty. It is unique, differing in "severity and finality" from every other punishment. While the death penalty may not be cruel and unusual punishment as such, its utilization requires the application of extensive substantive and procedural safeguards. *Gregg* reveals the Court's preference for leaving implementation of capital punishment to the guided discretion of judges and juries. The position taken by the Court in *Gregg* established the foundation for current judicial policy regarding the death penalty. *Barclay v. Florida* (463 U.S. 939: 1983) gave notice to sentencers that they cannot depart from statutory guidelines in determining aggravating circumstances for imposing the death penalty, however. This is not to say the Supreme Court will ignore statutory language which it deems vague and ambiguous. It struck down such language in *Godfrey v. Georgia* (446 U.S. 420: 1980). In *Zant v. Stephens* (462 U.S. 862: 1983), the Court underscored the jury's independence in determining aggravating circumstances where statutes are clear. The future dangerousness issue was also addressed by the Court in *Wainwright v. Goode* (464 U.S. 78: 1983), in which it used *Barclay* to uphold a death sentence against challenge that the trial judge had improperly considered the nonstatutory aggravating circumstance of the defendant's future dangerousness. The Court said the critical question was whether consideration of this factor "so infects the balancing process between aggravating and mitigating circumstances fashioned by the capital punishment statute that the sentence needs to be reversed." The Court was satisfied that the independent reweighing of factors by the required review process for the death sentence did not take the future dangerousness factor into account. Thus the *Wainwright* sentence was freed from Eighth Amendment prohibitions. The Court examined the issue of sympathy as a factor in the penalty phase of a capital murder trial in the case of *California v. Brown* (479 U.S. 538: 1987). Just prior to the jury's deliberation of sentence, its members were instructed by the court to consider the aggravating and mitigating factors of the crime. The judge said the jury "should not be swayed by mere sentiment, conjecture, sympathy, passion, prejudice, public opinion, or public feeling." The Supreme Court ruled that this instruction did not violate the Eighth Amendment. The Court felt it unlikely that jurors would focus on the term *sympathy* to the exclusion of the other terms accompanying it.

A number of states consider an aggravating circumstance to be a murder that is "especially heinous, atrocious, or cruel." The issue in *Maynard v. Cartwright* (486 U.S. 356: 1988) was whether such an aggravating factor is unconstitutionally vague. The Supreme Court unanimously held that it was. The notion that factual circumstances "in themselves" may characterize a murder as "especially heinous, atrocious, or cruel" is an approach which gives the sentencer impermissible discretion in the death penalty decision. Subsequently, the Court held in *Clemons v. Mississippi* (494 U.S. 738: 1990) that a state supreme court could eliminate a defective "especially heinous" aggravating factor and then reweigh the remaining factors. Prior conviction for a violent crime, including prior convictions from another state, is often used as such an aggravating circumstance. *Lowenfeld v. Phelps* (484 U.S. 231: 1988) raised an additional procedural issue. The question was whether a death sentence based on but one aggravating circumstance was proper when that circumstance of aggravation was identical to an element of the crime for which the defendant was convicted. Lowenfeld had been convicted of three counts of first-degree murder, an element of which was his intent to "kill or inflict great bodily harm upon more than one person." At the sentencing phase of the trial, the only aggravating circumstance found by the jury was that he "knowingly created a risk of death or great bodily harm to more than one person." Lowenfeld asserted that the overlap allowed the jury to "merely...repeat one of its findings in the guilt phase," and thus not to "narrow further" in the sentence stage the "class of death-eligible murderers." The Court rejected this contention. A constitutional scheme must "genuinely narrow" the class of persons eligible for the death penalty and must "reasonably justify" use of the comparatively more severe punishment. The narrowing function may be provided in two ways: (1) by narrow legislative definition or (2) where broadly defined offenses are narrowed by jurors, by identifying aggravating circumstances. Use of aggravating circumstances is not an "end in itself," but a means of channeling jury discretion. This function can be performed by a jury finding at "either the sentencing phase of the trial or the guilt phase."

The independent review required of state courts of last resort in capital punishment cases was before the Court in *Parker v. Dugger* (498 U.S. 308: 1991). Parker was convicted on two counts of first-degree murder. He presented nonstatutory mitigating evidence at his sentencing hearing. The jury recommended life sentences on both murder counts, finding the aggravating factors established by the state to be outweighed by the mitigating circumstances offered by Parker. The trial judge overrode the jury on one count and sentenced Parker to death. The judge said he found six aggravating circumstances, no statutory factors of mitigation, and that no mitigating circumstances outweighed the aggravating circumstances.

The Florida Supreme Court conducted its mandatory review and found sufficient evidence to support the trial judge's conclusions on four aggravating factors. It affirmed the death sentence on the ground that the trial judge had found no mitigating evidence to balance against the aggravating factors. The U.S. Supreme Court ruled the state supreme court had failed to adequately consider the nonstatutory mitigating evidence in conducting its review. While the trial judge did not explicitly explain what effect he gave Parker's mitigating evidence, the Supreme Court concluded from the trial judge's action that nonstatutory mitigating circumstances did exist, and that they were weighed by the judge before imposing sentence. The state supreme court's reweighing of the evidence, on the other hand, was inadequate because it relied exclusively on what it took for the trial judge to find no mitigating circumstances. The Florida Supreme Court's affirmation of Parker's death sentence thus deprived Parker of the "individualized treatment" to which he was entitled. Under Arizona law, in order to obtain a first-degree murder conviction, it must be shown that a killing was either premeditated or that it occurred in the course of committing a specified felony. In *Schad v. Arizona* (501 U.S. 624: 1991), the Court considered whether a jury in a capital murder case needs to unanimously agree on the underlying basis (premeditation or felony murder) for the offense. Schad was indicted for first-degree murder after being found in the possession of property belonging to a murder victim. The trial judge denied Schad's request to instruct the jury on theft as a lesser included offense. Instead, the judge instructed the jury on the lesser noncapital offense of second-degree murder. The trial court did not require the jury to agree on a single underlying theory of the first degree murder. In a 5–4 decision, the Supreme Court affirmed the conviction, although the majority could not agree on its reasons for doing so. Justice Souter's plurality opinion said that there is no one test for determining when two means by which a crime is committed are so different as to reflect two separate offenses. Rather, reviewing courts must examine the objectives of the state legislature in defining what constitutes a particular offense through the concept of due process. History and how widely a practice is used by the states are concrete reflections of the due process "demands for fairness and rationality." While it may have been desirable for Arizona to be more specific in defining capital murder, history and contemporary practice support Arizona's judgment to equate the mental states of premeditation and felony murder to prove the single offense of first-degree murder. Souter said there had never been a requirement that jurors agree upon the single means of committing a crime—the act itself. As long as jurors agree "upon the bottom line," it is acceptable that "different jurors may be persuaded by different pieces of evidence." Souter saw no reason why the principle that a jury need not agree on means of satisfying the *actus reus* element of an offense should not "apply equally to alternative means of satisfying the element of *mens rea*." Arizona could thus reasonably conclude that death in the course of a felony like robbery is the "moral equivalent of premeditation." Souter went on to say that courts ought to exercise restraint in cases like this. He felt a presumption of legislative competence applies in situations where judgments about what constitutes a crime are involved. These are value choices "more appropriately" made by legislatures. Justice White issued a dissent joined by Justices Marshall, Blackmun, and Stevens. White thought that felony murder was too different from premeditated murder to be linked under the capital murder statute. He thought it "particularly fanciful to equate an intent to do no more than rob with a premeditated intent to murder." It was the dissenters' view that a state could not convict Schad of first-degree murder by either of two "divergent routes possessing no elements in common except the fact of murder."

The Court considered capital case fair notice requirements in *Lankford v. Idaho* (500 U.S. 110: 1991). Lankford was charged with two counts of first-degree murder. He was told at his arraignment that if he was convicted on either count, he might be sentenced to the maximum penalty of death. He was convicted on both counts. Before his sentencing hearing, the trial court ordered the prosecution to disclose whether it would seek the death penalty. The prosecution indicated it would not. The subsequent sentencing hearing was confined to the discussion of alternative prison sentences. There were no arguments offered by either side on the death penalty. At the end of the hearing, the trial judge indicated he considered Lankford's crimes serious enough to warrant consideration of the death penalty notwithstanding the prosecution's judgment to seek a sentence of imprisonment. Indeed, the judge found five factors of aggravation present in Lankford's case and sentenced him to death. The state supreme court ruled that when Lankford was advised during his arraignment of the possibility of the death penalty, he was given sufficient notice. In a 5–4 ruling, the Supreme Court disagreed. Justice Stevens said for the majority that the concept of fair notice is the "bedrock of any constitutionally fair procedure." Fair procedure, in turn, is especially critical in capital cases because "death is a different kind of punishment." The critical issue was sufficiency of notice as to the real question before the trial court at the sentencing hearing. The trial court's presentencing order inquiring into the state's intent to seek the death sentence did not explicitly put limits on how Lankford's counsel prepared for the sentencing hearing. In the Court's view, however, it was reasonable for defense to assume that there was no real need to debate the death penalty. Orders that are "designed to limit the issues," said Stevens, "would serve no purpose if counsel acted at their peril when they complied with the order's limitations." The arraignment would have been sufficient had the trial court not issued the presentence order. The majority concluded that once the order was issued and the prosecutor responded in the negative, Lankford required specific advice that the trial court retained the death penalty as a sentence option in his case. More specifically, Lankford needed to know that the trial judge was considering the death penalty based on five specific aggravating circumstances. Arguments on these circumstances were not entered because defense counsel saw them as "entirely irrelevant" to a discussion "about the length of [Lankford's] possible incarceration." The dissenters, Justices Scalia, White, and Souter and Chief Justice Rehnquist, believed that Lankford had been sufficiently apprised of the death penalty possibility at the arraignment.

In *Dawson v. Delaware* (503 U.S. 159: 1992), the Court vacated a death sentence on First Amendment associational grounds. At Dawson's sentencing hearing, the prosecution read a stipulation referring to a white racist prison gang known as the "Aryan Brotherhood" that had a chapter in the Delaware prisons. Evidence was subsequently introduced to show that Dawson had the name of the gang tattooed on his hand. An eight-justice majority held that even though the First Amendment does not "erect a per se barrier to evidence concerning one's beliefs and associations," the narrowness of the stipulation left the reference to the gang irrelevant to Dawson's sentencing proceeding. The evidence about the Aryan Brotherhood was neither specifically tied to the murder committed by Dawson nor used to rebut any mitigating evidence offered by Dawson. The Court allowed that associational evidence might serve a legitimate purpose in representing a defendant's future dangerousness or in developing factors of aggravation. In this case, however, reference to the Aryan Brotherhood could do no more than represent "abstract beliefs" of the Delaware chapter of the gang and Dawson as an individual. The Court concluded that introduction of evidence about the prison gang and Dawson's membership was thus precluded by the First Amendment. Justice Thomas was the only dissenter, holding that Dawson's membership in the gang indicated his participation in forbidden prison activities and that membership evidence was relevant to a consideration of Dawson's character and his future dangerousness.

Mitigating Evidence

Penry v. Lynaugh, **492 U.S. 302, 106 L. Ed. 2d 256, 109 S. Ct. 2934 (1989)**
Ruled that capital punishment of convicted murderers who are mentally retarded is not necessarily cruel and unusual punishment. At the same

time, the Court reversed Penry's sentence in this case because the jury had not been properly instructed with respect to how it might give effect to his retardation and other mitigating factors. Under Texas law, a defendant convicted of capital murder is sentenced to death if a jury unanimously answers in the affirmative regarding three "special issues": (1) that the murder was committed deliberately and with the expectation that death would occur, (2) that the defendant would continue to pose a threat to society in the future, and (3) that the murder was an "unreasonable" response to victim provocation. Penry submitted various evidence in mitigation, including his IQ (between 50 and 63), his learning age (estimated as that of a 6- to 7-year old child), his social maturity (estimated as that of a 9-year old), and evidence that he had been severely abused as a child. Penry asked for jury instructions that defined the key terms in the three special issues in relation to the mitigating evidence he introduced. The trial court refused to provide those instructions, and the jury found in the affirmative on each of the special issues. Penry was then sentenced to death. Justice O'Connor, joined by Justices Brennan, Marshall, Stevens, and Blackmun, decided that Penry's death sentence must be vacated. An established principle for capital cases is that punishment must relate directly to the defendant's "personal culpability," said O'Connor. Failure to elaborate on or further define the key terms in the special issues to give effect to the defendant's mitigating evidence "compels the conclusion" that the jury was not fully enabled to give a "reasoned moral response" to the evidence submitted at the sentencing stage of the trial. The jury was required to find that the murder had been committed "deliberately." Penry requested special instructions that defined the term *deliberately* in a manner that would direct jurors to consider Penry's mitigating evidence as it pertains to moral culpability. Without the special instructions, a juror who was persuaded by the mitigating evidence that the death penalty should not be imposed would be unable to give effect to that judgment if the juror also believed the crime to have been committed deliberately. Penry's retardation and history of childhood abuse also furnished a "two-edged sword" with respect to the special issue of future dangerousness. On the one hand, those factors may diminish his "blameworthiness"; on the other, Penry's "inability to learn from his mistakes" because of his retardation and his history of abuse also indicate there is a "probability that he will be dangerous in the future." The same kind of defect existed on the final special issue of victim provocation. The Court did not find sufficient the broad instruction that the jury could simply decline to impose the death penalty on Penry. Such an instruction is too unfocused and gives the sentencing jury impermissibly "unbridled discretion." Chief Justice Rehnquist and Justices White, Scalia, and Kennedy joined O'Connor to hold that the Eighth Amendment does not categorically preclude execution of mentally retarded murderers. The Court agreed that "profoundly retarded" people lack the "capacity to appreciate the wrongfulness" of their conduct and cannot be sentenced to death. The profoundly retarded person is "unlikely" to face the prospect of the death penalty, however, because he or she is rarely found competent to stand trial or can advance an "insanity defense" based on "mental defect." Persons such as Penry do not fit this category. The jury found him competent to be tried and rejected his insanity defense, "reflecting the conclusion that he knew his conduct was wrong" and that he was "capable of conforming it to the requirements of law." The Court was unconvinced that there existed an "national consensus" against executing mentally retarded capital murderers. Indeed, only one state had enacted a prohibition of the practice. The Court agreed that retardation may diminish culpability and warrants consideration as a mitigating factor. Nonetheless, the Court concluded that not all retarded persons, by virtue of that "retardation alone," and separate from any individual consideration of personal responsibility, "inevitably lack the cognitive, volitional, and moral capacity to act with the degree of culpability associated with the death penalty." In other words, the Court found "insufficient basis" for a "categorical" Cruel and Unusual Punishment Clause ban on the death penalty for the retarded murderer. *See also* CRUEL AND UNUSUAL PUNISHMENT, p. 401.

Significance   *Penry* reflects the Rehnquist Court's reluctance to proscribe state capital punishment laws further with categorical restrictions. Mental retardation as such does not preclude imposition of the death sentence, but retardation is a mitigating factor that must be given full effect in the sentencing decision. Sentencers are required to make some very fine distinctions. The key process for doing so is the weighing of aggravating and mitigating factors. So long as these factors are given full consideration, the Rehnquist Court seems satisfied that these distinctions can by made by jurors in capital cases. Several cases further illustrate. In 1982, the Court ruled in *Enmund v. Florida* (458 U.S. 782) that a defendant could not be sentenced to death unless it could be shown that he or she killed, attempted to kill, or intended to kill. The ruling suggested that aiders and abetters could not be subjected to the death penalty. In *Tison v. Arizona* (481 U.S. 137: 1987), the Court rejected the *Enmund* framework, saying it dealt with two distinct subsets of felony murder: one in which a person is a minor actor and neither intended to kill nor was found to have any culpable mental state, and the other where the felony murderer actually killed, attempted to kill, or intended to kill. The *Tison* case was in neither of these categories. The Tison brothers aided in their father's prison escape and were with him when he killed four persons taken captive. Though the brothers claimed surprise at the killings, neither attempted to aid the victims and both continued their participation in the escape. They were subsequently captured, tried, convicted, and sentenced to death. The issue before the Court in *Tison* was whether the death penalty is precluded for a case between the polar extremes described in *Enmund*, a case in which a defendant's participation is minor and the defendant's mental state is one of reckless indifference to the value of human life. The Court said capital punishment was not appropriate in this intermediate category. *Enmund's* narrow focus on intent to kill was a "highly unsatisfactory means of definitively distinguishing the most culpable and dangerous murderers." Some nonintentional murderers may be among the most dangerous and inhumane of all, such as the person who tortures another without caring whether the victim lives or dies, or the robber who shoots someone in the course of a robbery, utterly indifferent to the fact that killing may be an unintended consequence of the desire to rob. The Court accordingly ruled that "reckless disregard for human life implicit in engaging in criminal activities known to carry a grave risk of death represents a highly culpable mental state." This mental state may be taken into account in making a capital sentencing judgment when that conduct causes its natural, though not inevitable, lethal result.

In *Mills v. Maryland* (486 U.S. 367: 1988), the Court considered whether the Maryland capital punishment law deprived a defendant of full consideration of mitigating factors. Under the law, the death sentence was required if jurors found an aggravating circumstance in the absence of a mitigating circumstance. Mills contended that the law as applied required jurors to agree unanimously on a particular mitigating circumstance. A death sentence using this approach, argued Mills, was unconstitutional because it could require capital punishment where unanimity did not exist on a particular mitigating factor even though all jurors believed some mitigating circumstance(s) existed. The Court agreed and vacated Mills's death sentence on the ground the unanimity issue interfered with the full consideration of possible mitigation. The Court saw a "substantial probability that reasonable jurors" may have thought they were "precluded from considering" mitigating evidence unless all the jury members agreed on the existence of a particular factor. Given the finality of the death sentence, the Court said that review of such cases requires "greater certainty that the jury's conclusions rested on proper grounds" than the finding of guilt itself. The Court acknowledged that there was no "extrinsic evidence" of what the jury thought in this case, but said the verdict form and jury instructions created "at least a substantial risk that the jury was misinformed." The Texas capital punishment law in effect until 1991 required that once a defendant was found guilty of murder, a jury had to find beyond a reasonable doubt that the killing was deliberate, and that the defendant represented a "continuing threat to society." The statute did not define the factors that might be offered in mitigation on the death sentence question. The *Penry* ruling required a special jury instruction when evidence offered in mitigation also supported the imposition of capital punishment. Dorsie Lee Johnson argued that the Texas law made youth a factor supporting the death penalty rather than diminish his culpability. The Supreme Court ruled in *Johnson v. Texas* (125 L. Ed. 2d 290: 1993) that the Texas capital sentencing system allowed the jury to sufficiently consider the effect of Johnson's youth as a possibe mitigating factor. Justice Kennedy spoke for the five-justice majority. The question in *Johnson* was identical to that presented in *Graham v. Collins* (122 L. Ed. 2d 260: 1993). The Court never reached the merits of Graham's claim because under terms of *Teague v. Lane* (489 U.S. 288: 1989), a "new" rule of law could not be applied to a case on federal habeas corpus review. *Johnson* was taken by the Court on direct review. The Court did not dispute that Johnson's youth is a relevant mitigating factor that "must be within the effective reach" of a capital sentencing jury. A lack of maturity and an underdeveloped sense of responsibility are commonly found in the young, and these qualities "often result in impetuous and ill-considered actions and decisions." The issue in this case is whether this factor was allowed adequate consideration without special jury instruction. The adequacy of the instruction given, said Kennedy, is not determined by a "technical parsing of the language of the instructions, but instead [we] approach the instructions in the same way that the jury would—with a 'commonsense understanding of the instructions in the light of all that has taken place at the trial.'" It was the Court's conclusion that there was "no reasonable likelihood" that the jury would have found itself "foreclosed" from considering the relevant aspects of Johnson's youth. Kennedy said that even on a "cold record, one cannot be unmoved" by the testimony of Johnson's father suggesting that his son's actions were largely due to his youth. It "strains credulity" to suppose that the jury would have evidence of Johnson's youth as "outside its effective reach" in considering the question of his future dangerousness. As long as any mitigating evidence is "within the effective reach of the sentencer," the Eighth Amendment requirements are met. The evidence of Johnson's youth was seen as outside the scope of *Penry*. Unlike Penry's mental retardation, which left Penry unable to learn from his mistakes, the "ill effects of youth that a defendant may experience are subject to change and, as a result, are readily comprehended as a mitigating factor in consideration of the second special issue [future dangerousness]." The rule sought by Johnson, in the Court's view, would require that the jury be able to give effect to mitigating evidence "in every conceivable manner in which the evidence might be relevant." The "fundamental flaw" in Johnson's argument is its failure to recognize the distinction between "rules that govern what factors the jury must be permitted to consider in making its sentencing decision and rules that govern how the State may guide the jury in considering and weighing those factors in reaching a decision." To rule for Johnson, the Court would have to require that a jury be instructed in a manner that leaves it "free to depart from the special issues in every case." Such a result would, said Kennedy, "remove all power on the part of the States to structure the consideration of mitigating evidence—a result we have been consistent in rejecting." Justices O'Connor, Blackmun, Stevens, and Souter dissented, believing that even if the jury could give some mitigating effect to youth on the future dangerousness issue, an additional instruction would still be required here. It was their view that under the Texas scheme, a jury could give effect to the most relevant aspect of youth without a special instruction—the relation of youth to a defendant's "culpability for the crime he committed."

Jonathan Simmons was convicted by a South Carolina jury of capital murder. He had a history of prior violent crimes that would have made him ineligible for parole if he were sentenced to a term of incarceration for the murder. The prosecution indicated prior to jury selection that it would oppose any mention of parole, including during the voir dire process. At the sentencing proceeding following Simmons's conviction, the state sought the death penalty on the grounds that Simmons represented a continuing danger to society. Simmons requested a jury instruction that he would never be paroled if sentenced to life imprisonment. In support of this request, Simmons offered a statement from the South Carolina Department of Probation, Parole and Pardons confirming his ineligibility for parole. He also submitted findings from opinion polling data that reflected a widely held belief among the public that a person sentenced to life imprisonment would eventually become eligible for parole. The trial judge rejected the jury instruction requested by Simmons. The jury began its deliberation on sentence and soon thereafter specifically asked the judge whether a life sentence included the possibility of parole. Over defense objection, the judge instructed the jury not to consider parole or parole eligibility in its deliberations on sentence. Twenty-five minutes after receiving this instruction, the jury returned and sentenced Simmons to death. He unsuccessfully appealed to the South Carolina Supreme Court. In a 7–2 decision, the Supreme Court invalidated the sentence in *Simmons v. South Carolina* (129 L. Ed. 2d 133: 1994). Justice Blackmun delivered an opinion joined by Justices Stevens, Souter, and Ginsburg. Justice O'Connor filed a concurring opinion joined by Chief Justice Rehnquist and Justice Kennedy. It was Blackmun's view that the Due Process Clause does not permit the execution of a prisoner on the basis of "information which he had no opportunity to deny or explain." Here, the sentencing jury could have reasonably believed that

Simmons could be released on parole if he were not executed. To whatever extent this misunderstanding "pervaded the jury's deliberations," it had the effect of "creating a false choice" between sentencing Simmons to death or a period of incarceration. This "grievous misunderstanding was encouraged by the trial court's refusal to provide the jury with accurate information regarding [Simmons's] parole eligibility, and by the State's repeated suggestion that [he] would pose a future danger to society if he were not executed." Blackmun suggested that because this was a capital case, many issues that are "irrelevant" to the guilt-innocence determination "step into the foreground and require consideration at the sentencing phase." As the jury considered Simmons's future dangerousness, the actual duration of the defendant's prison sentence is "indisputably relevant." The state, said Blackmun, "raised the specter of [Simmons's] future dangerousness generally, but then thwarted all efforts by [Simmons] to demonstrate that, contrary to the prosecutor's intimations, he would never be release on parole and thus...would not pose a future danger to society." As a general proposition, the Court will not "lightly second-guess" a decision whether or not to inform a jury about parole eligibility. If a state rests its case for imposing the death penalty at least in part on the premise that the defendant will be dangerous in the future, however, the fact that the "alternative sentence to death is life without parole will necessarily undercut the State's argument regarding the threat the defendant poses to society." Justices Scalia and Thomas felt that the practice of not informing the jury about Simmons's parole ineligibility was not a procedure "so incompatible with our national traditions of criminal procedure" as to violate the Due Process Clause. He characterized as "far-fetched" the possibility that the jury had imposed the death penalty "just in case" Simmons might be released on parole. Scalia was critical of the what he called the "death-is-different" jurisprudence where capital cases have different constitutional requirements than non-capital cases—requirements more demanding than what the Due Process Clause demands.

John Romano and a co-defendant were together convicted of murder and sentenced to death. Romano was later convicted for a second murder. At the sentencing phase of the second trial, the state introduced the first murder conviction and death sentence as evidence of aggravation. The jury recommended the death penalty in the second case. In *Caldwell v. Mississippi* (472 U.S. 320: 1985), the Court ruled that a jury in a capital case must understand that it has the sole responsibility for determining the defendant's sentence. Romano appealed his second sentence on the ground that the jury's knowledge that he was already facing a death sentence diminished any sense of singular responsibility for the sentencing decision in the second trial. The case was made more difficult by the fact that following sentencing in the second case, Romano's conviction for the first murder was reversed by the Oklahoma Appellate Court on the grounds that he should have been tried separately from his co-defendant. In *Romano v. Oklahoma* (129 L. Ed. 2d 1: 1994), the U.S. Supreme Court affirmed Romano's sentence in the second case by a 5–4 vote. To establish a *Caldwell* violation, a defendant must show that remarks to the jury "improperly describe the role assigned to the jury by local law." Romano contended that the evidence of his prior death sentence impermissibly undermined the sentencing jury's sense of responsibility in violation of the principle established in *Caldwell*. The Court disagreed. Here, said Chief Justice Rehnquist, the jury was not "affirmatively misled regarding its role in the sentencing process." The evidence presented to it was neither false at the time it was admitted nor did it directly pertain to the jury's sentencing role. Romano also contended that because the evidence of his previous death sentence was "inaccurate and irrelevant," the jury's consideration of it rendered his sentencing proceeding unreliable under the Eighth Amendment. The evidence may have been irrelevant as a matter of state law, Rehnquist said, but that "does not render its admission federal constitutional error." The core question was seen by the Court as whether the admission of evidence regarding Romano's prior death sentence "so infected the sentencing proceeding with unfairness" as to render the jury's decision to impose the death penalty a denial of due process. Using that standard, the Court concluded that Romano was not deprived of a fair sentencing proceeding. Justice Ginsburg, joined by Justices Blackmun, Stevens, and Souter, dissented. It was their view that the sentencing jury's consideration of Romano's previous conviction and death sentence "infected the jury's life-or-death deliberations" in violation of *Caldwell*. Revealing to the jurors that Romano was already condemned to die signaled that he faced execution regardless of their decision—that his fate "had been sealed" by the previous jury, and thus was not fully their responsibility.

Sentencers (jury or judge) in state capital cases are often required to balance or weigh aggravating and mitigating factors which may exist in a specific case. The prosecution must show at least one aggravating factor in order to obtain a death sentence. The Court has reviewed a number of cases where capital defendants have challenged the definition of certain aggravating factors on the grounds that the defining language is too vague or imprecise. While many states require sentencers to weigh aggravating and mitigating factors, only California instructs sentencers to consider various undesignated factors "if relevant." In these situations, the sentencer is left to determine whether any of these factors constitute evidence of aggravation or mitigation. The consolidated cases of *Tuilaepa v. California* and *Proctor v. California* (129 L. Ed. 2d 750: 1994) allowed the Court to consider challenges to the wording of three aggravating factors used in California. Both Proctor and Tuilaepa challenged an open-ended factor requiring the sentencer to consider the "circumstances of the crime." Tuilaepa further challenged factors which required the sentencer to consider the "presence or absence of criminal activity…which involved the use or attempted use of force or violence," and the age of the defendant at the time of the crime. The Court rejected these challenges in 8–1 decisions. The "circumstances of the crime" factor the Court found consistent with settled principles of capital jurisprudence. Indeed, consideration of the circumstances of a particular crime is an "indispensable part" of the process of imposing the death sentence. The Court would be "hard pressed," said Justice Kennedy, to "invalidate a jury instruction that implements what we have said the law requires." In the Court's view, the California factor instructs the jury to consider a "relevant subject matter and does so in understandable terms." Challenge of the factor which requires a sentencer to consider a defendant's previous criminal history similarly failed. The factor, Kennedy said, is phrased in "conventional and understandable terms." Both a "backward-looking and forward-looking inquiry" are permissible components of the sentencing process. Finally, Tuilaepa's challenge of the factor requiring considering the age of the defendant at the time of the crime was rejected. Consideration of age is a "factual inquiry…of the most rudimentary sort." The Court concluded that the arguments of Proctor and Tuilaepa would force the states to adopt a kind "mandatory sentencing scheme" requiring a sentencer to sentence a defendant to death if, for example, it found "a certain kind or number of facts, or found more statutory aggravating factors than statutory mitigating factors." The states, Kennedy concluded, "are not required to conduct the capital sentencing process in this manner." Justice Blackmun dissented, concluding that the three challenged factors "do not withstand a meaningful vagueness analysis…" and fail to effectively guide jury discretion.

Preventive Detention

Schall v. Martin, **467 U.S. 253, 81 L. Ed. 2d 207, 104 S. Ct. 2403 (1984)**
Upheld the preventive detention of juveniles. *Schall* examined a state statute which authorized pre-trial detention of a juvenile as long as it could be shown that there was "serious risk" of the juvenile's committing additional crimes if released. Martin brought suit claiming the statute was unconstitutional on due process and equal protection grounds. A U.S. district court found the law in violation of the Due Process Clause and ordered the release of all juveniles detained under the statute. The

Supreme Court reversed the district court in a 6–3 decision. The opinion of the Court was delivered by Justice Rehnquist. He said the question before the Court was whether preventive detention of juveniles is compatible with "fundamental fairness." Properly to address this issue, the Court felt two inquiries were necessary: is a legitimate state interest served by preventive detention, and are the procedural safeguards adequate to authorize the pre-trial detention. The Court said that crime prevention is a "weighty social objective," and a state's legitimate and compelling interest in protecting its citizenry from crime "cannot be doubted." That interest "persists undiluted in the juvenile context." The harm caused by crime is not dependent upon the age of the perpetrator, and the harm to society generally may be even greater given the high rate of recidivism among juveniles. In addition, the juvenile's liberty interest may be subordinated to the state's "parens patriae interest in preserving and promoting the welfare of the child." Rehnquist argued that society has a legitimate interest in protecting a juvenile from the consequences of his criminal activity. This includes the potential injury which may occur when a victim resists and "the downward spiral of criminal activity into which peer pressure may lead the child" persists. The Court saw the state interest as substantial and legitimate, a view "confirmed by the widespread use and judicial acceptance of preventive detention for juveniles." Rehnquist observed that "mere invocation of a legitimate purpose" will not justify particular restrictions and conditions of confinement amounting to punishment. The Court found the statute in question to have nonpunitive objectives, however. The detention specified was "strictly limited in time," and it entitled the juvenile to an expedited fact-finding hearing. The Court then addressed the procedural issue of whether there was "sufficient protection against erroneous and unnecessary deprivation of liberty." The Court found that the statute provided "far more predetention protection" than required for probable cause determinations for adults. While the initial appearance is informal, full notice is given and stenographic records are kept. The juvenile is accompanied by a parent or guardian and is informed of his or her constitutional rights, including the right to remain silent and be represented by counsel. Finally, the Court rejected the contention that the statute's standard for detention, serious risk of additional criminal conduct, was "fatally vague." Prediction of future criminal conduct is a judgment based on "a host of variables which cannot be readily codified." Nonetheless, the decision on detention is based on "as much information as can reasonably be obtained at the initial appearance," and is not impermissibly vague. Justices Marshall, Brennan, and Stevens dissented. They saw the statute as a violation of due process because it allowed punishment before final adjudication of guilt. They felt the crime prevention interest was insufficient justification for the infringement of the detainee's rights. *See also* BAIL, p. 387: DUE PROCESS CLAUSES, p. 405.

Significance   The Court's decision in *Schall v. Martin* was its first treatment of preventive detention. Prior to *Schall*, the Court had let preventive detention statutes stand without review, silently agreeing with their view of pre-trial release. While bail should have the effect of ensuring an appearance at subsequent proceedings, those persons released also constitute a continuing threat to society. The policy of preventive detention is aimed at confining defendants who present a serious threat of additional criminal conduct. Although such a policy may be effective as a crime prevention strategy, it also runs counter to the presumption of innocence. For many, it constitutes imposition of punishment before adjudication of guilt.

Congress enacted the Bail Reform Act of 1984 that authorized federal judges to order pre-trial detention of any person accused of serious crimes if appearance could not be reasonably assured and the person was deemed sufficiently dangerous to others. The preventive detention provisions of the act were upheld by the Supreme Court in *United States v. Salerno* (481 U.S. 739: 1987). The Court rejected the contention that the act was defective because it authorized punishment before trial. The history of the act "clearly indicates that Congress chose detention as a potential solution to the pressing societal problem of crimes committed by persons on release." Preventing danger to the community is a legitimate regulatory goal. Further, the incidents of detention are not excessive in relation to that goal. The Court then said unequivocally that the Due Process Clause did not prohibit pre-trial detention as a regulatory measure. The government's regulatory interest in public safety can, under certain circumstances, outweigh an individual's liberty interest. The Court said the act narrowly focuses on the acute problem of crime by arrestees in a situation where the governmental interest is overwhelming. In addition, the act contains extensive procedural safeguards which both limit the circumstances under which detention may be sought for the most serious crimes, and which furthers the accuracy of the likelihood of dangerousness determination. Finally, the Court said the act did not violate the Excessive Bail Clause. It simply permits bail to be set at an infinite amount for reasons not related to the risk of flight. Nothing in the clause, said the Court, limits the government's interest in setting bail solely for the prevention of flight. Where Congress has mandated detention on the basis of some other compelling interest—here, public safety—the Eighth Amendment does not require release on bail.

In *United States v. Montalvo-Murillo* (495 U.S. 711: 1990), the Court considered whether failure to provide a timely detention hearing under the Bail Reform Act of 1984 required release of a person who would otherwise be detained. The act provides that a detention hearing should occur "immediately" unless either side has "good cause" to obtain a continuance. Continuance on motion by the defendant is limited to five days while a government initiated continuance may not exceed three days. For several reasons, Montalvo's detention did not occur until thirteen days after his arrest. Because the statutory time limit had elapsed, the trial Court ruled that release was required. The Supreme Court disagreed. While the time limits of the act must be followed "with care and precision," the act "is silent" on the issue of remedy for violation. Nothing in the act "can be read to require, or even suggest, that a timing error must result in release of a person who should otherwise be detained." Furthermore, said Justice Kennedy, the act has been upheld as an "appropriate regulatory device to assure the safety of persons in the community and to protect against the risk of flight." Automatic release "contravenes the object of the statute." The end of "exact compliance" with the letter of the act "cannot justify the means of exposing the public to an increased likelihood of violent crimes by persons on bail, an evil the statute aims to prevent." The *Salerno* reasoning was subsequently advanced in a case involving detention of individuals acquitted of crimes on grounds of mental illness. The issue in *Foucha v. Louisiana* (118 L. Ed. 2d 437: 1992) was whether a state can continue to confine such individuals, even if recovered, until they can demonstrate that they are no longer a threat to their own or others' safety. In a 5–4 decision, the Court did not find the *Salerno* rationale sufficient to save the Louisiana law under review. Justice White said that, unlike the "sharply focused" pre-trial detention policy at issue in *Salerno,* the Louisiana scheme of confinement was "not carefully limited." In addition, under the Louisiana law, individuals such as Foucha were not entitled to a hearing at which the state carries the burden of demonstrating a potential community threat. To the contrary, "the State need prove nothing to justify continued detention" while shifting the burden to the detainee to prove he is not dangerous. *Salerno* was further distinguished in that detention was "strictly limited in duration." In this case, on the other hand, because Foucha was found to have an "antisocial personality that sometimes leads to aggressive conduct,...he may be held indefinitely." White said that by this reasoning, a state could be permitted to hold indefinitely any other recovered insanity acquittee who could be shown to have a personality disorder that may lead to criminal conduct. The same could be true of "any convicted criminal, even though he has completed his prison term." If allowed, such a policy would be "only a step away from substituting confinement for dangerousness for our present system which...incarcerates only those who are proved beyond reasonable doubt to have violated a criminal law." Justices Thomas, Rehnquist, Scalia, and Kennedy concluded that the Louisiana policy did not constitute a violation of due process.

Habeas Corpus Review

Coleman v. Thompson, **501 U.S. 722, 115 L. Ed. 2d 640, 111 S. Ct. 2546 (1991)** Examined whether a state prisoner could pursue federal habeas corpus review before a state appellate court had concluded its review. Under *Fay v. Noia* (372 U.S. 391: 1963), federal habeas corpus petitions could be granted even in cases where state appellate review had not taken place, unless the petitioner had "deliberately bypassed" the state appellate courts. The Court overruled *Fay v. Noia* in *Coleman*. In a 6–3 decision, the Court ruled that virtually any failure to satisfy state processes would constitute procedural default and preclude the prisoner from petitioning for federal habeas corpus review. Through Justice O'Connor, the Court made it clear the new rule reached cases where failure to pursue state review was the result of "inadvertent error" by defense counsel. Coleman's petition for state review had been dismissed because it had not been filed within the prescribed time period. The missed deadline was clearly outside the "deliberate bypass" provision of *Fay v. Noia*. O'Connor said the case was "about federalism," and the respect federal courts owe state court processes. It was necessary to overturn *Fay v. Noia* because that decision was "based on a conception of federal-state relations that undervalued the importance of state procedural rules." *Coleman* holds that federal courts can undertake habeas review only if the petitioner can show cause why state processes were not completed; mistakes of counsel acting as agents of the petitioner are insufficient cause. O'Connor said cause must be the consequence of something external to the petitioner, something that "cannot be fairly attributed to him." Justices Blackmun, Marshall, and Stevens dissented. Blackmun characterized the ruling as part of a "crusade" by the majority to limit the ability of state prisoners to access federal courts. He said the Court has created a "byzantine morass of arbitrary, unnecessary, and unjustifiable impediments to the vindication of Federal rights." *See also* HABEAS CORPUS, p. 419.

Significance The Rehnquist Court has examined a number of important habeas corpus issues in recent years. One such ruling was *McCleskey v. Zant* (499 U.S. 467: 1991). Part of the evidence against McCleskey was the testimony of a witness who occupied a jail cell next to him. After the conviction was affirmed by the Georgia Supreme Court, McCleskey unsuccessfully sought habeas corpus relief in the state courts. He argued that his incriminating statements to the informant in the adjoining cell were elicited in violation of his Sixth Amendment right to counsel under *Massiah v. United States* (377 U.S. 201: 1964). *Massiah* prohibits use of informants to elicit incriminating information after formal charges have been brought against a suspect. McCleskey then filed a federal habeas corpus petition. This petition did not include a *Massiah* claim since the evidence available to McCleskey's counsel at the time suggested such a claim could not be sufficiently supported. Rather, McCleskey argued that Georgia administered its death penalty law in a racially discriminatory manner. The case reached the Supreme Court, but the Court rejected McCleskey's discrimination claim (*see McCleskey v. Kemp*, 481 U.S. 279: 1987). McCleskey filed a second habeas corpus petition, this time asserting the *Massiah* claim. The petition was granted by the federal district court, but reversed by the Court of Appeals for the Eleventh Circuit. The Supreme Court affirmed the lower court. The principal issue in this case was whether McCleskey's failure to include the *Massiah* issue in his first petition precluded his raising that claim in a second petition. Key to resolving this issue was whether McCleskey's second petition constituted an abuse of the writ. McCleskey's position was that such abuse could only occur as a result of deliberately abandoning a claim in the first petition or through inexcusable neglect. In other words, McCleskey sought a nonrestrictive interpretation of the abuse of the writ standard. Georgia, on the other hand, argued that the standard requires prisoners to include all claims of which they were aware in the first petition. Justice Kennedy said doctrines such as abuse of the writ are based on concerns about the "significant cost" of federal habeas corpus review. First, the writ "strikes at finality." Perpetual disrespect for the finality of convictions, in turn, "disparages the entire criminal system." Second, habeas review burdens scarce federal judicial resources by threatening the "capacity of the system to resolve primary disputes." Habeas review may also give litigants "incentives to withhold claims for manipulative purposes." Kennedy then turned to the abuse of the writ standard. The majority sought to modify the abuse of writ doctrine to "curtail the abusive petitions that in recent years have threatened the integrity of the habeas corpus process." Under the new standard, habeas petitions following the first one will be dismissed unless a prisoner can demonstrate cause for not asserting the claim earlier. A mere showing of good faith was seen as insufficient to establish cause. Rather, the prisoner had to demonstrate "some external impediment preventing counsel from constructing or raising a claim." The Court said it was also necessary for the petitioner to demonstrate that he or she suffered "actual prejudice resulting from the errors of which he complains." The burden of disproving abuse of the petition falls to the prisoner once the state describes the prior petition(s) and isolates claims raised for the first time. In the absence of cause, a petition could be accepted only to prevent a "fundamental miscarriage of justice," something Kennedy said could occur only in "extraordinary instances." Even though the state had withheld evidence on the *Massiah* issue from McCleskey prior to the first petition, the Court concluded that omission of the Sixth Amendment claim from the first petition could not be excused.

Taken together, *Coleman* and *McCleskey* establish difficult hurdles for both initial and subsequent habeas corpus petitions of state prisoners. The Court continued to withdraw federal habeas corpus access from those convicted of state crimes in *Keeney v. Tamayo-Reyes* (118 L. Ed. 2d 318: 1992). Under standards that applied previous to *Keeney,* a state prisoner was entitled to habeas corpus review of evidence not adequately developed in state trial courts as long as the evidence was not deliberately withheld or "bypassed." In a 5–4 decision in *Keeney,* the Court ruled that federal *habeas corpus* review can take place only if "cause and prejudice" can be demonstrated. The prisoner must show cause for his failure to develop the evidence at trial and further demonstrate "actual prejudice resulting from that failure." The effect of the ruling was to make the standard for failing to develop a factual matter in a state court identical with the standard used to assert an appellate claim at the state level as required under *Coleman* and *McCleskey.* The new standard, said Justice White, "will appropriately accommodate concerns of finality, comity, judicial economy, and channeling the resolution of claims into the most appropriate forum." Under terms of *McCleskey v. Zant,* state prisoners are generally barred from submitting more than one petition for *habeas corpus* review. An exception to this prohibition exists if a prisoner can demonstrate "cause and prejudice." The would-be petitioner must show that a "miscarriage of justice" would occur if the petition were not permitted. Meeting this standard essentially means that a prisoner must demonstrate "actual innocence." The question in *Sawyer v. Whitley* (120 L. Ed. 2d 269: 1992) was how this exception applies to cases in which a prisoner asserts that he was erroneously sentenced to death. The Court retained the "cause and prejudice" framework and held that the miscarriage exception should extend to any prisoners who can demonstrate legal ineligibility for the death sentence. The more significant question of whether federal courts ought to make an independent examination of how state courts apply the Constitution to specific cases was raised in *West v. Wright* (120 L. Ed. 2d 225: 1992). The Court could not agree, however, on a response. Virginia, supported by the Bush administration, had argued that federal judges should not make such independent determinations. Only three justices—Rehnquist, Scalia, and Thomas—supported that position. The others, represented by four separate opinions, were of the view that federal courts need not be so deferential to state judgments on constitutional questions.

Herrera v. Collins, 506 U.S. __, 122 L. Ed. 2d 203, 113 S. Ct. 853 (1993)
Held that state prisoners are not entitled to federal habeas corpus review
on "actual innocence" claims. Leonel Herrera was convicted of murder
in Texas in 1982 and sentenced to death. He unsuccessfully sought to
have the conviction overturned at that time, including an attempt
through federal habeas review. Ten years after his conviction, Herrera
filed a second habeas petition, claiming that he was "actually innocent"
of the murder. The claim of innocence was supported by affidavits which
suggested that Herrera's brother (who had died during the ten-year
interim) had committed the crime. The principal question in *Herrera* was
whether his "actual innocence" claim, advanced in a second petition and
based on new evidence barred by Texas law, entitled him to federal habeas
relief. In a 6–3 decision, the Supreme Court ruled that Herrera was not
entitled to such relief. Chief Justice Rehnquist spoke for the majority. The
constitutional basis of Herrera's claim was the Eighth Amendment, which
he argued prohibited the execution of an innocent person. Though such
a proposition has "elemental appeal," Rehnquist said that the evidence
upon which Herrera's claim was based was "not produced at his trial, but
rather eight years later." The substance of his claim must be assessed in
light of the long history of the case. Rehnquist pointed out that Herrera
was afforded every constitutional protection directed toward "assuring
against the risk of convicting an innocent person." Herrera also received
the additional procedural safeguards that apply to capital cases. All of
these made it more difficult for the state to overcome the presumption of
innocence to which he was entitled. At the same time, said Rehnquist, due
process does not require that "every conceivable step be taken, at whatever
cost, to eliminate the possibility of convicting an innocent person." Once
a defendant has had a fair trial and been convicted, the "presumption of
innocence disappears." Another approach would "all but paralyze" our
criminal justice system. Rehnquist then reiterated the rule drawn from
Townsend v. Sain (372 U.S. 293: 1963) that claims of actual innocence
stemming from newly discovered evidence "have not provided a basis for
federal habeas relief absent an independent constitutional violation occurring in the underlying state criminal proceeding." The purpose of the
Townsend rule, Rehnquist said, is to ensure that federal habeas courts
"only determine whether individuals are imprisoned unconstitutionally,
but do not attempt to correct errors of fact." The "actual innocence" claim
is not itself a constitutional claim, but instead is a "gateway through which
a habeas petitioner must pass" before an otherwise barred constitutional
claim may be examined on the merits. Herrera claimed he was entitled
to habeas relief because newly discovered evidence showed that his
conviction was factually incorrect. The Court held, however, that this
placed Herrera outside the scope of federal habeas relief. Even the

"fundamental miscarriage of justice" exception is inapplicable in Herrera's case because it does not extend to "free-standing claims" of actual innocence absent an independent constitutional claim. A better avenue for a petitioner with an actual innocence claim is through executive clemency. Justice O'Connor concurred and focused her opinion on the presumption of innocence. Herrera is "no longer innocent in the eyes of the law." He had a trial, the "paramount event for determining guilt," and he was found guilty. As a result, he does not appear before the Supreme Court as "an innocent man on the verge of execution." Rather, he is a "legally guilty one who, refusing to accept the jury's verdict, demands a hearing in which to have his culpability determined once again."

Justice Blackmun, joined by Justices Stevens and Souter, dissented. He challenged the majority's concern that allowing Herrera to pursue his claim of innocence would disserve the objective of reliable trial outcomes. Such a concern, said Blackmun, "misses the point entirely." The question is not whether a retrial would be more reliable, but whether, in light of evidence not considered at the first trial, the result of the first trial "is sufficiently reliable for the State to carry out a death sentence." He also was critical of the Court's suggestion that executive clemency is a sufficient alternative. Blackmun was convinced that the possibility of clemency was not sufficient to satisfy the requirements of the Eighth and Fourteenth Amendments. The "vindication of rights guaranteed by the Constitution has never been made to turn on the unreviewable discretion of an executive officials of administrative tribunal." *See also* HABEAS CORPUS, p. 419.

Significance   In the broad range of habeas corpus questions reviewed by the Rehnquist Court, usually the objective has been to defer to judgments from state courts. Several cases are illustrative. Texas had a "special issue" capital punishment statute that required jurors to unanimously find that the defendant acted deliberately, constitutes a future danger to society, and was not provoked by the victim. Gary Graham was convicted of capital murder in 1981. The jury answered affirmatively on each of the "special issue" questions, and Graham was sentenced to death. Graham had argued at the sentencing phase of his trial that his youth—he was 17 at the time of the murder—and troubled childhood were mitigating factors. The Supreme Court previously ruled in *Penry v. Lynaugh* (492 U.S. 302: 1989) that a mentally retarded defendant was entitled to special jury instructions before deliberation of the "special issue" questions in order to give his mitigating evidence "full effect." Graham argued that his jury should have received similar special instructions. Following reconsideration of his case in light of the *Penry* decision, the court of appeals (sitting *en banc*) ruled that Graham's mitigating evidence was sufficiently examined as the three "special issue" questions were considered. Graham sought review by the Supreme Court. In *Graham v. Collins* (122 L. Ed. 2d 260: 1993), the Court held that Graham was not entitled to relief on federal habeas corpus grounds. The first question before the Court was whether granting Graham relief would create a "new rule" of constitutional law under the terms of *Teague v. Lane* (489 U.S. 288: 1989). Under *Teague*, the Court will not apply a new rule in cases on collateral review unless it falls under one of the two exceptions. The "new rule" principle adheres, said Justice White, "even if those good-faith interpretations are shown to be contrary to later decisions." Herrera could prevail with his claim if the judges hearing his claim at the time his conviction became final "would have felt compelled by existing precedent, to rule in his favor...." Otherwise, the Supreme Court is "barred from doing so now." Considering the "legal landscape" as it existed at the time Graham's conviction and sentence became final, the Court concluded that it would have been "anything but clear to reasonable jurists in 1984 that petitioner's sentence proceeding" was unconstitutional. Indeed, all the Court's decisions coming before *Penry* could reasonably be read to uphold the Texas "special issues" approach to capital sentencing. Furthermore, White indicated that *Penry* "did *not* broadly suggest the invalidity of [Texas's] special issues framework." Rather, *Penry* held only that the defendant was entitled to additional jury instructions. What Graham was seeking in this case, on the other hand, would require a new rule—it was "not commanded by the cases upon which *Penry* rested." Graham's evidence was "not placed beyond the jury's effective reach." In addition, Graham's jury could have responded in the negative to the special issues consistently with the instructions it received. The Court thus concluded that neither *Penry* nor any of its predecessors "dictates the ruling Graham seeks within the meaning required by *Teague.*" Even "with the benefit" of *Penry*, the Court was not convinced that "reasonable jurists would be of one mind in ruling on Graham's claim today." As a consequence, the Court concluded that the ruling Graham sought would be a "new rule" under *Teague*, and not retroactively applicable on collateral review. Justice Thomas concurred in the result, but expressed his view that *Penry* had been "wrongly decided." As the Court's "most extreme" statement on mitigating circumstances, *Penry* presents an "evident danger" to the objective of limiting the discretion of sentencers in capital cases. To require sentencers to consider mitigating evidence "whose relevance goes beyond the scope" of state sentencing criteria "renders meaningless any rational standards by which a State may channel or focus the jury's discretion." In dissent, Justices Stevens, Blackmun, O'Connor, and Souter felt that Graham was entitled under *Penry* to the special jury instructions he sought. It was their view that *Penry*, like other decision of the "mitigating" line, provides "critical protection against arbitrary and discriminatory capital sentencing," and protection that is "fully consonant with the principles of *Furman.*"

Doyle v. Ohio (426 U.S. 610: 1976) held that *Miranda* warnings contain an implicit assurance that silence will carry no penalty. As a result, the prosecutor may not call attention to a defendant's choice to remain silent after the administration of *Miranda*, even in the course of cross-examination. The question before the Court in *Brecht v. Abrahamson* (123 L. Ed. 2d 353: 1993) was the standard to be used to determine if a *Doyle* violation entitled a defendant to federal habeas corpus relief. The district court applied the standard from *Chapman v. California* (386 U.S. 18: 1967). Under *Chapman*, a conviction must be reversed if the error is not "harmless beyond a reasonable doubt." The lower courts had preferred the standard from *Kotteakos v. United States* (328 U.S. 750: 1946). Under the *Kotteakos* standard, a petitioner is entitled to federal habeas relief if the *Doyle* violation "had substantial and injurious effect or influence in determining the jury's verdict." In a 5–4 ruling, the Supreme Court held that the *Kotteakos* harmless error standard is "better tailored to the nature and purpose of collateral review" than the *Chapman* standard. Chief Justice Rehnquist disagreed with the court of appeals's characterization of *Doyle* as a "prophylactic rule." Rather, the Court saw *Doyle* error as "fit[ting] squarely into the category of constitutional violation which we have characterized as trial error." Trial error takes place in the presentation of a case to a jury, and lends itself to harmless error analysis because it may be "quantitatively assessed in the context of other evidence" in order to determine its effect on a trial. Rehnquist then returned to the theme of many recent habeas corpus rulings, the distinction between direct review and collateral review. Direct review is the "principal avenue" for challenging a conviction. While federal habeas proceedings are important in protecting constitutional rights, their role compared to direct review is "secondary and limited." Federal courts are not, concluded Rehnquist, "forums in which to relitigate state trials." State courts, said Rehnquist, "are fully qualified to identify constitutional error and evaluate its prejudicial effect on the trial process under *Chapman.*" The state court has a "superior vantage point" from which to assess the effects of trial error. It "scarcely seems logical to require federal habeas courts to engage in the identical approach to harmless error review that *Chapman* requires state courts to engage in on direct review." It was the Court's view that any additional deterrent effect from using *Chapman* on collateral review was outweighed by the costs of doing so. Reversing final and presumptively correct convictions on collateral review because states cannot demonstrate harmless error under *Chapman* undermines the states' "interest in finality and infringes on their sovereignty over criminal matters." Furthermore, Rehnquist saw the granting of federal habeas relief because there is a possibility that trial error affected the verdict as "at odds with the historic meaning of *habeas corpus*—to afford relief to those whom society has 'grievously wronged.'" The Court's cost-benefit analysis of applying *Chapman* on collateral review "counsels in favor of a less onerous standard on habeas review of constitutional error." The *Kotteakos* standard was seen as the better test. *Kotteakos* allows full review of constitutional claims, but petitioners are not entitled to relief based on trial error unless they can show that the error resulted in "actual prejudice." The *Kotteakos* standard was seen as "better tailored" to the unique purpose of collateral review, and more compatible with the Court's most recent habeas cases. The dissenters, Justices White, Blackmun and Souter, saw the central question as whether states may detain someone whose conviction was tarnished by a constitutional violation that is not harmless beyond a reasonable doubt. *Chapman* "dictates that they may not; the majority suggests that, so long as direct review has not corrected this error in time, they may."

The Supreme Court ruled in *Stone v. Powell* (428 U.S. 465: 1976) that federal habeas corpus review is not available to state prisoners asserting search or seizure violations when the state has afforded them a "full and fair" review of the Fourth Amendment claims. The Court ruled in *Withrow v. Williams* (123 L. Ed. 2d 407: 1993) that the *Stone* restriction does not apply to claims based on violations of *Miranda v. Arizona* (384 U.S. 436: 1966). The several opinions in *Withrow* effectively reflect the central habeas corpus positions currently represented on the Court. The State of Michigan (and the United States as *amicus*) argued that *Miranda*'s protections are not constitutional, but "merely prophylactic." As a consequence, they contended that federal habeas review should not extend to *Miranda*-based claims. While accepting that *Miranda* is prophylactic in character, the Supreme Court rejected the conclusion on habeas review. Characterizing *Miranda* protections as "prophylactic," said Justice Souter, is a "far cry from putting *Miranda* on all fours with *Mapp* [*v. Ohio* (367 U.S. 643: 1961)] or from rendering *Miranda* subject to *Stone*." Souter pointed to two substantial differences between *Mapp* and *Miranda*. *Mapp* can neither remediate the extrajudicial Fourth Amendment violation, nor improve on the reliability of evidence used at trial. On the other hand, *Miranda* safeguards a "fundamental trial right" by protecting a defendant's privilege against self-incrimination. Moreover, the trial right protected by *Miranda* furthers the end of "correct ascertainment of guilt." By reducing the possibility of unreliable statements during custodial interrogation, *Miranda* "serves to guard against the use of unreliable statements at trial." Moreover, Souter said that eliminating review of *Miranda* claims "would not significantly benefit the federal courts in their exercise of habeas jurisdiction, or advance the cause of federalism in any substantial way." Reducing or eliminating habeas review of *Miranda* issues would prompt "virtually all" *Miranda* claims to be recast into due process claims that convictions "rested on an involuntary confession." If that analysis is correct, Souter predicted, federal courts "would certainly not have heard the last of *Miranda* on collateral review." The Court concluded that "abdicating *Miranda's* bright-line...rules" for a totality-of-circumstances approach on habeas review would "not do much of anything to lighten the burdens placed on busy federal courts." Neither could the Court see how eliminating *Miranda* issues from federal habeas corpus "would go very far to relieve such tensions as *Miranda* may now raise between the two judicial systems." Finally, if one should question the need to use federal collateral review to maintain the "respect *Miranda* is due," Souter said, "the answer simply is that the respect is sustained in no small part by the existence of such review." Justice O'Connor, joined by Chief Justice Rehnquist, dissented. She focused on the distinction between direct and collateral review. When a case is on direct review, the damage to the "truth-seeking function is deemed an acceptable sacrifice for the deterrence and respect for constitutional values that the *Miranda* rule brings." On the other hand, when a case is on collateral review, the "balance between the costs and benefits shifts; the interests of federalism, finality, and fairness compel *Miranda's* exclusion from habeas." O'Connor said the benefit of enforcing *Miranda* through habeas is "marginal at best." Excluding involuntary statements is a task she thought could be "performed more accurately by adjudicating the voluntariness question directly." And because relief does not occur until years after the conviction, habeas enforcement of *Miranda* is of minimal value in deterring police misconduct. Justices Scalia and Thomas also dissented. In their view, both the Court and the O'Connor dissent overlooked the "most powerful equitable consideration: that Williams has already had a full and fair opportunity to litigate this claim." The question for them was whether, given the full review Williams was afforded at all levels of the Michigan court system, a federal habeas court should reopen the issue and assess the *Miranda* claim anew. The answer, said Scalia, "seems to be obvious: it should not." That would be the course followed by a federal habeas court reviewing a *federal* conviction; "it mocks our federal system to accord state convictions less respect."

A slightly different federalism issue is represented in *McFarland v. Scott* (129 L. Ed. 2d 666: 1994). The Congress chose death as penalty for certain federal drug offenses in the Anti-Drug Abuse Act of 1988. Section 848 (q)(4)(B) of the act provides that capital defendants are entitled to "qualified legal representation" in "any post-conviction proceeding" falling under Section 2254 (or 2255) of the federal habeas corpus statute. The question in *McFarland* was whether an unrepresented state capital defendant must file a federal habeas corpus petition in order to invoke the statutory right and to establish a federal court's jurisdiction to stay his execution. Frank McFarland was within 4 days of execution for murder in Texas when he petitioned a federal district court to appoint counsel under 848 (q)(4)(B) and stay his execution long enough to allow counsel time to file a habeas corpus petition. The district court ruled against McFarland concluding that because no post-conviction proceeding had been initiated, McFarland was not entitled to appointed counsel. The district court also ruled that it had no jurisdiction to stay his execution. The court of appeals affirmed and further ruled that McFarland's motion for a stay of execution and appointment of counsel was not comparable to a habeas petition. The Supreme Court held (6–3) that a defendant need not file a formal habeas petition in order to qualify for counsel under Section 848 (q)(4)(B). The Court ruled (5–4) that a formal petition for habeas corpus was not required for establishing a federal court's jurisdiction to stay an execution. An attorney's assistance prior to the filing of a capital defendant's habeas petition is critical because the "complexity of our jurisprudence in this area" makes its "unlikely" that capital defendants will be able to file successful petition on their own. Requiring an indigent capital defendant to proceed without counsel in order to have counsel appointed would "expose him to substantial risk that his habeas claims would never be heard on the merits." It was the view of Chief Justice Rehnquist and Justice Thomas that Congress intended to make legal counsel available to indigent defendants only after a habeas proceeding had been commenced by the filing of a petition for habeas relief. The dissenters agreed that legal assistance prior to filing a federal habeas petition could be "very valuable to a prisoner," but such does not "compel the conclusion that Congress intended the Federal Government to pay for it...." More troublesome to the dissenters was the "expan[sion of] the power of federal courts to interfere with States' legitimate interests in enforcing the judgments of their criminal justice systems." The dissenters embraced O'Connor's observations that by expanding the federal courts' power to grant stays of execution, the Court's decision "conflicts with the sound principle underlying our precedents that federal habeas review exists only to review errors of constitutional dimension."

6. Equal Protection and Privacy

Equal Protection

Right to Privacy

EQUAL PROTECTION
Desegregation Remedies

Board of Education of Oklahoma City v. Dowell, 498 U.S. 237, 112 L. Ed. 2d 715, 111 S. Ct. 630 (1991) Considered the terms under which a school district might be released from a busing order even though the district's schools may have become resegregated. Litigation in the Oklahoma City case began in the early 1960s. A district court found that Oklahoma City was operating a "dual" school system—one that is intentionally segregated. Desegregation efforts commenced at that point. In 1972, the district court found those efforts inadequate, and an order including busing was issued. After the busing order had been in effect for five years, the school district sought to close the case. The district court concluded that the objective of achieving a "unitary" district had been met and issued an order terminating the case. The original plaintiffs did not appeal. Then the demographics began to change, and the district considered reassignment of students. As more neighborhoods became integrated, more "stand alone" schools were established and inner-city black students needed to be bused further from their own homes to outlying white areas. The district eventually adopted a Student Reassignment Plan (SRP) in 1984 in part to alleviate the burden on the bused black students. While some busing continued under the SRP, it was contended that the plan had the effect of resegregating the school district. A motion was filed to reopen the case. The district court concluded that the prior decree should be vacated on the grounds that the underlying residential segregation was the result of "private decision making and economics, and that it was too attenuated to be a vestige of former school segregation." The court of appeals reversed, saying that an original decree must remain in effect until a school district can demonstrate a "grievous wrong evoked by new and unforseen conditions...that impose extreme and unexpectedly oppressive hardships." Applying this standard, the court of appeals ruled that conditions in the school district had not changed enough to justify modification of the initial decree. The Supreme Court reversed 5–3 (Justice Souter not participating), ruling that

141

the court of appeals applied the wrong standard. Through Chief Justice Rehnquist, the Court said that decrees such as those in the Oklahoma City case are not intended to "operate in perpetuity." Local control is preferable because it allows citizens to participate in decision making and permits adaptation of school programs to local needs. Displacement of local authority by injunctive decree can only occur when local officials are party to unlawful discrimination. Relinquishing federal authority by dissolving a desegregation decree should occur, said Rehnquist, "after the local authorities have operated in compliance with it for a reasonable period of time." Dissolving an order under those circumstances properly recognizes the value of local control of school systems, and reflects the proposition that a federal court's regulatory control of local systems "not extend beyond the time required to remedy the effects of past intentional discrimination." Rehnquist then turned to the standard to be used in deciding whether to modify or dissolve a decree. The court of appeals's test was seen as excessive, a test which would "condemn a school district, once governed by a board which intentionally discriminated, to judicial tutelage for the indefinite future." While courts should not accept at face value a district's profession that it would no longer discriminate in the future, compliance with previous court orders is a factor which is "obviously relevant." In addition to determining whether a district had made good faith compliance with a prior desegregation decree, a court also must determine whether the "vestiges of past discrimination have been eliminated" as far as "practicable." *See also* EQUAL PROTECTION CLAUSE, p. 313; *SWANN v. CHARLOTTE-MECKLENBURG BOARD OF EDUCATION* (402 U.S. 1: 1971), p. 329.

Significance   *Brown v. Board of Education I* (347 U.S. 483: 1954) ruled that a racially segregated or "dual" school system violated the Equal Protection Clause. Under terms of *Brown v. Board of Education II* (349 U.S. 294: 1955), a large number of American school districts have operated under the supervision of federal courts for the purpose of establishing "unitary" systems. In 1991, the Supreme Court ruled in *Dowell* that a school district may achieve unitary status if the district has complied in good faith with any desegregation order for a "reasonable period" of time. *Dowell* further said that school districts need address unlawful discrimination only as long as it is "practicable." The question raised in *Freeman v. Pitts* (118 L. Ed. 2d 108: 1992) was whether federal court supervision may be withdrawn in stages as local districts desegregate particular aspects of their operations. The Supreme Court unanimously ruled that lower federal courts could relinquish remedial control incrementally as particular district operations are found to be unitary in character. A district court "need not retain active control over every aspect of school administration" until a district has shown "unitary status in all facets of its system." Justice Kennedy spoke for the Court, saying that in addition to remediating the violation, lower courts must also "restore state and local authorities to the control of a school system that is operating in compliance with the Constitution." Returning schools to local control at the "earliest practicable date is essential to restore their true accountability." Kennedy acknowledged that the potential for discrimination remains in our society, and the states and their subdivisions must "ensure that such forces do not shape or control the politics of its schools systems." Kennedy pointed to several factors that lower courts must examine when considering partial withdrawal from supervision of a school district. They include (1) whether there has been "full and satisfactory compliance with the decree in those aspects of the system where supervision is to be withdrawn," (2) when retention of control is still needed to "achieve compliance with the decree in other facets of the school system," (3) and whether the local district has shown to the public and those among the "once disfavored race" that its good-faith commitment to the "whole of the court's decree and to those provisions of the law and the Constitution that were the predicate for judicial intervention in the first place." Racial imbalance, said Kennedy, "is not to be achieved for its own sake." Rather, it is pursued only in response to a constitutional violation. Once a de jure violation has been remedied, a district is "under no duty to remedy imbalance that is caused by demographical factors." Resegregation produced by private choices rather than state action "does not have constitutional implications." It is "beyond the authority and...practical ability" of federal courts to try to "counteract these kinds of continuous and massive demographic shifts." To pursue such an end would require "ongoing and never-ending supervision by the courts of school districts simply because they were once de jure–segregated." Finally, Kennedy said that while vestiges of past discrimination are a "stubborn fact of history" that we cannot escape, neither should federal courts "overstate" history's consequences in fixing legal responsibilities. The vestiges of segregation under review by federal courts may be "subtle and intangible but nonetheless they must be so real that they have a causal link to the de jure violations being remedied." As de jure violations become "more remote in time," and as demographic changes occur, the likelihood a student assignment imbalance is a vestige of a previous de jure violation is lessened. Further, the causal link between any current imbalance and prior violations is "even more attenuated if the school district has demonstrated its good faith."

Mississippi's eight public colleges and universities were segregated by law for almost a decade after *Brown I.* In 1962, James Meredith was admitted to the previously all-white University of Mississippi by force of a federal court order. While both black and white students were subsequently admitted to each of the schools historically designated for students of either the black or white race, the numbers of cross-enrolled students were sufficiently low that each of the school remained racially identifiable. A class action was brought by a number of black residents of Mississippi charging both constitutional and statutory violations by the state through its perpetuation of a dual system of higher education. The federal government eventually intervened in the case and pursued its own appeal of the court of appeals ruling in the case of *United States v. Fordice* (120 L. Ed. 2d 575: 1992). The case gave the Supreme Court its first opportunity to examine the issue of desegregating educational institutions at the university level. The court of appeals had ruled that Mississippi had met its constitutional obligation to eliminate all discrimination by adopting good faith policies that gave both black and white students "unfettered choice" of schools to attend. The Supreme Court, however, remanded the case, finding several aspects of Mississippi's system to be "constitutionally suspect." A state does not fulfill its constitutional obligations, said Justice White, "until it eradicates policies and practices traceable to its prior de jure system that continue to foster segregation." The adoption of race-neutral policies such as the "freedom of choice" approach does not "alone suffice to demonstrate that the state has completely abandoned its prior dual system." Attendance by choice is determined, White pointed out, "not simply by admissions policies, but also by many other factors." The case was remanded for specific reconsideration of admissions standards, the mission statements of each of the eight institutions, duplication of programs among the black and white universities, and whether Mississippi needed all eight institutions.

Gender: Employment

United Auto Workers v. Johnson Controls, Inc., **499 U.S. 187, 113 L. Ed. 2d 158, 111 S. Ct. 1196 (1991)** Ruled that women may not be excluded from jobs that might endanger a developing fetus or a fetus a woman might conceive in the future. Johnson Controls manufactures batteries. One of the primary ingredients of the batteries is lead. Exposure to lead carries health risks including the risk of endangering any fetus carried by a female employee. Johnson Controls first established a fetal protection policy in 1977 in which it suggested that women who expected to have a child should not choose a job which would include exposure to lead. The company changed its policy in 1982 to one which excluded all women "capable of bearing children" from jobs which could expose them to lead. An exception was made for women who could medically document they could no longer bear children. A class action was brought claiming the

144

policy violated Title VII of the Civil Rights Act of 1964. Johnson Controls won summary judgment in the district court. The Court of Appeals affirmed, finding the policy to be justified as both a "business necessity" and a "bona fide occupation qualification (BFOQ)." The Supreme Court reversed. Under terms of Johnson Controls' policy, fertile men are given a choice as to whether they wish to assume reproductive health risks for a particular job. Women do not have the same choice. A unanimous Supreme Court found the bias in Johnson's policy "obvious." The policy, said Justice Blackmun, "excludes women with childbearing capacity from lead-exposed jobs and so creates a facial classification based on gender." The policy concerns itself only with the "harms that may befall the unborn offspring of its female employees." Johnson's use of the words "capable of bearing children" is an explicit classification based on potential for pregnancy. The Pregnancy Disability Act of 1978 (PDA) provides that such a classification must be regarded, for Title VII purposes, in the "same light" as explicit sex discrimination. Johnson's choice to treat all female employees as potentially pregnant "evinces discrimination" on the basis of gender. The lower court's assumption was that because Johnson's objective of protecting women's unconceived offspring was "ostensibly benign," the policy did not constitute sex-based discrimination. The Supreme Court disagreed. Absence of a malevolent motive "does not convert" a facially discriminatory policy into a neutral policy with a discriminatory effect. Whether an employment practice involves disparate treatment through explicit facial discrimination, said Blackmun, "does not depend on why the employer discriminates but rather on the explicit terms of the discrimination." Unless pregnant employees differ from others in their "ability or inability to work," they must be treated the same. The Court acknowledged the health risks, especially late in pregnancy, but said Congress decided that an employer must take into account "only the woman's ability to get her job done." Women as capable of doing their jobs as their male counterparts "may not be forced to choose between having a child and having a job." See also COUNTY OF WASHINGTON v. GUNTHER (450 U.S. 907: 1981), p. 361; EQUAL PROTECTION CLAUSE, p. 313; GROVE CITY COLLEGE v. BELL (465 U.S. 555: 1984), p. 123 (Supplement 1).

Significance   Some decisions such as *Grove City College v. Bell* (465 U.S. 555: 1984) limited the scope of Title IX, so much so that Congress was prompted to modify some of the Court's rulings. Concern over the issue of sexual harassment once again raised questions about the reach of Title IX. The Court ruled in *Franklin v. Gwinnett County Public Schools* (503 U.S. 60: 1992) that Title IX could serve as the basis of actions by school and college students seeking damages for various forms of sex discrimination. Franklin had filed a lawsuit against Gwinnett County schools claiming that she had been subjected to ongoing sexual harassment by a teacher. Her complaint was dismissed on the ground that damage remedy is not available under Title IX. In a unanimous decision, the Supreme Court disagreed. While Title IX does not specify damages as a remedy, Justice White said that it presumes "availability of all appropriate remedies unless Congress has expressly indicated otherwise." It had been urged by the Gwinnett County schools, supported by the Bush administration, that Title IX remedies be confined to back pay or injunctions directed at ending any violations. Such a limitation on remedies would have left Franklin "remediless," said White, in that she was no longer a student in the school system, and the teacher was no longer employed by the school system. The Court also noted that Congress had clearly indicated intent not to limit the remedies available under Title IX by subsequent adoption of language amending Title IX.

Gender: Sexual Harassment

Harris v. Forklift Systems, Inc., 510 U.S. __, 126 L. Ed. 2d 295, 114 S. Ct. 367 (1993)   Title VII of the Civil Rights Act of 1964 prohibits discrimination in the workplace on the basis of such factors as race and gender. The Supreme Court ruled in *Meritor Savings Bank v. Vinson*, 477 U.S. 57 (1986), that actions can be brought under Title VII where sexual harassment is sufficiently severe as to "alter the conditions of the victim's employment and create an abusive working environment." Teresa Harris filed a sexual harassment claim against her employer, but was unsuccessful in the lower courts because she had not demonstrated that she suffered psychological injury from the employer's conduct. The Court granted review in *Harris v. Forklift Systems, Inc.* to determine whether proof of psychological injury was the appropriate standard by which to qualify sexual harassment as actionable under Title VII. A unanimous Court reaffirmed the standard contained in *Meritor* that "takes a middle path between making actionable any conduct that is merely offensive and requiring the conduct to cause a tangible psychological injury." Justice O'Connor sought to clarify the *Meritor* standard. Conduct that is not pervasive enough to create an "objectively hostile or abusive work environment," an environment a "reasonable person would find hostile or abusive," is outside the reach of Title VII. Similarly, if the victim does not "subjectively perceive the environment to be abusive," there is no conduct which has actually altered the victim's working conditions and no Title VII violation. On the other hand, said O'Connor, Title VII "comes into play before the harassing conduct leads to a nervous breakdown." A abusive workplace environment, even one that does not "seriously affect employees' psychological well-being," can and often will "detract from employees' job performance, discourage employees from remaining on the job, or keep them from advancing in their careers." Even without regard to what O'Connor characterized as "tangible effects" of workplace discrimination, conduct which is so severe as to create an abusive workplace environment "offends Title VII's broad rule of workplace equality." The Court said the lower courts erred in Harris's case by "needlessly focus[ing] the factfinder's attention on concrete psychological harm," an element not required under Title VII. Certainly conduct that seriously affects an employee's psychological well-being violates Title VII, but the statute, said O'Connor, "is not limited to such conduct." As long as the workplace environment is reasonably perceived as hostile or abusive, there "is no need for it also to be psychologically injurious." O'Connor acknowledged that there is no "mathematically precise" test to apply to claims of sexual harassment. Determination of whether a workplace environment is hostile or abusive requires examination of "all the circumstances." Psychological harm, like any other relevant factor, may be taken into account, "but no single factor is required." Justice Scalia concurred, but expressed concern about the imprecision of the standard contained in O'Connor's opinion. As a practical matter, he suggested, the ruling "lets virtually any unguided juries decide whether sex-related conduct engaged in (or permitted by) an employer is egregious enough to warrant an award of damages." He favored an inquiry that would focus more attention on job performance, but agreed that Title VII cases should not be confined to that consideration. He joined the majority because he knew of "no alternative to the course the Court today has taken." *See also* CIVIL RIGHTS ACT OF 1964, p. 393; EQUAL PROTECTION CLAUSE, p. 313.

Significance   The problem of sexual harassment in the workplace has been highly visible recently. *Harris* set standards for bringing Title VII to bear on on such conduct. The Rehnquist Court looked at another harassment case during the 1994 Term. The question in *Landgraf v. USI Film Products* (128 L. Ed. 2d 229: 1994) was whether provisions of the Civil Rights Act of 1991 apply retroactively to cases already in progress prior to the effective date of the law. Under Title VII of the 1964 Civil Rights Act, victims of job discrimination were able to obtain job reinstatement and back pay, or an order prohibiting future discriminatory conduct. The 1991 act added trial by jury in employment discrimination cases, and it provided the opportunity to obtain compensatory and punitive damages. Barbara Landgraf brought a Title VII action claiming that she had been forced from her job because of unlawful sexual harassment. The trial court found that her employer had taken sufficient corrective action that Landgraf's resignation was unrelated to any unlawful harassment. The act became law while Landgraf's case was on appeal. The Court of Appeals for the Fifth Circuit rejected the contention that Landgraf was entitled to benefit from provisions of the new law. Over the lone dissent of Justice Blackmun, the Supreme Court agreed. Justice Stevens said the Court starts with a "presumption against statutory retroactivity." The presumption is "deeply rooted in our Jurisprudence, and embodies a legal doctrine centuries older than our Republic." There is, however, no conflict between the presumption and statutory language which "unambiguous[ly]" provides for retroactivity. The presumption will set aside only if there is "clear evidence" that Congress intended retroactive application. Absent such clear evidence, the Court has no legal basis except to apply statutory language prospectively. Requiring clear evidence of intent assures that Congress has "affirmatively considered the potential unfairness of retroactive application and determined that it is an acceptable price to pay for the countervailing benefits." No such clear evidence of congressional intent for retroactivity was found here. To the contrary, the relevant legislative history of the 1991 act "discloses some frankly partisan statements" about the effective date language and could not "plausibly be read as reflecting any general agreement." Further, the Court compared the language of the 1991 act with language from the civil rights bill which passed both Houses of Congress the preceding year. The 1990 bill explicitly called for application of many of its provisions to cases arising before its effective date. The bill was vetoed by President Bush, at least in part because of the "unfair retroactivity rules." Congress failed to override the veto. When the 1991 bill was introduced, it did not contain comparable retroactivity language. It is possible, suggested Stevens, that because Congress "was unable to resolve the retroactivity issue with the clarity of the 1990 legislation, Congress viewed the matter as an open issue to be resolved by the courts." The Court also rejected Landgraf's textual arguments. Given the "high stakes" of the retroactivity question, Stevens said, it would "be surprising for Congress to have chosen to resolve the question through negative inferences drawn from [the] two provisions [asserted by Landgraf] of quite limited effect." In dissent, Justice Blackmun indicated that provisions of the act ought to apply to cases pending when the law took effect even without specific legislative instruction to do so. At no time in the last generation "has an employer had a vested right to engage in or to permit sexual harassment; 'there is no such thing as a vested right to do wrong.'" In his view, the retroactivity presumption should not apply to remedial legislation that "does not proscribe any conduct that was previously legal."

Age

Massachusetts Board of Retirement v. Murgia, **427 U.S. 307, 49 L. Ed. 2d 520, 96 S. Ct. 2562 (1976)** Upheld a mandatory retirement age of fifty for uniformed police officers against Fourteenth Amendment challenge. *Murgia* illustrates the rationality test for invalidating classifications. In reviewing challenged classification schemes, the Supreme Court has used different evaluative criteria or standards, the least stringent of which is the rationality test. It would invalidate classifications only if they are arbitrary and have no demonstrable justification. The rationality test is typically used in reviewing age-based classifications. In *Murgia,* a provision of state law required that uniformed state police officers retire at age fifty. Key to the Court's holding in the case was the criteria used to assess the mandatory retirement policy. Murgia argued that the age classification was a "suspect class" and entitled to a "strict scrutiny" review, a more stringent review than that associated with the rationality test. The Court disagreed, holding that Murgia did not belong to a suspect class. His claim could be reviewed using the rationality test. In a 7–1 decision, Justice Stevens not participating, the Court upheld the mandatory retirement law and determined that the strict scrutiny approach should be used only when the classification impermissibly interferes with the exercise of a fundamental right or operates to the particular disadvantage of a suspect class. In the Court's view, the Massachusetts policy involved neither situation. It proceeded using the rational basis standard, a relatively relaxed criterion reflecting the Court's awareness that the drawing of lines creating distinctions is peculiarly and unavoidably a legislative task. The legislature's actions are presumed to be valid under this approach, and "perfection in making the necessary classification is neither possible nor necessary." In this instance, the legislature sought "to protect the public by assuring the physical preparedness of its uniformed police." Given the fact that physical ability generally declines with age, the Court found the mandatory retirement policy rationally related to the state's objective. It concluded by saying the choice of policy by Massachusetts may not be the best means, or a more just and humane system could not be devised, but under the rational basis test the enactment did not deny equal protection. Justice Marshall dissented from the use of the less demanding test because of its failure sufficiently to safeguard equal protection interests. He would have preferred a flexible standard that would have examined more carefully the means chosen by Massachusetts. To Justice Marshall, the means chosen "forced retirement of officers at age fifty and is therefore so overinclusive that it must fall." *See also* CLASSIFICATION, p. 394; EQUAL PROTECTION CLAUSE, p. 313; FOURTEENTH AMENDMENT, p. 412.

Significance   *Murgia* held that a mandatory retirement policy for uniformed police officers was rational. Soon after *Murgia,* the Court upheld a mandatory retirement policy for Foreign Service officers in *Vance v. Bradley* (440 U.S. 93: 1979). Again the Court found a retirement policy rationally related to the legislative goal of assuring the professional capacity of persons holding critical public service positions. In this case, Foreign Service officers have to undergo special rigors associated with overseas duty. Justice Marshall dissented and reiterated his call for a more demanding standard in reviewing such legislation. Not all age discrimination suits have been unsuccessful, however. In *Trans World Airlines, Inc. v. Thurston* (469 U.S. 111: 1985), the Court unanimously held that an airline's policy of not permitting the automatic transfer of age-disqualified captains to other positions with the company was a violation of the Age Discrimination in Employment Act of 1967 (ADEA), which prohibits employer discrimination against any employee or potential employee because of age. The *Thurston* decision was soon followed by several other important rulings on the same federal law. In *Western Air Lines, Inc. v. Criswell* (472 U.S. 400 1985), the Court unanimously held that an airline could not require mandatory retirement of flight engineers at age 60. Unlike the situation of pilots and copilots, where age was considered a bona fide occupational qualification, the Court felt that flight engineers could be individually assessed rather than subjected to blanket early retirement rules. In *Johnson v. Mayor & City Council of Baltimore* (472 U.S. 353: 1985), a unanimous Court also refused to permit a municipality to require mandatory retirement of firefighters at age 55. Key to this decision was the Court's rejection of Baltimore's contention that Congress had approved mandatory retirement when it retained such a policy for federal firefighters at the time it amended the statute in 1978. The Court held that retention of the provision was only for expediency and did not reflect a legislative judgment that youth was a bona fide qualification for the job. In *Equal Employment Opportunity Commission v. Wyoming* (460 U.S. 226: 1983), the Court ruled that state and local governments are not immune from provisions of the Age Discrimination in Employment Act. The Court made it clear, however, that the judgment did not compel a state to abandon policies that can demonstrate age as a bona fide occupational qualification. Central to the decisions in both *Murgia* and *Bradley* was the holding that compulsory retirement would better insure good job performance by limiting the age of employees. Both cases sought to maximize the physical capabilities of persons performing certain lay functions.

The Missouri Constitution establishes 70 as the mandatory retirement age for state judges. The Court upheld the mandatory retirement provision in *Gregory v. Ashcroft* (501 U.S. 452: 1991) against challenges brought by a number of state judges who were subject to the requirement. The judges asserted that the requirement violated both the ADEA and the Equal Protection Clause of the Fourteenth Amendment. The Court ruled on Tenth Amendment grounds that there was no ADEA violation. Justice O'Connor spoke for the majority and said the authority of the people of a state to set qualifications of government officials "lies at the heart of representative government." Making such a decision is one of the "most fundamental sort for a sovereign entity." Because congressional interference with Missouri's decision would "upset the usual constitutional balance of federal and state powers," courts must be certain that congressional intent to do so is "unmistakably clear." No such level of certainty existed here. The Court also rejected the Equal Protection Clause challenge. In order to overturn the mandatory requirement provision, it must be demonstrated that the classification is so unrelated to a legitimate objective as to be irrational. The Court said that it is quite rational that the people of a state could conclude that the risk of mental and/or physical deterioration at age 70 is sufficiently great, in the absence of effective alternatives, to warrant mandatory retirement. The Court saw the interest in maintaining a capable judiciary as not only legitimate, but "compelling."

Hazen Paper Co. v. Biggins (123 L. Ed. 2d 338: 1993) involved a different age-based problem—the termination of an employee prior to his vesting in a company's pension program. Thomas Biggins was fired by Hazen Paper after almost ten years' employment. He was 62 when terminated, and was just short of the time in service needed for his pension benefits to vest. A jury found a "willful" violation of the ADEA and awarded damages to Biggins. In affirming the lower court, the court of appeals concluded that the jury could reasonably have found that age was "inextricably intertwined" with Hazen Paper's decision to terminate Biggins. The Supreme Court considered two questions in reviewing this case. The first was whether interference with the vesting of pension benefits violates the ADEA. In a disparate treatment case such as this, said Justice O'Connor, liability "depends on whether the protected trait (under the ADEA, age) actually motivated the employer's decision." Regardless of the employer's decision-making process, a disparate treatment claim "cannot succeed unless the employee's protected trait actually played a role in that process and had a determinative influence on the outcome." When, however, an employer's decision is motivated by factors other than age, the "problem of inaccurate and stigmatizing stereotypes disappears." This is true "even if the motivating factor is correlated with age, as pension status typically is." The Court saw age and years of service as "analytically distinct"; an employer could "take account of one while ignoring the other." Thus, the Court concluded that it is "incorrect to say that a decision based on years of service is necessarily 'age-based.'" A decision to fire an older employee solely because of years of service would "not constitute discriminatory treatment on the basis of age," said O'Connor. A years-of-service decision to fire would not be the result of an "inaccurate and denigrating generalization about age, but would rather represent an accurate judgment about the employee—that he is close to vesting." Firing an employee in order to prevent his benefits from vesting may violate provisions of the Employment Retirement Income Security Act of 1974 (ERISA) but does not violate ADEA. ADEA requires employers to ignore the age of employees but "does not specify *further* characteristics that an employer must ignore." The Court concluded that it was necessary to remand the case to the court of appeals for reconsideration of whether the jury had sufficient basis for awarding damages under ADEA. The decision to remand gave rise to the second issue addressed in *Hazen Paper*, the meaning of a "willful" ADEA violation that is required to award damages. It would be a "wholly circular and self-defeating interpretation of the ADEA to hold that, in cases where an employer more likely knows its conduct to be illegal, knowledge alone does not suffice for liquidated damages." The Court went on to reaffirm that the definition of "willful" established in *Thurston* applies to all ADEA disparate treatment cases— "that the employer either knew or showed reckless disregard for the matter of whether its conduct was prohibited by statute."

Voting Rights

South Carolina v. Katzenbach, **383 U.S. 301, 15 L. Ed. 2d 769, 86 S. Ct. 803 (1966)** Upheld the Voting Rights Act of 1965. *South Carolina v. Katzenbach* explored how the Fifteenth Amendment protects the right to vote and provides Congress with authority to enact appropriate legislation to further that objective. The Voting Rights Act of 1965 abolished devices such as the literacy test and accumulated poll taxes, by which citizens had been disqualified from voting. The act also provided for extensive federal supervision of elections and required that any new conditions of voter eligibility be reviewed by the Attorney General before implementation. Provisions of the act were triggered if less than 50 percent of citizens of voting age were registered to vote or where fewer than 50 percent of the voting age population had participated in the 1964 presidential election. Chief Justice Warren wrote the opinion of the Court. He noted that the purpose of the act was "to banish the blight of racial discrimination in voting, which has infected the electoral process in parts of our country for nearly a century." The Court accorded great deference to an act dedicated to such a purpose even if Congress had exercised power in an inventive manner. Referring to the stringent remedies and their implementation without prior adjudication, the Court said that litigation was inadequate when discrimination was widespread and persistent. Following nearly a hundred years of systematic resistance to the Fifteenth Amendment, Congress might well decide to shift the advantage of time and inertia from the perpetrators of the evil to its victims. The targeted nature of the act's coverage was a reasonable legislative option. Congress determined that voting discrimination "presently occurs in certain sections of the country. In acceptable legislative fashion, Congress chose to limit its attention to the geographic areas where immediate action seemed necessary." In sum, the Court viewed the act as an array of potent weapons marshalled to combat the evil of voting discrimination. They were weapons that constitute, "a valid means for carrying out the commands of the Fifteenth Amendment." *See also BAKER v. CARR* (369 U.S. 186: 1962), p. 343; FIFTEENTH AMENDMENT, p. 412; *SHAW v. RENO* (125 L. Ed 2. 511: 1993), Supplement 3.

Significance   In upholding the Voting Rights Act of 1965 in *South Carolina v. Katzenbach,* the Court targeted voting practices involving non–English-speaking voters for the first time. The act had provisions intended for the large Spanish-speaking Puerto Rican population in New York. They were upheld on equal protection grounds in *Katzenbach v. Morgan* (384 U.S. 641: 1966). The act had a five-year limitation but was extended in 1970, 1975, and 1982. The 1970 extension banned the use of literacy tests. The same extension also set the minimum voting age at 18 throughout the country. The Court held in *Oregon v. Mitchell* (400 U.S. 112: 1970), however, that Congress could only establish age qualifications for federal elections. States retained control over state and local elections. Ratification of the Twenty-Sixth Amendment in 1971 superseded the Court's decision in *Oregon v. Mitchell.* Primary elections also have attained constitutional status. After several decisions to the contrary, the Court held in *United States v. Classic* (313 U.S. 299: 1941), that the federal government could regulate primaries because of their integral role in the overall election process. In *Smith v. Allwright* (321 U.S. 649: 1944), the Court found that political parties conducting racially exclusive primaries were acting as an agent of the state and thus were in violation of the Fifteenth Amendment. The Court also outlawed the poll tax for state elections in *Harper v. Virginia State Board of Elections* (383 U.S. 663: 1966), holding that such a tax discriminated in an invidious fashion.

Two issues stemming from provisions of the Voting Rights Act were before the Court in the 1990–1991 Term. As amended in 1982, Section 2 of the Voting Rights Act prohibits practices and procedures that result in "denial or abridgement," on the basis of race, of the right to vote. The question in *Chisom v. Roemer* (501 U.S. 380: 1991) was whether the "results test" contained in the 1982 amendment protects the right to vote in state judicial elections. In a 6–3 decision, the Court ruled that judicial elections are covered by the act as amended. Prior to 1982, Section 2 was not violated absent a showing of discriminatory intent. The 1982 amendment substituted the results standard. Congress established that a violation occurs if portions of the electorate have less opportunity than others to "participate in the political process and to elect representatives of their choice." The question in *Chisom* rested on whether judges are "representatives." The Court concluded they are. Justice Stevens noted that the Voting Rights Act had been enacted for the "broad remedial purpose" of eliminating racial discrimination in voting. Accordingly, the act should be interpreted in a manner that provides the "broadest possible scope in combatting racial discrimination." When each of several judges of a court must live in separate districts and be elected by the voters of those districts, it "seems both reasonable and realistic to characterize the winners as representatives of that district." Justice Scalia issued a dissent that was joined by Chief Justice Rehnquist and Justice Kennedy. They were critical of the Court's refusal to distinguish judges from other elective officers for purposes of the act.

Section 5 of the Voting Rights Act requires "preclearance" by the federal government when a state covered by the act attempts to change any "practice or procedure with respect to voting." The issue before the Court in *Presley v. Etowah County Commission* (502 U.S. 491: 1992), and in a companion case *Mack v. Russell County Commission,* was whether a shifting of authority away from an elected official to another body was subject to the preclearance requirement. Prior to 1986, members of the Etowah and Russell County Commissions had been elected at-large but required to live in different districts. Each commissioner individually controlled all county bridge and road maintenance expenditures within his or her district. In the early 1980s, the at-large election process was found to impermissibly dilute minority electoral influence, and the counties were ordered to move to a single-member district system. The election conducted in 1986 brought about the election of one black commissioner in Etowah County and two in Russell County. During the same period, both counties transferred control over bridge and road funds from individual commissioners to the county commissions as a whole. This meant that funds over which individual commissioners previously had full control were now pooled into a single county-wide fund with expenditures governed by majority vote. This reassignment of function was made without Justice Department approval. In a 6–3 decision, the Supreme Court ruled that the reorganization of the county commissions was not covered by Section 5 of the Voting Rights Act, and thus did not require federal preclearance. Justice Kennedy noted that the Court had given Section 5 "broad construction" in previous cases. Those prior decisions, however, had recognized for Section 5 purposes only those changes that have a "direct relation to voting and the election process." While the restructuring of commissioners' authority had the "effect of altering" county commission practices, the change had "no connection to voting procedures" or the "substance of voting power." Rather, the change "concerns the internal operations of an elected body." Application of Section 5 to such situations, said Kennedy, "would work an unconstrained expansion of its coverage." Because virtually any governmental decision "implicates voting," Kennedy expressed concern that no workable standard could be found to define the reach of Section 5 if extended beyond voting itself. Justice Stevens, joined by Blackmun and White, dissented. They felt that the reallocation of authority under the circumstances present in these cases had the "same potential for discrimination" as changes from district to at-large voting or the gerrymandering of district boundaries. In their view, the decision left states free to "evade" the requirements of Section 5, and to "undermine" the objectives of the act "simply by transferring the authority of an elected official, who happens to be black, to another official or group controlled by the majority."

Reapportionment and Race

Mobile v. Bolden, 446 U.S. 55, 64 L. Ed. 2d 47, 100 S. Ct. 1490 (1980)
Upheld a municipal at-large election process against claims that such a system diluted minority group voting influence. *Mobile v. Bolden* considered whether malapportionment of legislative districts violated the Equal Protection Clause of the Fourteenth Amendment because it debased the value of an individual's vote. A federal district court found a constitutional violation in the election process in Mobile, Alabama, and ordered that a single-member district structure replace the current at-large system. The Supreme Court found the at-large plan to be constitutionally adequate and reversed the district court in a 6–3 decision. Critics of the at-large or multimember district approach argue that some elements of the electorate are unrepresented. The Court noted that criticism of the at-large election is rooted in its winner-take-all aspect and its tendency to submerge minorities. The specific question posed in *Bolden* was whether the at-large scheme had been established for the purpose of reducing the impact of black voters. No finding was made by the trial court that black voters had been deprived of the privilege of voting or hampered in the registration process. The Court had previously found in such cases as *White v. Regester* (412 U.S. 755: 1973), that the multimember election system was not unconstitutional per se. Constitutional violations occur in apportionment systems only "if their purpose were invidiously to minimize

or cancel out the voting potential of racial or ethnic minorities." To demonstrate such a violation, a plaintiff must prove that the disputed plan was conceived or operated as a purposeful device to further racial discrimination. A showing that a particular group has not elected representatives in proportion to its members is not sufficient. The Court said that while black candidates in Mobile have been defeated, that fact alone does not work a constitutional deprivation. The Court also rejected the relevance of discrimination by the city in the context of municipal employment and the dispensing of public services. Evidence of possible discrimination by city officials in other contexts is "tenuous and circumstantial evidence of the constitutional invalidity of the electoral system under which they attained their offices." The Burger Court concluded that past cases show "the Court has sternly set its face against the claim, however phrased, that the Constitution somehow guarantees proportional representation." Justices Brennan, Marshall, and White dissented. They argued that a sufficient discriminatory impact had been shown. Justice Marshall said the Court's decision meant that "in the absence of proof of discrimination by the State, the right to vote provides the politically powerless with nothing more than the right to cast meaningless ballots." *See also* APPORTIONMENT, p. 384; *REYNOLDS v. SIMS* (377 U.S. 533: 1964), p. 344; *SHAW v. RENO* (125 L. Ed. 2d 511: 1993), Supplement 3; *SOUTH CAROLINA v. KATZENBACH* (383 U.S. 301: 1966), p. 348.

Significance   *Mobile v. Bolden* held that discriminatory intent must be demonstrated before an electoral system can be found constitutionally defective. But what if the intent is benevolent? What if an apportionment plan is designed to make more likely the electoral success of minorities? The Court upheld such a plan in *United Jewish Organizations of Williamsburgh, Inc. v. Carey* (430 U.S. 144: 1977) where district lines in New York were redrawn to enhance the possibility of electing racial minorities to the state legislature. The plan split a group of Hasidic Jews, formerly concentrated in a single state Assembly and Senate district, into two districts. Suit was brought claiming voter reassignment had been based on race. The Court upheld the redistricting plan, finding that other voters in the county involved were not denied an opportunity to participate in the political process. The Court also held that considerations of race could be made in an attempt to comply with provisions of the Voting Rights Act of 1965, as in *South Carolina v. Katzenbach* (383 U.S. 301: 1966). As long as reasonable considerations of race were directed toward the achievement of racial equality, they were permissible. Plans which actually disenfranchise are clearly unconstitutional, however. In *Gomillion v. Lightfoot* (364 U.S. 339: 1960), the Court held that a plan which restructured the boundaries of a city so that most black residents were placed outside the city limits was in violation of both the Fourteenth and Fifteenth Amendments. The Voting Rights Act of 1965 also requires that any change in voting procedures or conditions which impact on voting practices are subject to preclearance by the Attorney General of the United States. The full impact of this requirement was seen in *City of Pleasant Grove v. United States* (479 U.S. 462: 1987). Pleasant Grove, a nearly all-white city in Alabama, was denied preclearance to annex a then uninhabited area on the ground that it had refused to annex adjacent black neighborhoods despite petitions by the neighborhood residents. The Supreme Court said an annexation is subject to preclearance under the law. Even the annexation of vacant land on which residential development is anticipated must be precleared. In the Court's view, to allow a state to circumvent the preclearance requirement when annexing vacant land intended for white development would disserve congressional intent to reach the subtle as well as the obvious official actions which have the effect of denying voter groups based on race. Pleasant Grove argued that there were no black voters in the city at the time the annexation decision was made, so the proposals did not deny or reduce existing black voter representation. The Court rejected this contention, saying it was based on an incorrect assumption that relevant provisions of the act can only relate to present circumstances. Its provisions look not only at present effects, but at future effects as well. Annexation cannot be used as a means of preventing integration. An obvious means of thwarting integration is to provide for the growth of a monolithic white voting block, thereby effectively diluting the black vote in advance. This is just as impermissible an objective as the dilution of present black voting strength.

A provision of the Missouri Constitution authorized creation of a board empowered to reorganize city and county governments in St. Louis. The constitutional provision limited membership on the board to "freeholders," owners of real estate. The restriction was challenged as a violation of equal protection. A unanimous U.S. Supreme Court held in *Quinn v. Millsap* (491 U.S. 95: 1989) that the board of freeholders was not exempt from the reach of the Equal Protection Clause. The Clause "protects the right to be considered for public service without the burden of individually discriminatory disqualifications." Membership on the board of freeholders was viewed as a form of public service even though the board did not enact laws directly. The Court then considered whether the land ownership requirement could withstand Equal Protection scrutiny, and ruled the requirement was a form of invidious discrimination even using the least demanding rational basis test.

Following the 1990 Census, the Court reviewed two cases raising questions about the scope of federal judicial power in responding to redistricting challenges. In *Voinovich v. Quilter* (122 L. Ed. 2d 500: 1993), a federal district court had ordered the revision of an Ohio plan that created several minority-dominated state legislative districts. The plan had been challenged under Section 2 of the Voting Rights Act on the ground that it "packed" minority voters in a minimum number of districts. Unlike typical voting power dilution challenges, where fragmentation of a minority group occurs, this case claimed dilution of voting strength by concentration of minority voters within districts. The Supreme Court unanimously reversed the judgment of the federal district court on two grounds. First, Section 2 targets exclusively the "consequences of apportionment." As a result, a federal court must first determine what the consequences of a plan would be before ruling on the validity of the plan itself. The district court had erred in not doing so in this case. Second, the Supreme Court held that the district court had erred in requiring state authorities to carry the burden of proof in support of the reapportionment plan. Furthermore, the Supreme Court ruled that states may create majority-minority districts even in the absence of the need to remedy a violation of federal law. As a result, federal courts cannot intervene in state apportionment unless a federal violation exists because "it is the domain of the States, and not the federal courts, to conduct apportionment in the first place."

Growe v. Emison (122 L. Ed. 2d 388: 1993) presented two different issues: whether the U.S. district court had intervened before the state had sufficient opportunity to redistrict itself, and whether the district court had exceeded its authority to remedy vote-dilution claims brought under Section 2 of the Voting Rights Act of 1965. In this case, the lower federal court enjoined a proceeding in a state court following an unsuccessful resolution of the matter by the state legislature. A unanimous Supreme Court reversed. Justice Scalia said that principles of federalism and comity require federal judges to defer consideration in redistricting disputes where state legislatures or state courts have begun to "address that highly political task [themselves]." In the absence of evidence that either state branch will fail to discharge its redistricting responsibilities in a timely manner, federal courts "must neither affirmatively obstruct state reapportionment nor permit federal litigation to be used to impede it." Here, the federal court erred in deferring only to the state legislature and not the state courts. Scalia pointed out that either the state legislature *or* the state courts are preferred over federal courts as "agents of apportionment." The federal court's intervention was not a "last-minute...rescue," but rather a "race to beat...[state authorities] to the finish line." In responding to the Voting Rights Act claim, the district court had created a "super majority-minority" state senate district by linking several "separately identifiable minority groups." The Supreme Court reversed, finding that the preconditions for such intervention, as established in *Thornburg v. Gingles*

(478 U.S. 30: 1986), were "unattainable." In particular, Scalia pointed to the failure of the district court to demonstrate sufficient political cohesiveness or a bloc voting history among the "distinct language and ethnic minority groups" combined under the order.

Racial Gerrymandering

Shaw v. Reno, **509 U.S. __, 125 L. Ed. 2d 511, 113 S. Ct. 2816 (1993)**
Congressional districts were reapportioned following the 1990 Census. The process resulted in a gain of one congressional seat for North Carolina in the U.S. House of Representatives. The North Carolina General Assembly fashioned a plan establishing twelve congressional districts. The plan contained one majority-black district. The plan was submitted to the Justice Department for preclearance as required under Section 5 of the Voting Rights Act. A Section 5 objection was made by the Justice Department on the grounds that, despite including one majority-black district, the plan still underrepresented minority voting strength in the state. In response to the objection, the General Assembly revised the plan by adding a second majority-black district. The first majority-black district (CD #1) is a "somewhat hook-shaped" district centered in northeast North Carolina. The district moves southward until it "tapers to a narrow band; then with finger-like extensions," it reaches into the southernmost part of the state near the South Carolina border. The second district (CD #12) is "even more unusually shaped." This district is approximately 160 miles long, and for much of its length "no wider than the I-85 corridor." The district "winds in snake-like fashion through tobacco country, financial centers, and manufacturing areas until it gobbles in enough enclaves of black neighborhoods...." The Justice Department approved the revised plan containing these two majority-black districts. A black member of Congress was elected in each of these districts in November 1992. A challenge to the revised plan was brought by the North Carolina Republican Party and several white voters residing in the state. They claimed the plan was based on unconstitutional political gerrymandering. The political gerrymander claim was dismissed, but a second claim was heard by a three-judge district court on the grounds that North Carolina had created an unlawful racial gerrymander. The district court rejected the challengers' contention that race-conscious redistricting "to benefit minority voters is per se unconstitutional." In addition, the district court upheld the North Carolina plan containing the two majority-black districts. Direct appeal was taken to the Supreme Court which reversed in a 5–4 decision in the case of *Shaw v. Reno* (125 L. Ed. 2d 511: 1993). It was the Court's conclusion that the challengers' claim was one for which

Equal Protection Clause relief could be granted. The case was remanded to allow the white voters an opportunity to demonstrate that the districting plan was an unconstitutional racial gerrymander. Justice O'Connor said it is "unsettling how closely the North Carolina plan resembles the most egregious racial gerrymanders of the past." The challengers did not claim dilution of white voting strength. Rather, their claim focused the constitutional right to "participate in a 'color-blind' electoral process." Their objection to the redistricting plan is that it is so "extremely irregular on its face" that it can be viewed "only as an effort to segregate the races for purposes of voting, without regard for traditional districting principles and without sufficiently compelling justification." In the Court's view, the Equal Protection Clause could provide relief in such a situation. O'Connor referred to such traditional principles as compactness, contiguity, and political subdivision boundaries as "objective factors" that might provide the basis for setting aside claims of racial gerrymandering. Apportionment is an area where, said O'Connor, "appearances do matter." A reapportionment plan that includes in a district individuals of one race, but who are otherwise "widely separated by geographical and political boundaries, and who may have little in common with one another but the color of their skin, bears an uncomfortable resemblance to political apartheid." Racial classifications of "any sort pose the risk of lasting harm to our society." Such classifications reinforce the belief that individuals should be judged on the basis of race. Racial classifications with respect to voting "carry particular dangers." Racial gerrymandering, even for remedial purposes, she concluded, "may balkanize us into competing racial factions; it threatens to carry us further from the goal of a political system in which race no longer matters...."

Justices White, Blackmun, Stevens, and Souter dissented. Souter said the decision recognizes a new cause of action under which a redistricting plan with a configuration "so bizarre" that it cannot be viewed as anything but an attempt to place voters into districts on the basis of race requires strict judicial scrutiny. Such an approach departs from prior decisions, and Souter felt there was no justification for the departure. Justice White observed that members of the white majority can "not plausibly argue that their influence over the political process has been unfairly canceled or that such had been the State's intent." Similarly, it was Blackmun's view that no Equal Protection Clause violation exists unless the redistricting plan has the effect of unduly minimizing a particular group's voting strength. He found it "particularly ironic" that the Court chose a case to recognize an "analytically distinct" constitutional claim was a challenge by white voters to a plan under which North Carolina "has sent black representatives to Congress for the first time since Reconstruction." Justice Stevens discounted the "bizarre" shape of the district saying that there is "no independent constitutional requirement of compactness or contiguity." He also saw drawing districts for the purpose of facilitating election of a second black member of Congress as justifiable. The difference between constitutional and unconstitutional gerrymanders has nothing to do with whether they are based on assumptions about the groups they affect, but whether their purpose is to "enhance the power of the group in control of the districting process at the expense of any minority group, and thereby to strengthen the unequal distribution of electoral power." *See also* APPORTIONMENT, p. 384; *SOUTH CAROLINA v. KATZENBACH* (383 U.S. 301: 1966), p. 348.

Significance   Section 2 of the Voting Rights Act essentially prohibits use of a qualification to vote or a "standard, practice, or procedure" that abridges the right to vote on the basis of race or membership in a language minority. Dilution of minority voting strength violates Section 2. The test for determining whether minority voting strength is illegally diluted was set forth by the Court in *Thornburg v. Gingles* (478 U.S. 30: 1986). Section 2 is violated if a minority group can demonstrate that its voters are "sufficiently numerous and compact" that they would constitute a majority in a district of a multi-member body. There are two other *Gingles* preconditions: that whites vote as a bloc in a "manner sufficient to defeat the black preferred candidate," and that blacks are "politically cohesive."

The case of *Holder v. Hall* (129 L. Ed. 2d 687: 1994) considered whether the *Gingles* criteria apply to single official electoral situations. Bleckley County, Georgia operates with a single commissioner form of county government: a single commissioner possesses all legislative and executive authority. In 1985, the state legislature authorized the county to move to a five-member commission, but the proposal was defeated in a referendum. Black voters filed an action claiming that the sole-commissioner system was maintained to limit the political influence of the minority population—77 percent of the county's population was white. A federal district court found no violation, but the Court of Appeals for the Eleventh Circuit reversed, and ordered the district court to reconsider ordering a five-member commission with one district created to facilitate the election of a minority commissioner. In a 5–4 decision, the Supreme Court reversed. The Court held that the size of a governing body is not subject to a vote dilution challenge under Section 2 of the Voting Rights Act. Before a court can find a Section 2 violation, it must determine whether the *Gingles* preconditions, supported by a totality of other circumstances, are met. Beyond that, a court must find a "reasonable alternative practice as a benchmark against which to measure the existing voting practice." There is no "objective and workable standard," said Justice Kennedy, "in cases where the challenge is brought to the size of a governing authority;

there is no reason why one size should be selected over another." In this case, the challengers to the single-commissioner structure offered no convincing reasons why the benchmark should be a five member commission. Justices Thomas and Scalia also voted to overturn the lower court. Their reasoning, expressed in Justice Thomas' concurring opinion of almost 60 pages in length, differed substantially from that of Justice Kennedy. They felt that the size of a governing body was not a "standard, practice, or procedure" within the meaning of Section 2. That section of the Voting Rights Act covers only those practices that affect ballot access by minority voters; districting systems and election processes that affect the "weight" given a vote are "simply beyond the purview of the act." They urged that *Thornburg v. Gingles* be overruled because it interprets Section 2 as reaching vote dilution. By allowing consideration of dilutive electoral practices, federal courts have become "immersed" in a "hopeless project of weighing questions of political theory." Worse than that, Thomas continued, the Court has devised remedial mechanisms that "[encourage] federal courts to segregate voters into racially designated districts to ensure minority electoral success." In doing so, the Court has "collaborated on what may be called the racial 'balkanization' of the Nation." Thomas said he no longer joined a reading of the Voting Rights Act that has produced "such a disastrous misadventure in judicial policymaking." Justices Blackmun, Stevens, Souter, and Ginsburg strongly dissented. They concluded that the sole-commissioner system had the effect of diluting minority voting strength. It was their view that the Voting Rights Act had to be interpreted to effectively confront "subtler, more complex means of infringing minority voting strength."

The Rehnquist Court reviewed a second case, involving the redistricting of the Florida legislature. A group of Hispanic voters including Miguel DeGrandy filed a complaint in federal court in 1992 against various Florida officials, claiming that the Florida House of Representatives and Senate districts were discriminatorily apportioned. The complaint specifically alleged that the districts failed to properly reflect changes in the population during the ten years since the most recent redistricting. A special redistricting session of the legislature was called and a joint resolution redistricting both the House and Senate was adopted and subsequently approved by the Florida Supreme Court. The plaintiffs then amended their original complaint, claiming Voting Rights Act violations. These claims were consolidated with those made by African American voters and the United States. A three-judge district court ruled that both the House and Senate plans diluted Hispanic votes. The court then ordered the number of Hispanic majority districts be raised to 11 (from 9) of the 20 Dade County districts. The court also concluded that the Senate districting diluted both Hispanic and African American votes.

(Subsequent hearings on possible district changes led the court to decide that the original plan was fairest to all ethnic communities after all). The U.S. Supreme Court unanimously overturned the district court's order modifying the state plan for the House of Representatives in *Johnson v. DeGrandy* (129 L. Ed. 2d 775: 1994). Justice Souter delivered the opinion of the Court. Unlike the district court, the Supreme Court found no Section 2 violation. Despite some evidence of ongoing discrimination and racial bloc voting, Hispanic voters "form effective voting majorities" in a number of Florida House districts "roughly proportional to their respective shares in the voting-age population." While proportionality is not wholly dispositive, it is relevant to the totality of circumstances analysis in determining whether minority voters have less opportunity to elect representatives of their choice. Meeting the *Gingles* preconditions, in itself, is not "necessarily sufficient." A court must assess the probative significance of the *Gingles* factors after considering all circumstances arguably related to the question of political opportunity. The trial court in this case "misjudged" the relative importance of the *Gingles* factors and historical discrimination by equating dilution with failure to maximize the number of majority-minority districts. A finding of vote dilution "cannot be inferred from the mere failure to guarantee minority voters maximum political influence."

RIGHT TO PRIVACY
Abortion Regulations

Webster v. Reproductive Health Services, **492 U.S. 490, 106 L. Ed. 2d 410, 109 S. Ct. 3040 (1989)** *Webster* provided the Court with an opportunity to fully reconsider and possibly overrule the controversial ruling of *Roe v. Wade* (410 U.S. 113: 1973). The Court rendered a decision in *Webster* which substantially modified *Roe,* but did not explicitly overrule it. The origin of the case was a Missouri statute enacted in 1986. Several components of the statute were challenged in federal court by a number of doctors and nurses and two nonprofit medical corporations, one of which was Reproductive Health Services (RHS). The challenged provisions included: (1) a preamble that states that life begins at conception, and that the "unborn" have life interests requiring protection, (2) a requirement that before an abortion can be performed on any woman a physician has "reason to believe" is 20 or more weeks pregnant, the physician must determine whether the fetus is "viable" by performing specified medical examinations and tests, (3) an informed-consent requirement which included information on abortion alternatives, and (4) prohibitions on use of public funds, public facilities, or public employees in "performing or assisting" an abortion. This restriction included public employees counseling pregnant women to have nontherapeutic abortions. A U.S. district court upheld only the viability testing, but in doing so eliminated many of the viability tests specified in the law. Missouri, through its attorney general William Webster, challenged each element of the district court decision except for that portion which struck down the informed-consent requirement. The Court of Appeals for the Eighth Circuit affirmed the district court relying on *Roe v. Wade.* In a fragmented 5–4 decision, the Supreme Court allowed the restrictions, but did not explicitly reverse *Roe.* The opinion of the Court was delivered by Chief Justice Rehnquist. The Court did not rule on the preamble. The preamble was seen as an "abstract proposition" rather than an operating regulation. Since the preamble did not restrict the activities of RHS in "some concrete way," the Court concluded RHS had no standing to challenge the preamble language. This ruling was a rejection of Reproductive Health Services' argument that the preamble was an "operative part" of the statute intended to "guide the interpretation of other provisions of the Act." Rehnquist then turned to the ban on the use of public funds, facilities, and employees. The court of appeals had seen this regulation as possibly preventing a woman's doctor from performing an abortion if the doctor did not have privileges in another hospital. Increased costs and possible delay also were attributed to the regulation. The Supreme Court disagreed, using much of the same analysis as can be found in the Medicaid cases such as *Maher v. Roe* (432 U.S. 464: 1977) and *Harris v. McRae* (448 U.S. 297: 1980). As with those cases, the Court recognized the state's decision to "encourage childbirth over abortion," and that policy preference "places no governmental obstacle in the path of a woman who chooses to terminate her pregnancy." Missouri's refusal to allow public employees to perform abortions or to allow abortions to be performed in public facilities leaves a pregnant woman "with the same choices as if the State had chosen not to operate any public hospitals at all." Having already ruled that state refusal to fund abortions (in *Maher* and *Harris*) does not violate *Roe v. Wade,* it "strains logic to reach a contrary result for the use of public facilities and employees." Rehnquist then turned to the most critical aspect of the decision, the viability-testing requirements.

Rehnquist said the statute required physicians to perform "only those tests that are useful to making subsidiary findings as to viability." Key, however, was the presumption of viability at twenty weeks which must be directly rebutted by viability test results before an abortion can be performed. The *Roe v. Wade* decision is based on a concept of trimesters. Under *Roe,* the interests of the fetus are not recognized until the final trimester which occurs about 24 weeks into the pregnancy. Specification in the Missouri law of methods for determining viability "does superimpose state regulation on the medical determination of viability." This section was struck down by the court of appeals on this basis. The Supreme Court was less convinced that the law was flawed, however. Rather, the problem, said Rehnquist, was the "rigid trimester analysis of the course of a pregnancy enunciated in *Roe.*" The "rigid *Roe* framework is hardly consistent with the notion of a Constitution cast in general terms." The Court simply should not function as the "country's *ex officio* medical board with powers to approve or disapprove medical and operative practices and standards...." Thus, the "web of legal rules" developed through application of *Roe* could be loosened. More important, the Court did not see "why the State's interest in protecting potential human life should come into existence only at the point of viability," and that there should be a "rigid line allowing state regulation after viability but prohibiting it before viability." The Court acknowledged that the tests "increase the expense of abortion and regulate the discretion of the physician in determining viability of the fetus." Nonetheless, the Court was "satisfied" that the requirement "permissibly furthers the State's interest in protecting potential human life" and is constitutional. Justice O'Connor agreed that the viability testing requirement was constitutional, but came to that conclusion because she did not see the requirement as incompatible with *Roe v. Wade.* Justice Scalia was also among the majority, but said, in his concurring opinion, that *Roe* had been effectively overruled. Indeed, he was critical of Rehnquist for not acknowledging that result. By hanging on to *Roe,* Scalia said the Court "needlessly" prolonged its "self-awarded sovereignty over a field where it has little proper business" since responses to most of the critical questions are "political and not juridical."

Justices Blackmun, Brennan, Marshall, and Stevens dissented. Blackmun, the author of the *Roe v. Wade* opinion, was most outspoken in criticizing the decision. He spoke of the "feigned restraint" of the plurality opinion claim that it "leaves *Roe* undisturbed." "But this disclaimer is totally meaningless." The plurality opinion, he contended, is "filled with winks, nods, and knowing glances to those who would do away with *Roe* explicitly." Blackmun was very troubled by the viability testing and what it meant to the *Roe* trimester framework. He was even more troubled by Rehnquist's decision to uphold viability testing, because it "permissibly furthers the State's interest in protecting potential human life." The "newly minted" standard is "circular and totally meaningless." Whether a challenged regulation "permissibly furthers" a legitimate interest is the "question that courts must answer" in abortion cases, not the "standard for courts to apply." The standard has "no independent meaning," and consists of "nothing other than what a majority of this Court may believe at any given moment in any given case." *See also* RIGHT OF PRIVACY, p. 316; *ROE v. WADE* (410 U.S. 113: 1973), p. 379.

Significance   *Webster* signaled state legislatures that the Court would be receptive to additional restrictions on abortion. Two additional abortion regulation cases were decided during the 1989–1990 Term. *Hodgson v. Minnesota* (497 U.S. 417: 1990) and *Ohio v. Akron Center for Reproductive Services* (497 U.S. 502: 1990) examined parental notification statutes from Minnesota and Ohio. The Minnesota statute had two key parts. First, the state required notification of both biological parents when a minor daughter sought an abortion. In a 5–4 decision, the Court struck down this requirement. The statute contained contingency language that if a court enjoined enforcement of the notification requirement, the statute would be amended automatically to provide a judicial bypass as an alternative to parental notification. This alternative allowed a minor to petition a court for permission to obtain an abortion without notifying her parents. The Court upheld this alternative, again by a 5–4 vote, with Justice O'Connor providing the decisive vote in both instances. She joined Justices Marshall, Brennan, Blackmun, and Stevens in striking down the statute without judicial bypass. She was joined by Chief Justice Rehnquist and Justices Kennedy, White, and Scalia in upholding the alternative. The Ohio statute required notification of only one parent. It also contained judicial bypass language, but the Court upheld the one-parent notice requirement on its own by a 6–3 vote—Justice Stevens joining the five justices who had upheld the Minnesota alternative. The defect with the Minnesota statute absent the judicial bypass arose from the fact that only about half of Minnesota's minors resided with both biological parents. Justice Stevens spoke of the "particularly harmful effects" of the two-parent notification requirement on "both the minor and custodial parent when parents were divorced or separated." In addition, the Court concluded the requirement "does not reasonably further any legitimate state interest." The principal justification for notification is that it "supports the authority of a parent who is presumed to act in the minor's best interest and thereby assures that the minor's decision to terminate her pregnancy is knowing, intelligent, and deliberate." To the extent "such an interest is legitimate," it could be "fully served" by the notification of one parent who can then seek counsel from the other parent or anyone else. The state has no legitimate interest in questioning the one parent's judgment on whether to seek wider counsel. The Court concluded that the two-parent requirement actually "disserves" any state interest in protecting a minor in "dysfunctional families." Two-parent notice in such situations is "positively harmful to the minor and her family." As in cases involving judicial hearings as an alternative to securing parental consent for an abortion, the Court found the bypass alternative constitutionally sufficient for notification as well. The judicial bypass feature allows a minor to demonstrate she is fully capable of making the abortion decision. The Court decided the Ohio case without actually ruling on whether the judicial bypass provision is necessary in the one-parent notice situation. Rather, it upheld the one-parent notification requirement as a "rational way" for a state to assist a pregnant minor who is considering abortion. "It would deny all dignity to the family," said Justice Kennedy, "to say that the State cannot take this reasonable step...to ensure that, in most cases, a young woman will receive guidance and understanding from a parent."

Several provisions of the Pennsylvania Abortion Control Act were before the Court in *Planned Parenthood of Southeastern Pennsylvania v. Casey* (120 L. Ed. 2d 674: 1992). The act required that a woman seeking an abortion must give "informed consent." To that end, the woman must be provided with certain information at least 24 hours before an abortion. A minor must obtain the informed consent of one of her parents. As in parental consent requirements upheld by the Court in previous cases, judicial bypass was allowed if the minor did not wish to seek or could not secure parental consent. Further, the act required a married woman to inform her husband of the intended abortion. Finally, the act established certain reporting requirements for facilities that perform abortions. As with several other cases in recent years, most notably *Webster,* this case provided the Court with an opportunity to reconsider the basic question of whether an abortion is constitutionally protected—whether to overturn the ruling of *Roe v. Wade.* A coalition of five justices—Blackmun, Stevens, O'Connor, Kennedy, and Souter—said "the essential holding of *Roe v. Wade* should be retained and once again reaffirmed." These same five justices struck down the portion of the act requiring notification of the husband. Over the dissents of Blackmun and Stevens, the other seven justices upheld the remaining four restrictions contained in the Pennsylvania law. Justices O'Connor, Kennedy, and Souter issued a decisive joint opinion. They identified three underlying principles from *Roe v. Wade* that must be retained. First, women have a right to an abortion at any time before fetal viability and must be free to obtain it "without undue interference from the States." Prior to viability, they said, a state's interests are not strong enough to support either a prohibition on abortion or to impose any "substantial obstacle to the woman's effective right to elect an abortion." Second, they confirmed a state's power to regulate abortions after fetal viability as long as the regulation "contains exceptions for pregnancies which endanger a woman's life or health." Third, a state has a legitimate interest in protecting a woman's health and the "life of the fetus that may become a child" from the "outset" of the pregnancy. These principles, they concluded, "do not contradict one another; and we adhere to each." They referred to abortion as a "unique act," and although it is conduct, a state is not entitled to "proscribe it in all instances." This is because the liberty of a woman "is at stake in a sense unique to the human condition and so unique to the law." The right is qualified, however. Women must be able to "make the ultimate decision," although the right to an abortion does not permit her to be "insulated from all others in doing so." As a result, regulations that only create a structural mechanism by which the state, or the parent or guardian of a minor, may "express profound respect for the life of the unborn" are permissible if they do not create a "substantial obstacle to the woman's exercise of the right to choose." Similarly, regulations intended to foster the health of a pregnant woman "are valid if they do not constitute an undue burden." In addition to expressing agreement with at least the "essence" of *Roe*, the joint opinion argued that *Roe* needed to be retained on stare decisis grounds. To overrule *Roe* while "under fire," in the absence of the "most compelling reason to reexamine a watershed decision would subvert the Court's legitimacy beyond any serious question." Reversal of *Roe's* essential holding would occur "at the cost of both profound and unnecessary damage to the Court's legitimacy, and to the Nation's commitment to the rule of law." Justice Blackmun expressed strong support for the reaffirmation of *Roe*, and acknowledged as an "act of personal courage and constitutional principles" the positions taken by O'Connor, Kennedy, and Souter. At the same time, he expressed a "fear for the darkness as four Justices anxiously await the single vote necessary to extinguish the light." He noted his age (83), and said he and his vote could not "remain on this Court forever…." He predicted a serious confirmation battle for that vote upon his decision to step down.

Chief Justice Rehnquist and Justice Scalia issued dissents. Each signed the dissent of the other, and Justices White and Thomas signed both. Rehnquist said *Roe* was "wrongly decided" and should be overruled. He would have substituted the approach of the plurality in *Webster.* Following what he called a "newly minted variation on stare decisis," Rehnquist said the majority had retained only the "outer shell" of *Roe.* In his view, the majority had beaten a "wholesale retreat from the substance of that case." What was left of *Roe,* said Rehnquist, was a "sort of judicial Potemkin Village, which may be pointed out to passers by as a monument to the importance of adhering to precedent." Behind the "facade" of stare decisis, he charged that the Court had resorted to an "entirely new method of analysis, without any roots in constitutional law," to be used when reviewing state abortion regulations. Neither stare decisis nor an interest in judicial legitimacy was well served by such an approach. To Scalia, the question in *Casey* was not whether the "power of a woman to abort her unborn child is a 'liberty' in the absolute sense; or even whether it is a liberty of great importance to many women." Scalia acknowledged both as true. Rather, he maintained, the "issue is whether it is a liberty protected by the Constitution of the United States." His answer was, "I'm sure it is not." His conclusion was not based on "anything so exalted" as his own concept of existence or the "mystery of life." Instead, it was based on two simple facts: "(1) the Constitution says absolutely nothing about it, (2) the longstanding traditions of American society have permitted it to be legally proscribed." Scalia was also critical of the majority's claim that *Roe* had been a workable response to the abortion controversy. Compromise on the issue had been possible before *Roe*, he said, but not after. *Roe's* mandate for "abortion-on-demand destroyed the compromises of the past, rendered compromises impossible for the future, and required the entire issue to be resolved uniformly, at the national level." Furthermore, *Roe* "created a vast new class of abortion consumers and abortion proponents by eliminating the moral opprobrium that had attached to the act."

Abortions and Protests

Bray v. Alexandria Women's Health Clinic, **506 U.S. __, 122 L. Ed. 2d 34, 113 S. Ct. 753 (1993)**   The issue in *Bray* was whether federal judges have authority under an 1871 statute to enjoin anti-abortion demonstrators from preventing entry to abortion clinics. The statute, known as the Ku Klux Klan Act, has been frequently used to protect clinics from disruptive demonstrations. The law bans conspiracies to deprive persons or classes of persons of equal protection. In order to prove a conspiracy in violation of the law, plaintiffs need to show that the conspirators were motivated, at least in part, by a "class-based invidiously discriminatory animus." Plaintiff would further need to show that the conspiracy was designed to interfere with rights protected against encroachment by private parties. It was asserted by the abortion clinics that because only women can have abortions, the demonstrators discriminated against women as a class by interfering with access to legal abortions. The Supreme Court ruled in a 6–3 decision that the plaintiffs did not prove a private conspiracy in violation of the statute. Absent such a finding, the federal courts are without power to restrict demonstrations such as those involved here. Justice Scalia, on behalf of the majority, rejected the contention that women seeking abortions constitute a "class" within the meaning of the law. The term, he said, "unquestionably connotes something more than a group of individuals who share a desire to engage in conduct...the defendant disfavors." The Court also rejected the contention that the demonstrators' actions were directed toward women in general. The Court did not see in the record any indications that the abortion protesters were motivated by a purpose directed at women as a class. Rather, the Court pointed to the district court finding that the protesters define their "rescues" as interventions between "abortionists and innocent victims." Opposition to voluntary abortion, said Scalia, "cannot possibly be considered...an irrational surrogate for opposition to (or paternalism toward) women." Regardless of one's position on abortion, it "cannot be denied that there are common and respectable reasons for opposing it, other than hatred of or condescension toward (or indeed any view at all concern) women as a class, as is evident from the fact that men and women are on both sides of the issue, just as men and women are on both sides of petitioners' unlawful demonstrations." As a result, the position of the legal clinics comes down to the proposition that "intent is legally irrelevant; that since voluntary abortion is an activity engaged in only by women, to disfavor it is ipso facto to discriminate invidiously against women as a class. Our cases do not support that proposition."

Justice Stevens, in dissent, suggested the majority ignored the objective of the federal statute. He said it was designed to protect the country's citizens from "what amounts to the theft of their constitutional rights by organized and violent mobs across the country." It was his view that the statute could be activated if a conspiracy was found to be motivated "at least in part by its adverse effects upon women." Stevens also felt that the demonstrators' conduct was motivated at least partially by the "invidious belief that individual women are not capable of deciding whether to terminate a pregnancy, or that they should not be allowed to act on such a decision." He disagreed with the Court's "unstated and mistaken assumption that this is a case about opposition to abortion. It is not. It is a case about the exercise of Federal power to control an interstate conspiracy to commit illegal acts." Justice O'Connor's dissent also focused on the class-based effect of the demonstrations. Those victimized by the protests are "linked by their ability to become pregnant and by their ability to terminate their pregnancies, characteristics unique to the class of women." She recognized the sincerity of the demonstrators' opposition to abortion. In examining their motivation, however, the "sincerity of their opposition cannot surmount the manner in which they have chosen to express it." Justice Blackmun joined both dissents. It is possible that the effects of this decision will be limited by congressional action.

Significance   Title X of the Public Health Service Act of 1970 authorizes federal funding for public and private nonprofit agencies providing family planning services. Section 1008 of the act specifies that none of the funds appropriated under Title X can be used for programs where "abortion is a method of family planning." Until 1988, this phrase was interpreted as precluding Title X grantees from actually performing abortions as opposed to providing information about abortion as an option. In 1988, the Secretary of Health and Human Services issued new regulations that imposed significant conditions on grant recipients. First, Title X projects cannot counsel about abortion or provide referrals for abortions. Instead, pregnant clients must be referred to agencies providing "appropriate" prenatal services. Recipient agencies are explicitly forbidden to refer a client to an abortion provider even on specific request. Second, a Title X project cannot engage in activities that "encourage, promote or advocate abortion as a method of family planning." Finally, recipient agencies must be organized in such a way as to be wholly independent from any abortion-related activities. Activities supported by federal funds must take place in separate facilities and use personnel independent from any agency personnel involved in providing abortion services.

A number of Title X grantees and physicians associated with recipient agencies sought to prevent implementation of the new regulations. In *Rust v. Sullivan* (500 U.S. 173: 1991), the Supreme Court ruled 5–4 that the secretary's regulations were permitted under terms of the act, and that the regulations did not violate the First or Fifth Amendment rights of recipient agencies or their clients. The constitutionality of abortion as such was not directly before the Court in this case. Chief Justice Rehnquist spoke for the majority and said the secretary's interpretation of the meaning of Section 1008 must be accorded substantial deference not only because his agency administers the statute, but because the evidence as to congressional intent is "ambiguous." In addition, the Court thought the secretary's regulations reflected a "plausible construction" of the statute. The secretary's interpretation was clearly not one that would lead the Court to conclude that Congress had not intended regulations of this kind. Focus was then turned to the First Amendment issue. The principal contention of the challengers was that because Title X funds speech in a way that is not "evenhanded with respect to views and information about abortion, it invidiously discriminates on the basis of viewpoint." Rehnquist agreed that the secretary's regulations represented a value choice preferring childbirth to abortion, but he said the government may make that policy decision and "implement that judgment by the allocation of public funds." Unequal subsidization, however, is not unconstitutional. When government believes it in the public interest to fund a program to "encourage certain activities" but does not fund an alternate program, government has not "discriminated on the basis of viewpoint; it has merely chosen to fund an activity to the exclusion to the other." In the Court's view, the essence of the challengers' argument was that "if the Government

The Constitutional Law Dictionary

chooses to subsidize one protected right, it must subsidize analogous counterpart rights." Rehnquist said that proposition had been "soundly rejected" in previous Court decisions. Rather, when government appropriates public funds to establish a program, it is entitled to define the limits of that program. Furthermore, the regulations do not require Title X recipients to forego abortion-related speech. Instead, the regulations "merely require that the grantee keep such activity separate and distinct from Title X activities." Finally, the Court concluded that the regulations did not violate a woman's Fifth Amendment right of choice. Citing *Webster*, Rehnquist said the government has no "constitutional duty to subsidize an activity merely because the activity is constitutionally protected and may validly choose to fund childbirth over abortion." That funding decision does not create obstacles for the woman wishing to terminate her pregnancy. The woman has the same choices she would have if the government had chosen to fund no family planning services at all. Nor did the Court find the regulations to interfere with the patient/physician relationship or the woman's right to have certain options discussed by her physicians. Access to abortion-related information remained "unfettered outside the context of the Title X project." This conclusion was unaffected by the fact that most Title X clients are precluded by indigence from seeing a physician besides the Title X grantee. Inability of indigent women to "enjoy the full range" of the protected freedom of choice was seen as a product of her indigence and not restrictions under the regulations. Justices Blackmun, O'Connor, Marshall, and Stevens dissented. Blackmun said the regulation was "viewpoint suppression of speech solely because it is imposed on those dependent on the Government for economic support." The purpose and result of the regulations is to "deny women the ability voluntarily to decide their procreative destiny." Justice O'Connor said in dissent that the Court should have simply ruled the regulations were unreasonable under the statute. This would have avoided the need to address any constitutional issues, and it would have returned the question to Congress for clarification of what it intended under the statute.

The Racketeer-Influenced and Corrupt Organizations Act (RICO) makes it a federal crime to conduct the "affairs" of an "enterprise" through "patterned" racketeering activity—a pattern of federal and/or state felonies. The National Organization for Women (NOW) attempted to use RICO in an action against the Pro-Life Action Network (PLAN), an anti-abortion coalition including such groups as Operation Rescue. NOW claimed that PLAN had engaged in criminal conspiracy to close down abortion clinics through patterned use of intimidation and extortion. RICO provides for triple damages and payment of attorney fees if a plaintiff prevails in such a case. The lower federal courts dismissed this action on the ground that RICO applied only to those activities that were economically motivated. The lower court found the actions of PLAN to be political rather than economic. A unanimous Supreme Court reversed in *National Organization for Women (NOW) v. Scheidler* (127 L. Ed. 2d 99: 1994). The Court focused on the wording of RICO to determine whether the law could be used as the basis for suits seeking damages against anti-abortion protesters. The provision of RICO in question here was Section 1962, subsection (c). This subsection makes it unlawful for any-one employed or associated with "any enterprise...to conduct or partici-pate...in the conduct of such enterprise's affairs through a pattern of racketeering activities...." Reference to "enterprise" in subsection (c), said Chief Justice Rehnquist, "connotes generally the vehicle through which the unlawful pattern of racketeering activity is committed, rather than the victim of the activity." Since the enterprise in subsection (c) is not being acquired, it was the Court's view that it "need not have a property interest that can be acquired nor an economic motive for engaging in illegal activity; it need only be an association in fact that engages in a pattern of racketeering activity." In ruling that an economic motive was required, the lower courts (and the respondents) had over-looked the fact that predicate acts, such as the alleged extortion, "may not benefit the protesters financially but still may drain money from the economy by harming businesses such as the clinics...." The Court found the requirement of economic motive to be neither expressed nor fairly implied in RICO. While the act may have been passed to combat organ-ized crime, Congress enacted a more general statute; it "was not limited in application to organized crime." The case was remanded to allow NOW to attempt to demonstrating their claims for damages under RICO. The case did not involve abortion rights as such nor did it take up First Amendment expression questions. It was noted by the Court that RICO actions could affect protected expression.

The Court considered a similar issue in *Madsen v. Women's Health Center, Inc.* (129 L. Ed. 2d 593: 1994). A number of Florida abortion clinics including Women's Health Center, Inc. sought an injunction from a state court prohibiting certain actions by certain individuals and anti-abortion organizations such as Operation Rescue. A permanent injunction was issued in late 1992 prohibiting such activities as trespassing on clinic property, blocking access to clinics, and harassing persons associated with the clinics. In April 1993, a more extensive injunction was issued. The second injunction created "buffer zones" of 36 and 300 feet from the clinics. The abortion protesters were forbidden to approach persons seeking clinic services inside the 300-foot zone. An exception was allowed for potential clinic patients who consented to talk with the protesters. Nonthreatening communication and the passing out of printed literature

173

could occur within the 300-foot zone until the 36-foot boundary was reached, at which time all interaction between the prospective patients and protesters was prohibited. The amended injunction also prohibited making sounds that could be heard inside the clinics, and prohibited the exhibiting of "images observable" to patients of the clinic. The amended injunction was upheld by the Florida Supreme Court. Shortly before the Florida Supreme Court decision was announced, the U.S. Court of Appeals for the Eleventh Circuit struck down the injunction in a separate case. In a 6–3 decision, the U.S. Supreme Court upheld the 36-foot buffer zone, but struck down the restrictions within the 300-foot zone. Chief Justice Rehnquist began with the question on which the two lower courts had differed—whether the injunction was content neutral or content based. The Court rejected the protesters' contention that because the injunction prohibits only the speech of the protesters, it is necessarily viewpoint or content based. To accept their claim, said Rehnquist, would be to classify "virtually every injunction" as content based because by its very nature, it applies only to particular individuals and perhaps their speech. Content neutrality hinges on the purpose of the regulation—a purpose chosen without reference to the content of the regulated speech. The injunction was issued here because the protesters "repeatedly violated" the court's original order. That the protesters all shared the same view on abortion did not in itself demonstrate a viewpoint-based purpose. Rather, the order reflects that the group "whose *conduct* violated the court's order happen to share the same opinion regarding abortions being performed at the clinic." Injunctions, however, carry greater risks for "censorship and discriminatory application than do general ordinances." Accordingly, a standard must obtain that is more rigorous than used for time, place, and manner analysis. The challenged injunction must "burden no more speech than necessary" to serve a significant government interest. Here, the state had a strong interest in "protecting a woman's freedom to seek lawful medical or counseling services in connection with her pregnancy." The state also had a strong interest in ensuring the public safety and order, promoting the free flow of traffic, and protecting property rights. The Court concluded that the state had "few other options to protect access given the narrow confines around the clinic," and upheld the 36-foot buffer zone. The Court also noted that an even narrower order was issued originally, and that it had failed to protect clinic access. The Court also upheld the limited noise restrictions. The First Amendment, said Rehnquist, "does not demand that patients at a medical facility undertake Herculean efforts to escape the cacophony of political protests." If overamplified loudspeakers "assault the citizenry, government may turn them down." Here the Court distinguished the sound restrictions from the restrictions on "images observable." This restriction was too broad—it was more burdensome than necessary to achieve the purpose of limiting threats to clinic patients or their families. Similarly, the Court found insufficient justification for creating the 300-foot buffer zone; the desired result could have been accomplished with less burdensome restrictions. Justice Scalia, joined by Justices Kennedy and Thomas, dissented. It was their view that the injunction was "profoundly at odds with our First Amendment precedents and traditions." The order was unconstitutional because it was content based; it targeted a particular group which had broken no laws and imposed restrictions on only that group. The danger with such restrictions, said Scalia, is that "they may be designed and used precisely to suppress the ideas in question rather than to achieve any other proper governmental aim."

APPENDIX C: JUSTICES OF THE SUPREME COURT

CHIEF JUSTICES CAPITALIZED

	TENURE	APPOINTED BY	REPLACED
JOHN JAY	1789–1795	Washington	
John Rutledge	1789–1791	Washington	
William Cushing	1789–1810	Washington	
James Wilson	1789–1798	Washington	
John Blair	1789–1796	Washington	
James Iredell	1790–1799	Washington	
Thomas Johnson	1791–1793	Washington	Rutledge
William Paterson	1793–1806	Washington	Johnson
JOHN RUTLEDGE	1795	Washington	Jay
Samuel Chase	1796–1811	Washington	Blair
OLIVER ELLSWORTH	1796–1800	Washington	Rutledge
Bushrod Washington	1798–1829	John Adams	Wilson
Alfred Moore	1799–1804	John Adams	Iredell
JOHN MARSHALL	1801–1835	John Adams	Ellsworth
William Johnson	1804–1834	Jefferson	Moore
Brockholst Livingston	1806–1823	Jefferson	Paterson
Thomas Todd	1807–1826	Jefferson	(new judgeship)
Gabriel Duval	1811–1835	Madison	Chase
Joseph Story	1811–1845	Madison	Cushing
Smith Thompson	1823–1843	Monroe	Livingston
Robert Trimble	1826–1828	John Q. Adams	Todd
John McLean	1829–1861	Jackson	Trimble
Henry Baldwin	1830–1844	Jackson	Washington
James Wayne	1835–1867	Jackson	Johnson
ROGER B. TANEY	1836–1864	Jackson	Marshall
Phillip P. Barbour	1836–1841	Jackson	Duval
John Catron	1837–1865	Jackson	(new judgeship)
John McKinley	1837–1852	Van Buren	(new judgeship)
Peter V. Daniel	1841–1860	Van Buren	Barbour
Samuel Nelson	1845–1872	Tyler	Thompson
Levi Woodbury	1846–1851	Polk	Story
Robert C. Grier	1846–1870	Polk	Baldwin
Benjamin R. Curtis	1851–1857	Fillmore	Woodbury
John A. Campbell	1853–1861	Pierce	McKinley
Nathan Clifford	1858–1881	Buchanan	Curtis
Noah H. Swayne	1862–1881	Lincoln	McLean
Samuel F. Miller	1862–1890	Lincoln	Daniel
David Davis	1862–1877	Lincoln	Campbell
Stephen J. Field	1863–1897	Lincoln	(new judgeship)
SALMON CHASE	1864–1873	Lincoln	Taney
William Strong	1870–1880	Grant	Grier
Joseph P. Bradley	1870–1892	Grant	Wayne
Ward Hunt	1872–1882	Grant	Nelson
MORRISON R. WAITE	1874–1888	Grant	Chase
John Marshall Harlan	1877–1911	Hayes	Davis
William B. Woods	1880–1887	Hayes	Strong
Stanley Matthews	1881–1889	Garfield	Swayne
Horace Gray	1881–1902	Arthur	Clifford
Samuel Blatchford	1882–1893	Arthur	Hunt

	TENURE	APPOINTED BY	REPLACED
Lucius Q. C. Lamar	1888–1893	Cleveland	Woods
MELVILLE W. FULLER	1888–1910	Cleveland	Waite
David J. Brewer	1889–1910	Harrison	Matthews
Henry B. Brown	1890–1906	Harrison	Miller
George Shiras, Jr.	1892–1903	Harrison	Bradley
Howell E. Jackson	1893–1895	Harrison	Lamar
Edward D. White	1894–1910	Cleveland	Blatchford
Rufus W. Peckham	1895–1909	Cleveland	Jackson
Joseph McKenna	1898–1925	McKinley	Field
Oliver Wendell Holmes	1902–1932	T. Roosevelt	Gray
William R. Day	1903–1922	T. Roosevelt	Shiras
William H. Moody	1906–1910	T. Roosevelt	Brown
Horace H. Lurton	1909–1914	Taft	Peckham
Charles Evans Hughes	1910–1916	Taft	Brewer
EDWARD D. WHITE	1910–1921	Taft	Fuller
Willis VanDevanter	1910–1937	Taft	White
Joseph R. Lamar	1910–1916	Taft	Moody
Mahlon Pitney	1912–1922	Taft	Harlan
James McReynolds	1914–1941	Wilson	Lurton
Louis D. Brandeis	1916–1939	Wilson	Lamar
John H. Clark	1916–1922	Wilson	Hughes
WILLIAM H. TAFT	1921–1930	Harding	White
George Sutherland	1922–1938	Harding	Clarke
Pierce Butler	1922–1939	Harding	Day
Edward T. Sanford	1923–1930	Harding	Pitney
Harlan F. Stone	1925–1941	Coolidge	McKenna
CHARLES EVANS HUGHES	1930–1941	Hoover	Taft
Owen J. Roberts	1932–1945	Hoover	Sanford
Benjamin N. Cardozo	1932–1938	Hoover	Holmes
Hugo L. Black	1937–1971	F. Roosevelt	Van Devanter
Stanley F. Reed	1938–1957	F. Roosevelt	Sutherland
Felix Frankfurter	1939–1962	F. Roosevelt	Cardozo
William O. Douglas	1939–1975	F. Roosevelt	Brandeis
Frank Murphy	1940–1949	F. Roosevelt	Butler
James F. Byrnes	1941–1942	F. Roosevelt	McReynolds
HARLAN F. STONE	1941–1946	F. Roosevelt	Hughes
Robert H. Jackson	1941–1954	F. Roosevelt	Stone
Wiley B. Rutledge	1943–1949	F. Roosevelt	Byrnes
Harold H. Burton	1945–1958	Truman	Roberts
FRED M. VINSON	1946–1953	Truman	Stone
Tom C. Clark	1949–1967	Truman	Murphy
Sherman Minton	1949–1956	Truman	Rutledge
EARL WARREN	1954–1969	Eisenhower	Vinson
John M. Harlan	1955–1971	Eisenhower	Jackson
William J. Brennan	1957–1990	Eisenhower	Minton
Charles E. Whittaker	1957–1962	Eisenhower	Reed
Potter Stewart	1959–1981	Eisenhower	Burton
Byron R. White	1962–1993	Kennedy	Whittaker
Arthur J. Goldberg	1962–1965	Kennedy	Frankfurter
Abe Fortas	1965–1969	Johnson	Goldberg
Thurgood Marshall	1967–	Johnson	Clark
WARREN E. BURGER	1969–1986	Nixon	Warren
Harry A. Blackmun	1970–1994	Nixon	Fortas

Justices of the Supreme Court-Continued

	TENURE	APPOINTED BY	REPLACED
Lewis F. Powell	1971–1988	Nixon	Black
William H. Rehnquist	1971–	Nixon	Harlan
John Paul Stevens	1975–	Ford	Douglas
Sandra Day O'Connor	1981–	Reagan	Stewart
WILLIAM H. REHNQUIST	1986–	Reagan	Burger
Antonin Scalia	1986–	Reagan	Rehnquist
Anthony M. Kennedy	1988–	Reagan	Powell
David H. Souter	1990–	Bush	Brennan
Clarence Thomas	1991–	Bush	Marshall
Ruth Bader Ginsburg	1993–	Clinton	White
Stephen G. Breyer	1994–	Clinton	Blackmun

APPENDIX D: COMPOSITION OF THE SUPREME COURT SINCE 1900

The table below represents the members of the Supreme Court since 1900. By locating the term in which a particular case was decided, the names of the justices on the Court at the time of the decision may be readily determined.

THE FULLER COURT (1900–1909)

1900–1901	Fuller	White	Gray	Peckham	Brown	Shiras	Brewer	Harlan	McKenna
1902	Fuller	White	Holmes	Peckham	Brown	Shiras	Brewer	Harlan	McKenna
1903–1905	Fuller	White	Holmes	Peckham	Brown	Day	Brewer	Harlan	McKenna
1906–1908	Fuller	White	Holmes	Peckham	Moody	Day	Brewer	Harlan	McKenna
1909	Fuller	White	Holmes	Lurton	Moody	Day	Brewer	Harlan	McKenna

THE WHITE COURT (1910–1920)

1910–1911	White	VanDevanter	Holmes	Lurton	Lamar	Day	Hughes	Harlan	McKenna
1912–1913	White	VanDevanter	Holmes	Lurton	Lamar	Day	Hughes	Pitney	McKenna
1914–1915	White	VanDevanter	Holmes	McReynolds	Lamar	Day	Hughes	Pitney	McKenna
1916–1920	White	VanDevanter	Holmes	McReynolds	Brandeis	Day	Clarke	Pitney	McKenna

THE TAFT COURT (1921–1929)

1921	Taft	VanDevanter	Holmes	McReynolds	Brandeis	Day	Clarke	Pitney	McKenna
1922	Taft	VanDevanter	Holmes	McReynolds	Brandeis	Butler	Sutherland	Pitney	McKenna
1923–1924	Taft	VanDevanter	Holmes	McReynolds	Brandeis	Butler	Sutherland	Sanford	McKenna
1925–1929	Taft	VanDevanter	Holmes	McReynolds	Brandeis	Butler	Sutherland	Sanford	Stone

THE HUGHES COURT (1930–1940)

1930–1931	Hughes	VanDevanter	Holmes	McReynolds	Brandeis	Butler	Sutherland	Roberts	Stone
1932–1936	Hughes	VanDevanter	Cardozo	McReynolds	Brandeis	Butler	Sutherland	Roberts	Stone
1937	Hughes	Black	Cardozo	McReynolds	Brandeis	Butler	Sutherland	Roberts	Stone
1938	Hughes	Black	Cardozo	McReynolds	Brandeis	Butler	Reed	Roberts	Stone
1939	Hughes	Black	Frankfurter	McReynolds	Douglas	Butler	Reed	Roberts	Stone
1940	Hughes	Black	Frankfurter	McReynolds	Douglas	Murphy	Reed	Roberts	Stone

continued

181

THE STONE COURT (1941–1945)

Years									
1941–1942	Stone	Black	Frankfurter	Byrnes	Douglas	Murphy	Reed	Roberts	Jackson
1943–1944	Stone	Black	Frankfurter	Rutledge	Douglas	Murphy	Reed	Roberts	Jackson
1945	Stone	Black	Frankfurter	Rutledge	Douglas	Murphy	Reed	Burton	Jackson

THE VINSON COURT (1946–1952)

Years									
1946–1948	Vinson	Black	Frankfurter	Rutledge	Douglas	Murphy	Reed	Burton	Jackson
1949–1952	Vinson	Black	Frankfurter	Minton	Douglas	Clark	Reed	Burton	Jackson

THE WARREN COURT (1953–1968)

Years									
1953–1954	Warren	Black	Frankfurter	Minton	Douglas	Clark	Reed	Burton	Jackson
1955	Warren	Black	Frankfurter	Minton	Douglas	Clark	Reed	Burton	Harlan
1956	Warren	Black	Frankfurter	Brennan	Douglas	Clark	Reed	Burton	Harlan
1957	Warren	Black	Frankfurter	Brennan	Douglas	Clark	Whittaker	Burton	Harlan
1958–1961	Warren	Black	Frankfurter	Brennan	Douglas	Clark	Whittaker	Stewart	Harlan
1962–1965	Warren	Black	Goldberg	Brennan	Douglas	Clark	White	Stewart	Harlan
1965–1967	Warren	Black	Fortas	Brennan	Douglas	Clark	White	Stewart	Harlan
1967–1969	Warren	Black	Fortas	Brennan	Douglas	Marshall	White	Stewart	Harlan

THE BURGER COURT (1969–1985)

Years									
1969	Burger	Black	Fortas	Brennan	Douglas	Marshall	White	Stewart	Harlan
1969–1970	Burger	Black	Blackmun	Brennan	Douglas	Marshall	White	Stewart	Harlan
1970	Burger	Black	Blackmun	Brennan	Douglas	Marshall	White	Stewart	Harlan
1971–1974	Burger	Powell	Blackmun	Brennan	Douglas	Marshall	White	Stewart	Rehnquist
1975–1980	Burger	Powell	Blackmun	Brennan	Stevens	Marshall	White	Stewart	Rehnquist
1981–1985	Burger	Powell	Blackmun	Brennan	Stevens	Marshall	White	O'Connor	Rehnquist

THE REHNQUIST COURT (1986–)

Years									
1986	Rehnquist	Powell	Blackmun	Brennan	Stevens	Marshall	White	O'Connor	Scalia
1987–1989	Rehnquist	Kennedy	Blackmun	Brennan	Stevens	Marshall	White	O'Connor	Scalia
1990	Rehnquist	Kennedy	Blackmun	Souter	Stevens	Marshall	White	O'Connor	Scalia
1991	Rehnquist	Kennedy	Blackmun	Souter	Stevens	Thomas	White	O'Connor	Scalia
1993	Rehnquist	Kennedy	Blackmun	Souter	Stevens	Thomas	Ginsburg	O'Connor	Scalia
1994	Rehnquist	Kennedy	Breyer	Souter	Stevens	Thomas	Ginsburg	O'Connor	Scalia

INDEX

Cross-references to dictionary entries are provided throughout the text at the end of each definition paragraph. Page references for all subjects and cases discussed in this volume are provided below. Page references in boldface indicate cases for which a definitional section has been prepared. All other references are to cases or subjects discussed within an entry for another case.

Index

Index

Index

Index